VOL. 6

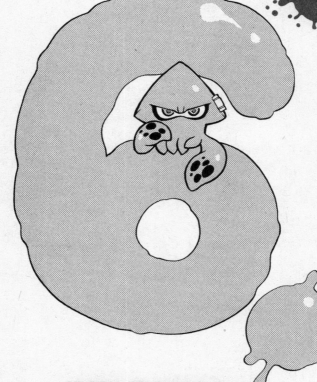

STORY AND ART BY
Sankichi Hinodeya

CONTENTS

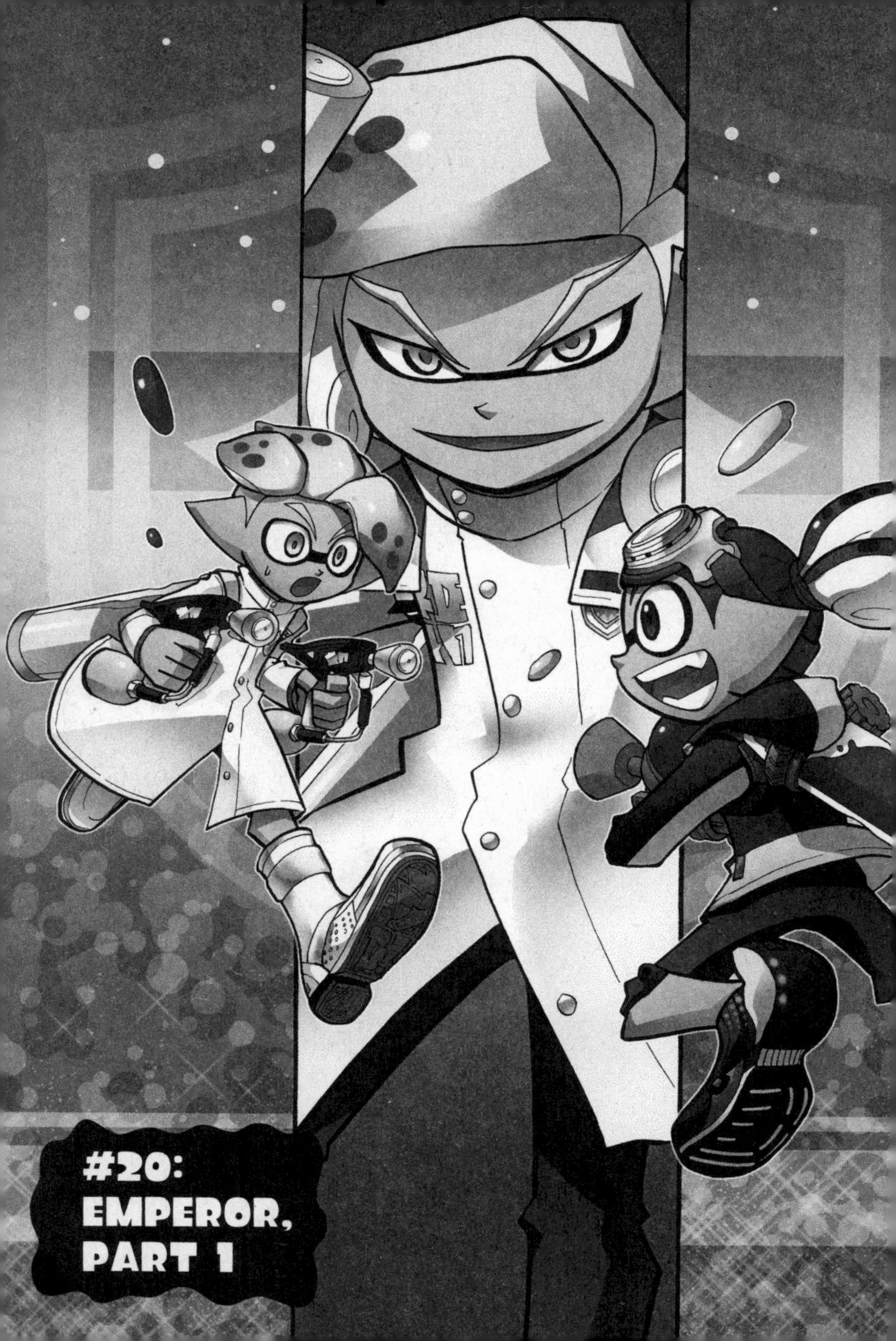
#20:
EMPEROR,
PART 1

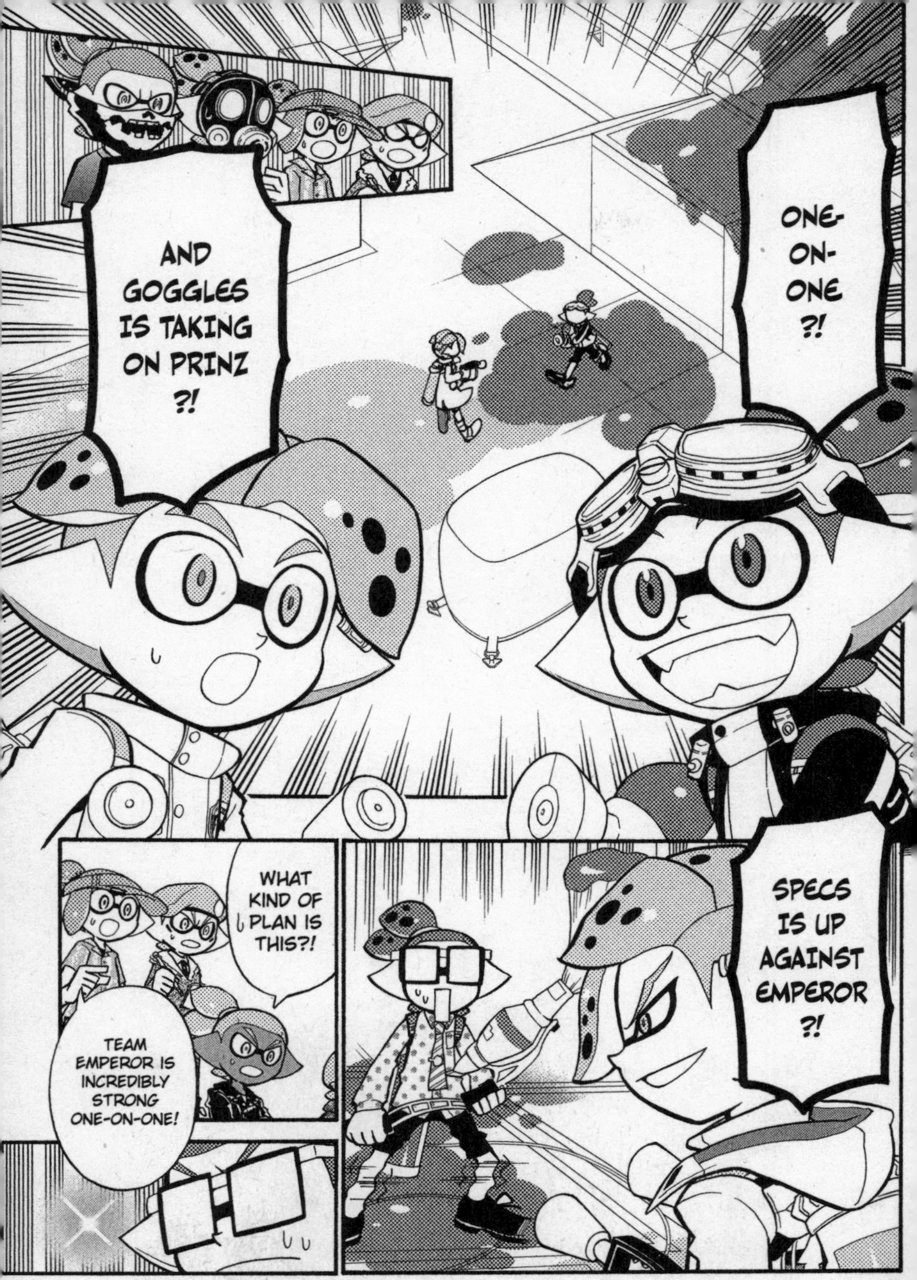
ONE-ON-ONE ?!
AND GOGGLES IS TAKING ON PRINZ ?!
SPECS IS UP AGAINST EMPEROR ?!
WHAT KIND OF PLAN IS THIS?!
TEAM EMPEROR IS INCREDIBLY STRONG ONE-ON-ONE!

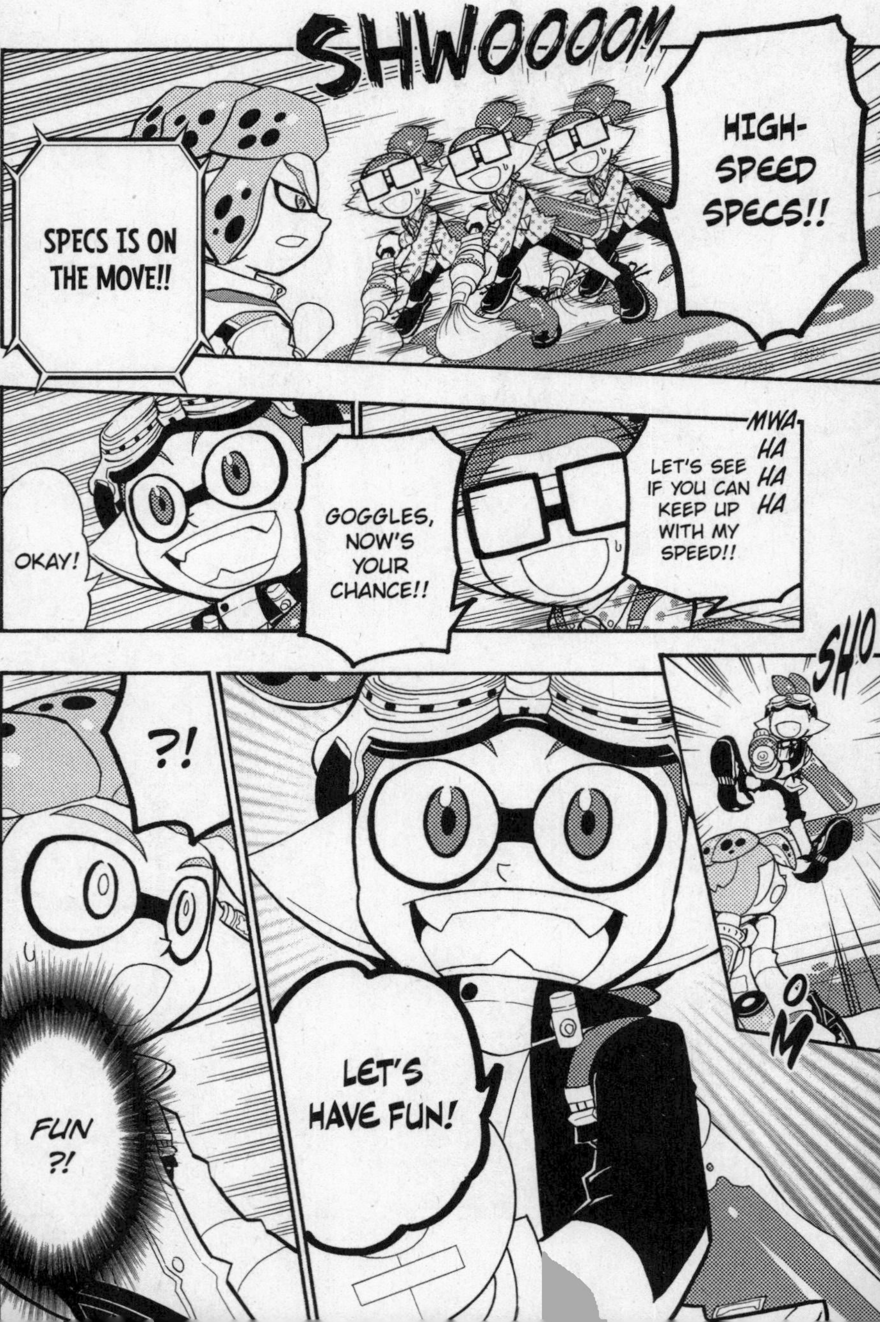
SHWOOOOM
HIGH-SPEED SPECS!!
SPECS IS ON THE MOVE!!
MWA-HA HA HA
LET'S SEE IF YOU CAN KEEP UP WITH MY SPEED!!
GOGGLES, NOW'S YOUR CHANCE!!
OKAY!
SHOOM
LET'S HAVE FUN!
?!
FUN ?!

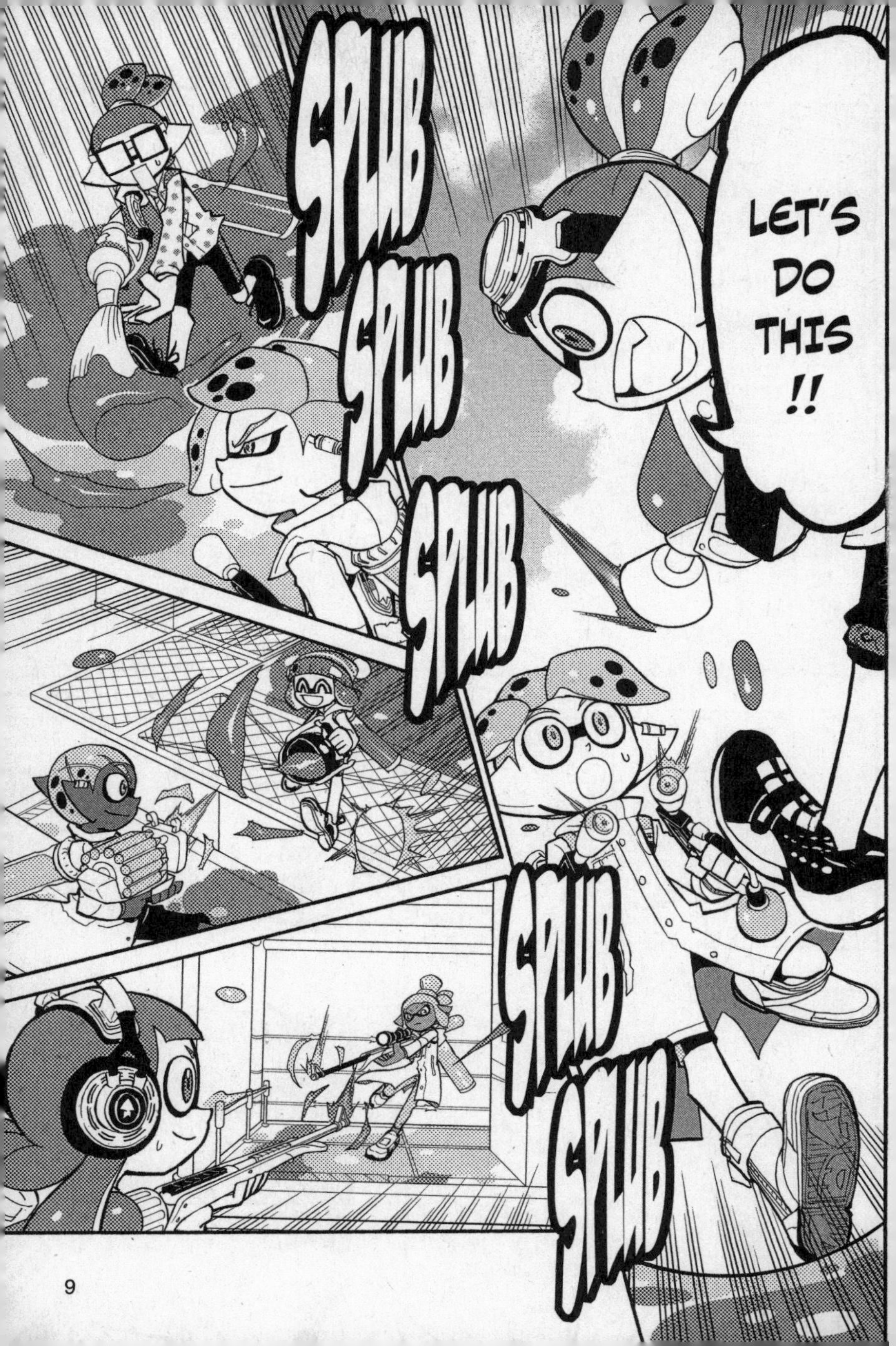
LET'S DO THIS!!
SPLUB
SPLUB
SPLUB
SPLUB
SPLUB

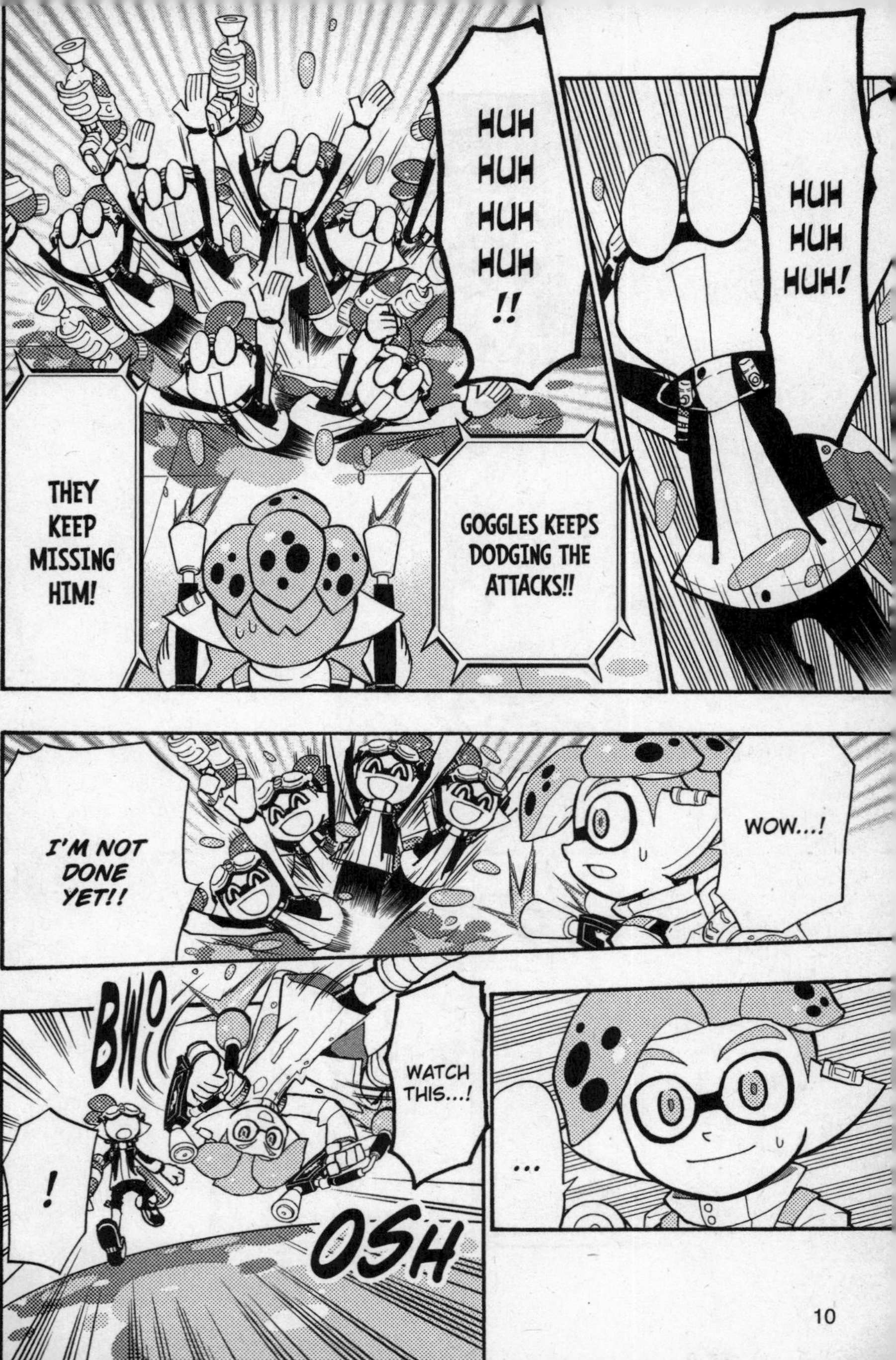
HUH HUH HUH!
HUH HUH HUH HUH !!
GOGGLES KEEPS DODGING THE ATTACKS!!
THEY KEEP MISSING HIM!
WOW...!
I'M NOT DONE YET!!
...
WATCH THIS...!
BWOOSH
!

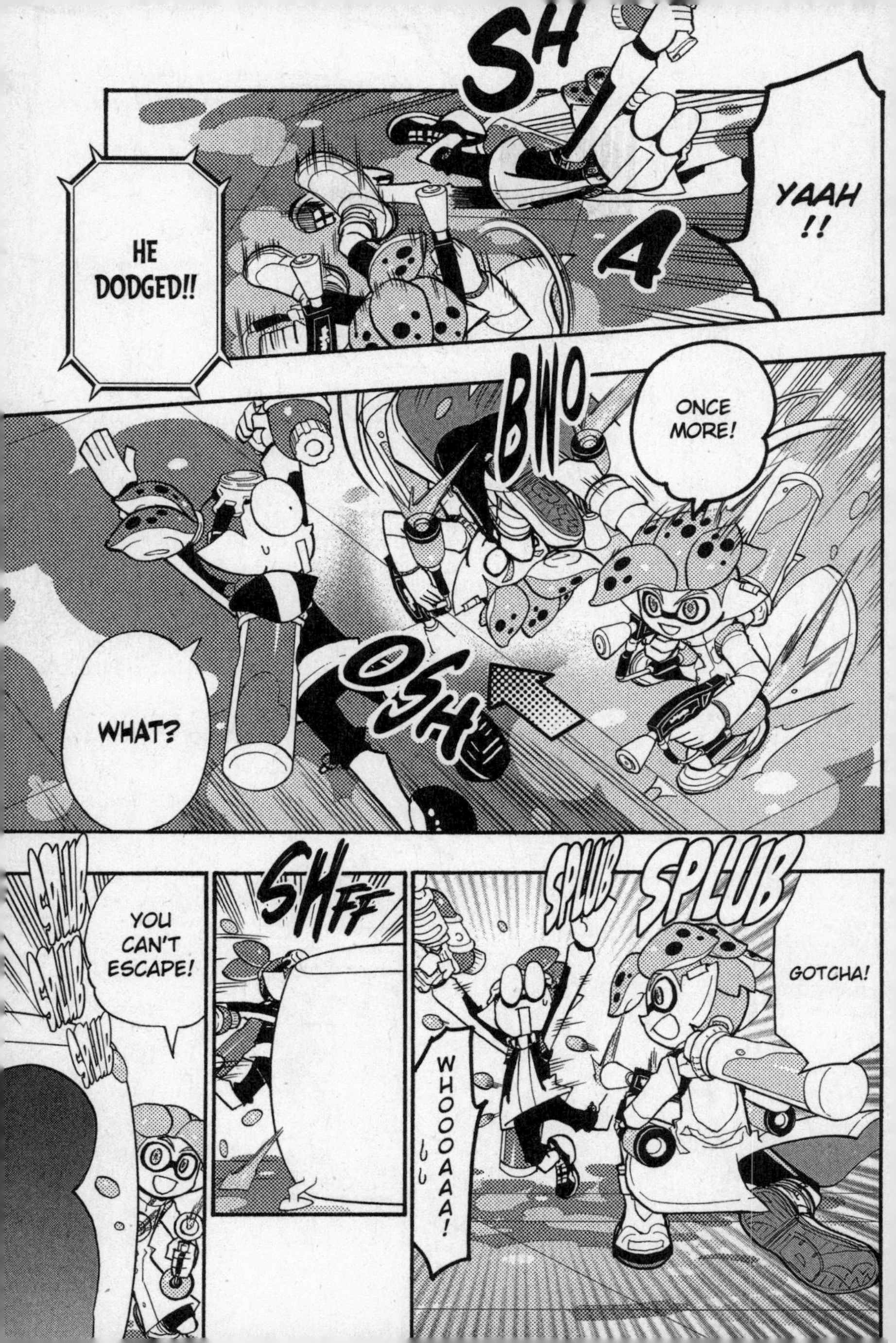
SH
YAAH!!
A
HE DODGED!!
ONCE MORE!
BWO
OSH
WHAT?
SPLUB
SPLUB
GOTCHA!
WHOOOAAA!
SHFF
YOU CAN'T ESCAPE!
SPLUB
SPLUB
SPLUB

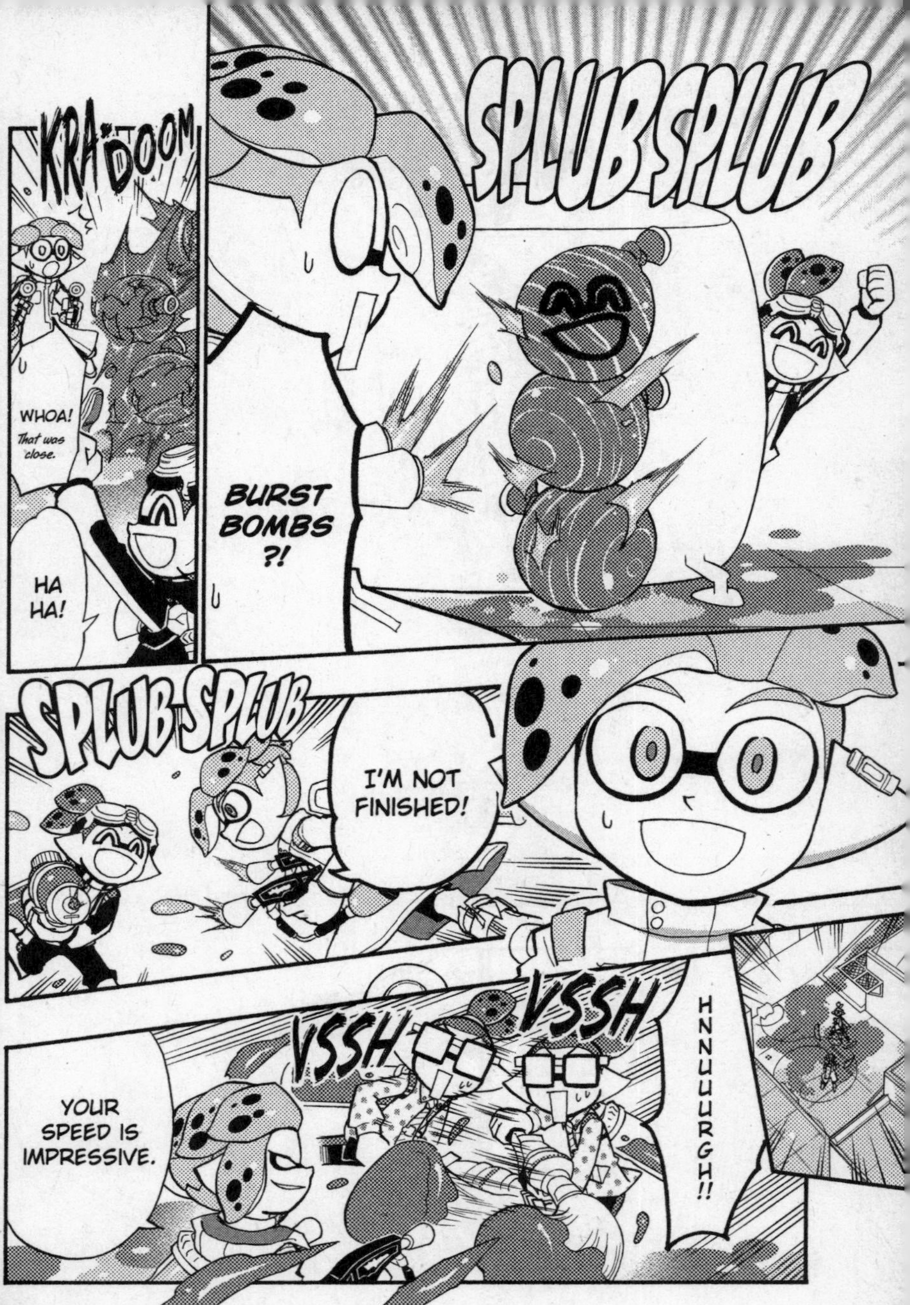

SPLUB SPLUB
BURST BOMBS ?!
KRA-DOOM
WHOA! That was close.
HA HA!
I'M NOT FINISHED!
SPLUB SPLUB
HNNUUURGH!!
VSSH
VSSH
YOUR SPEED IS IMPRESSIVE.

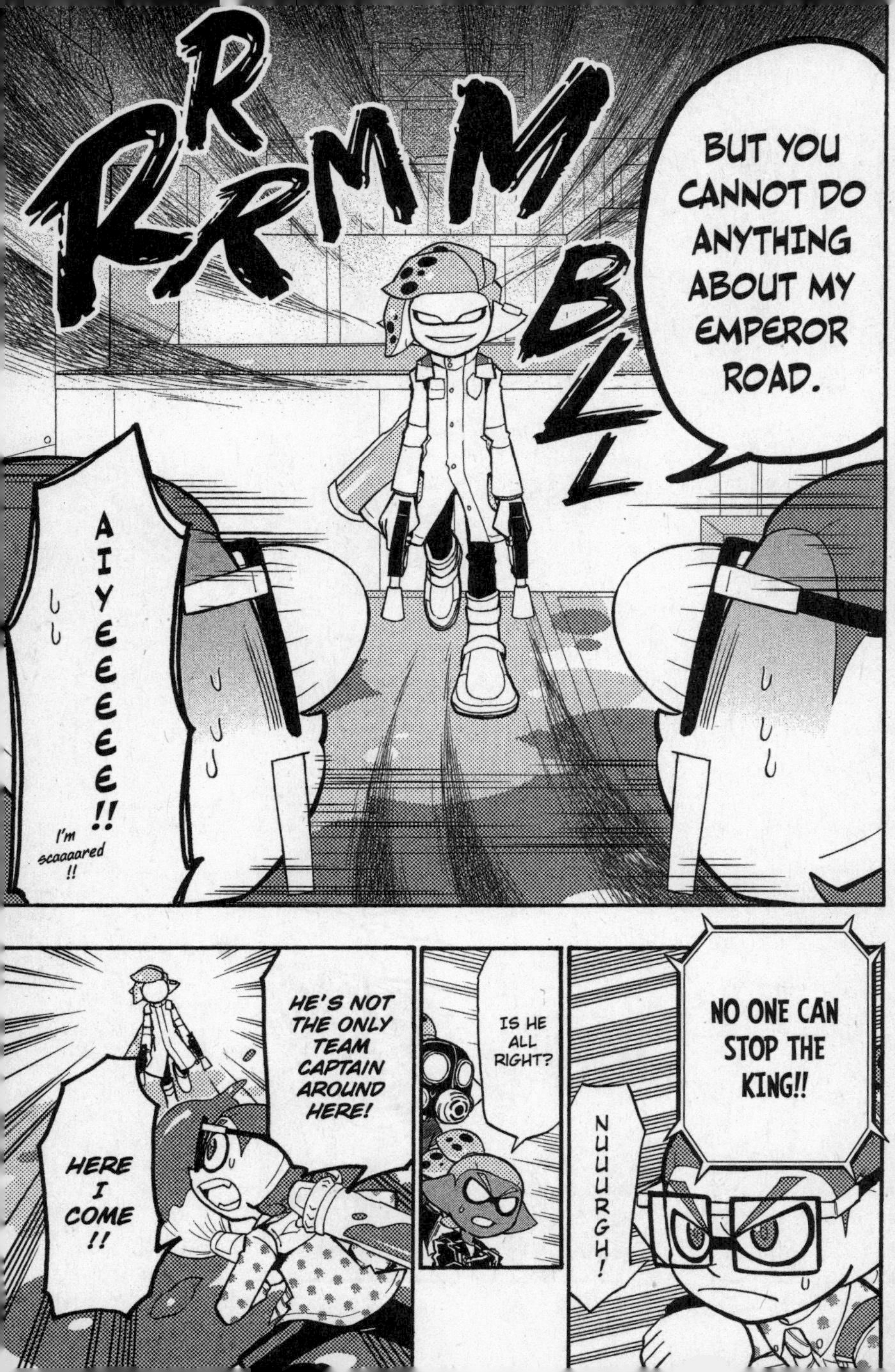

BUT YOU CANNOT DO ANYTHING ABOUT MY EMPEROR ROAD.
RRRMMBLL
AIYEEEEEE!!
I'm scaaaared !!
NO ONE CAN STOP THE KING!!
NUUURGH!
IS HE ALL RIGHT?
HE'S NOT THE ONLY TEAM CAPTAIN AROUND HERE!
HERE I COME!!

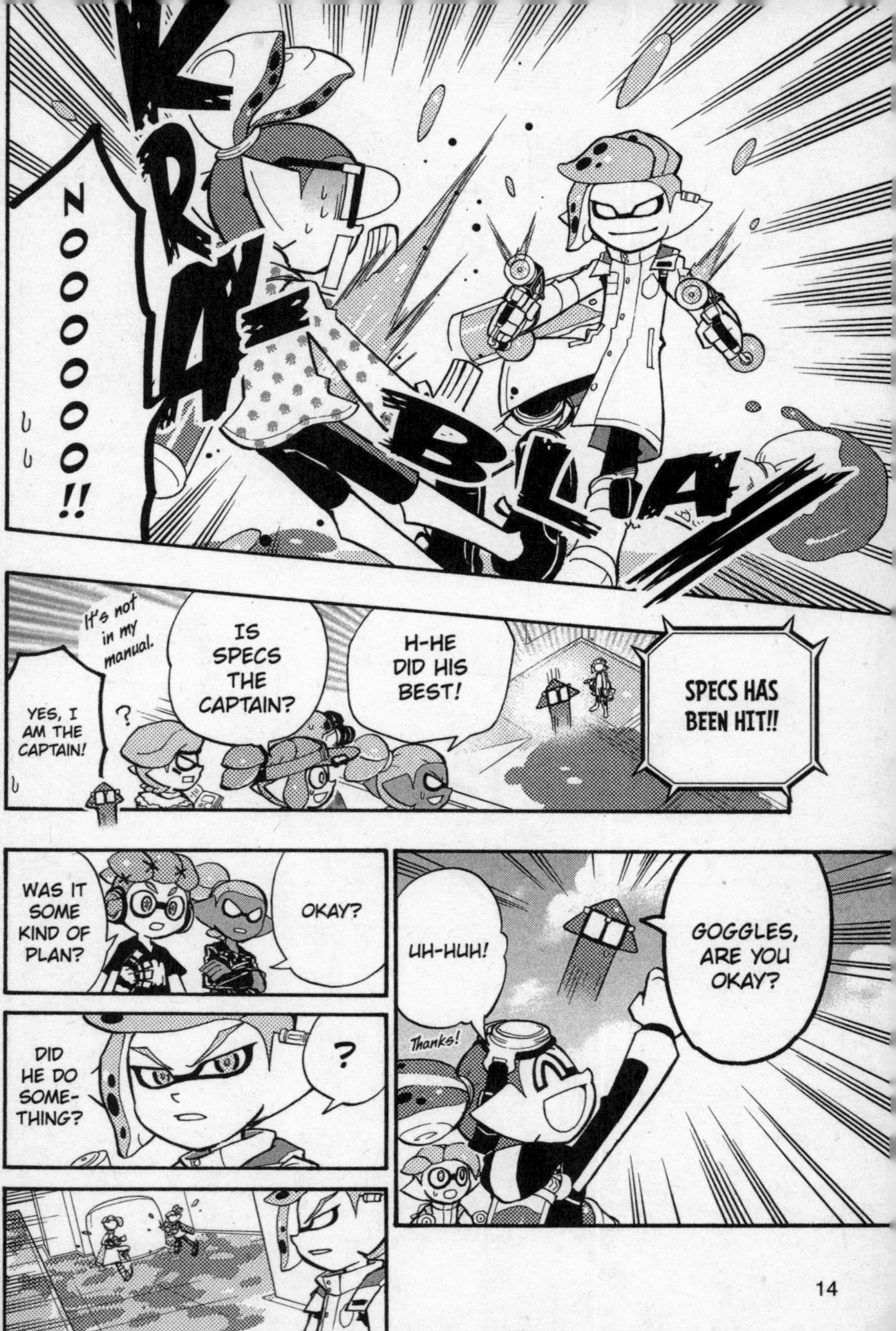
NOOOOOOOO!!
SPECS HAS BEEN HIT!!
H-HE DID HIS BEST!
IS SPECS THE CAPTAIN?
It's not in my manual.
YES, I AM THE CAPTAIN!
?
GOGGLES, ARE YOU OKAY?
UH-HUH!
Thanks!
OKAY?
WAS IT SOME KIND OF PLAN?
?
DID HE DO SOMETHING?

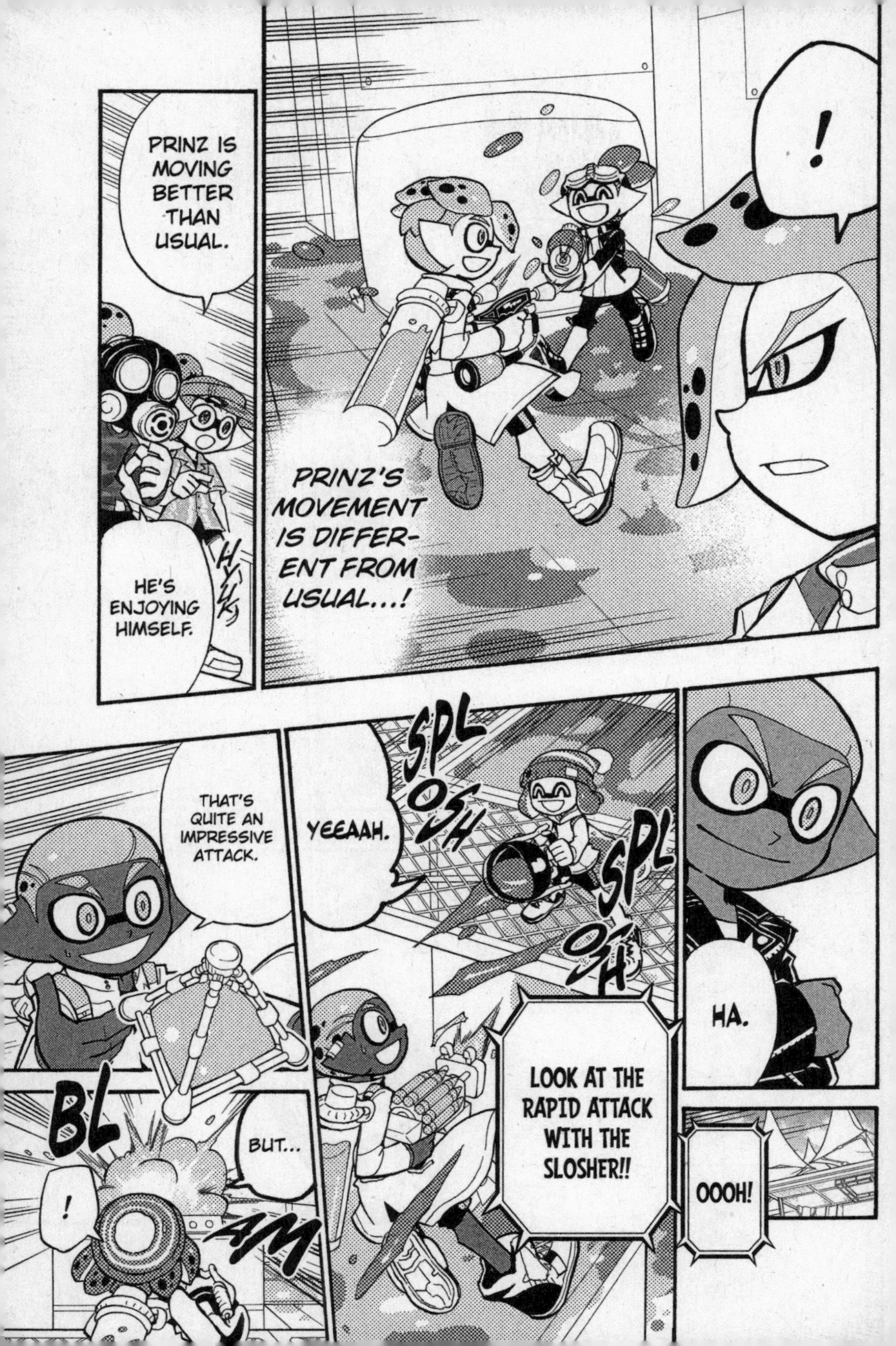
!
PRINZ'S MOVEMENT IS DIFFERENT FROM USUAL...!
PRINZ IS MOVING BETTER THAN USUAL.
HYUK
HE'S ENJOYING HIMSELF.
HA.
OOOH!
SPLOOSH
YEEAAH.
SPLOOSH
LOOK AT THE RAPID ATTACK WITH THE SLOSHER!!
THAT'S QUITE AN IMPRESSIVE ATTACK.
BUT...
BLAM
!

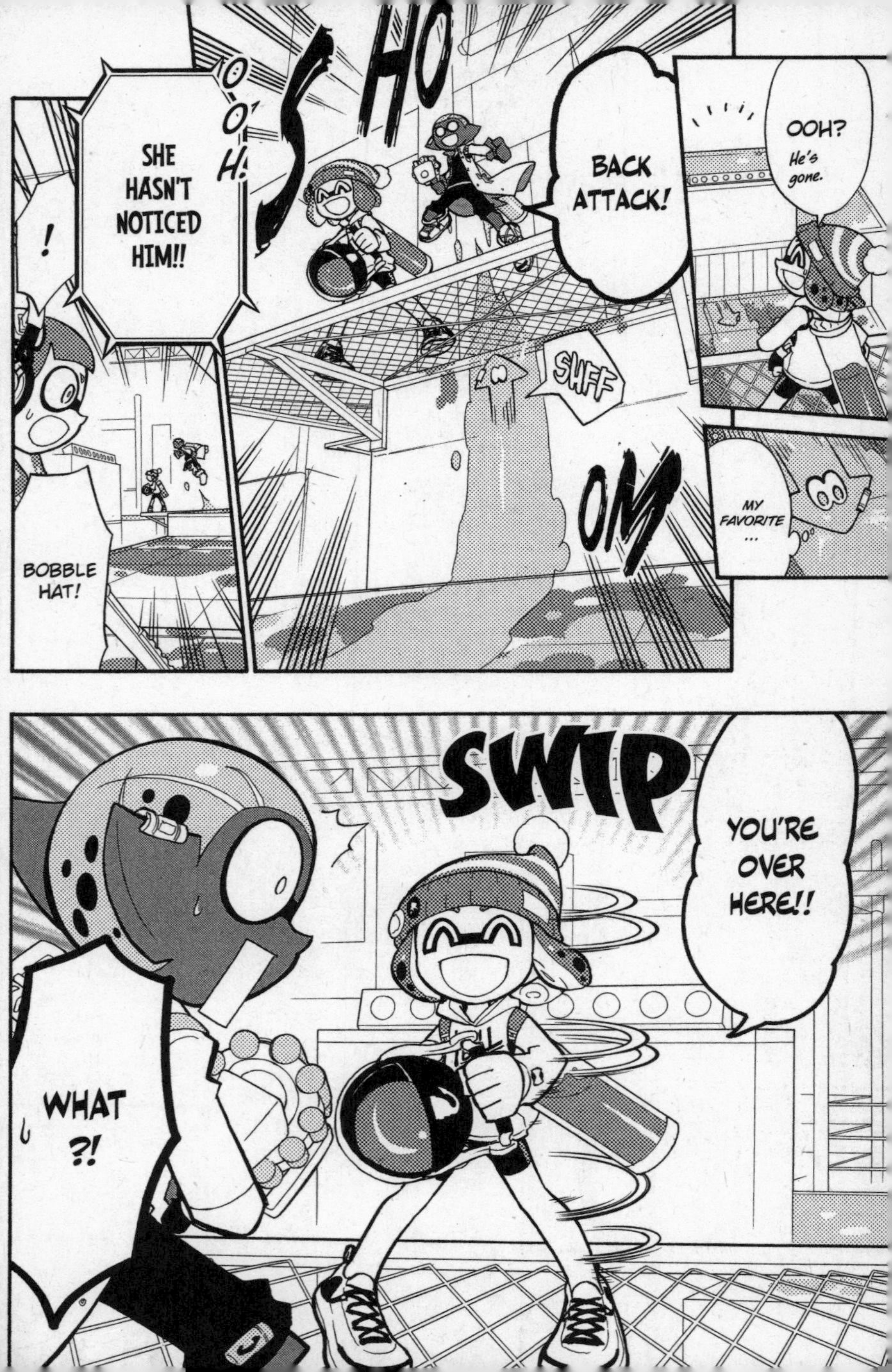

OOH?
He's gone.
MY FAVORITE ...
BACK ATTACK!
SHO
OM
SUFF
OOOH!
SHE HASN'T NOTICED HIM!!
!
BOBBLE HAT!
SWIP
YOU'RE OVER HERE!!
WHAT ?!

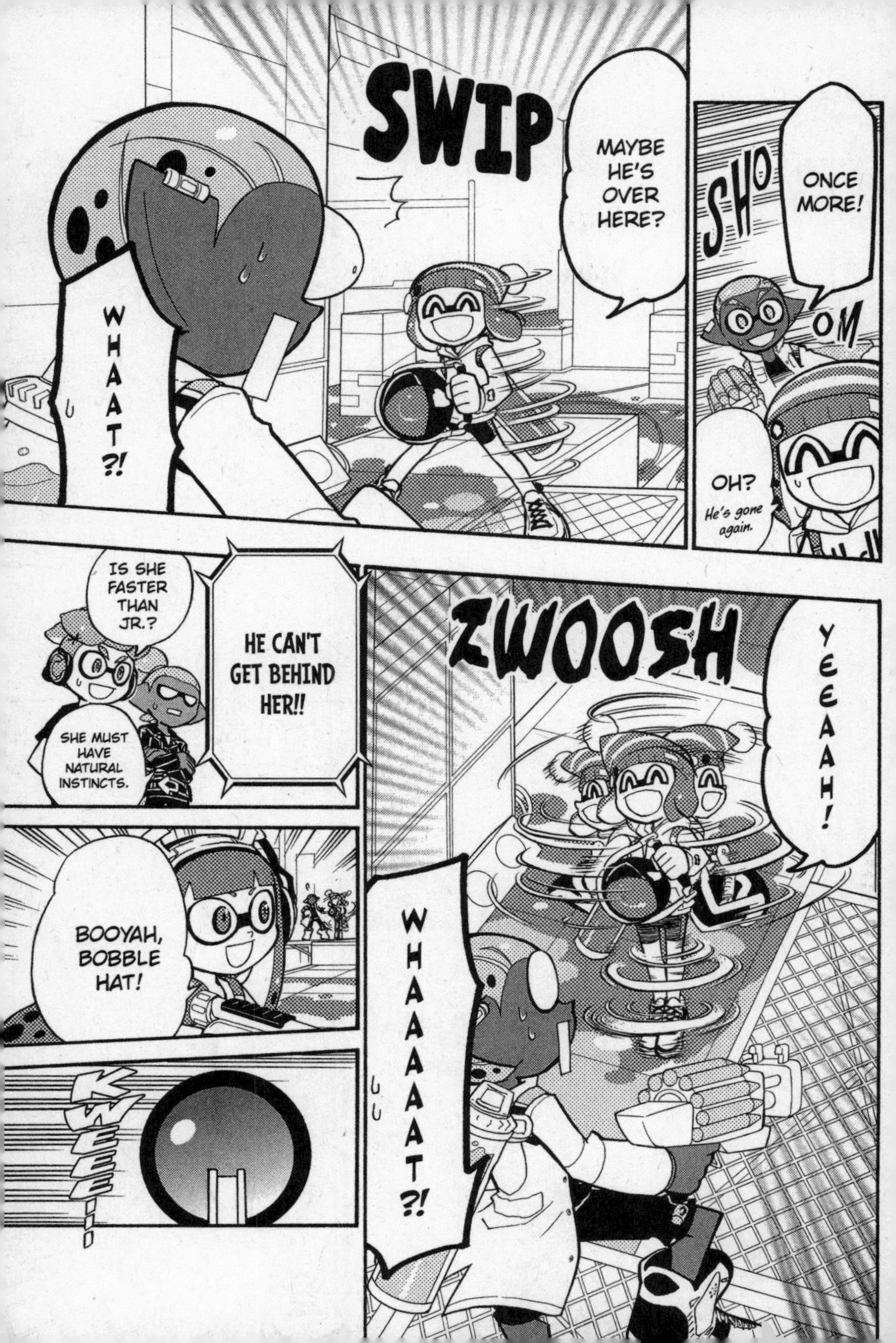
ONCE MORE!
SHOOM
OH?
He's gone again.
SWIP
MAYBE HE'S OVER HERE?
WHAAT?!
ZWOOSH
YEEAAH!
WHAAAAAAT?!
HE CAN'T GET BEHIND HER!!
IS SHE FASTER THAN JR.?
SHE MUST HAVE NATURAL INSTINCTS.
BOOYAH, BOBBLE HAT!
KWEEEE

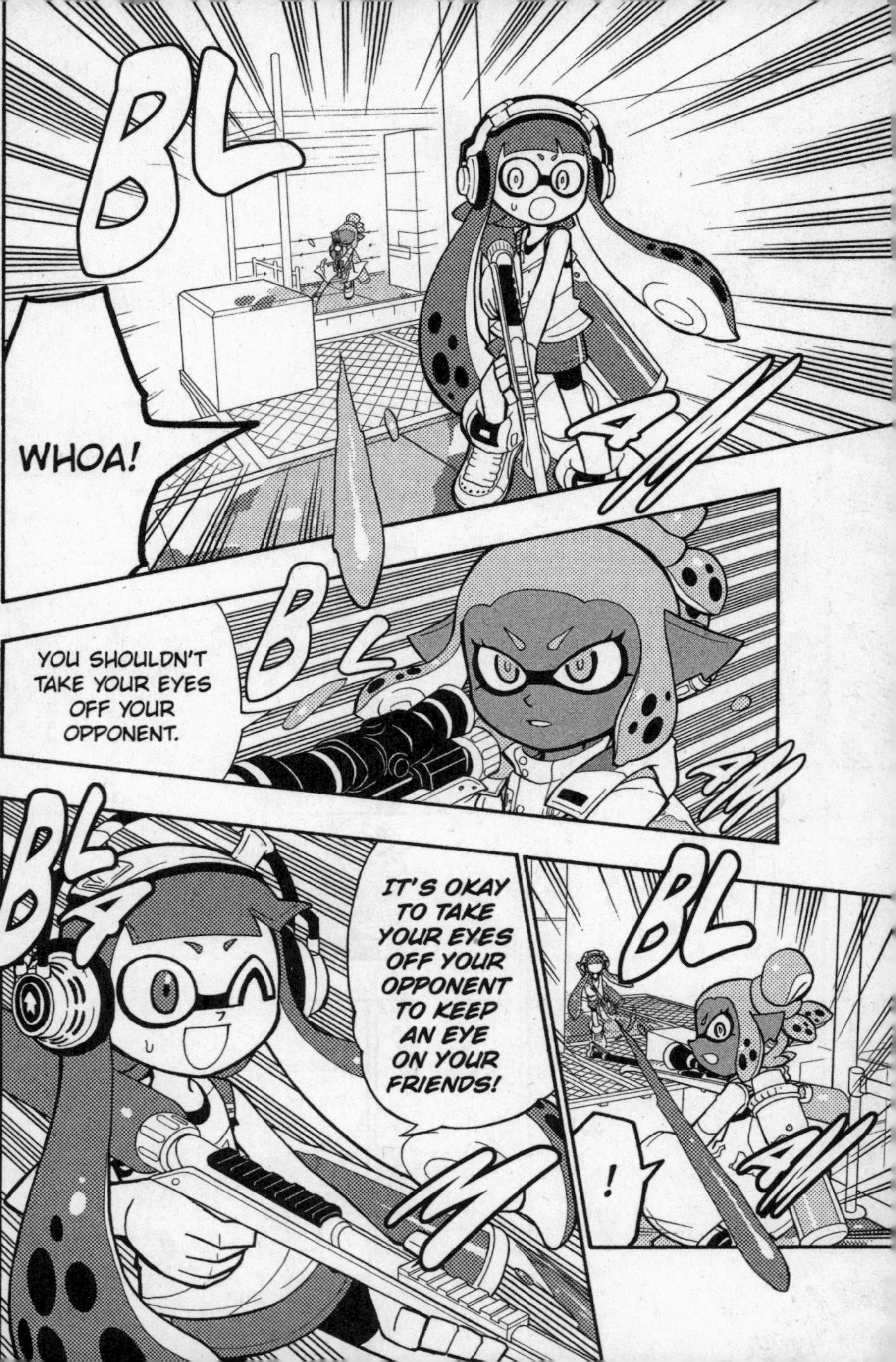
BL
AM
WHOA!
BL
AM
YOU SHOULDN'T TAKE YOUR EYES OFF YOUR OPPONENT.
BL
AM
!
BLA
M
IT'S OKAY TO TAKE YOUR EYES OFF YOUR OPPONENT TO KEEP AN EYE ON YOUR FRIENDS!

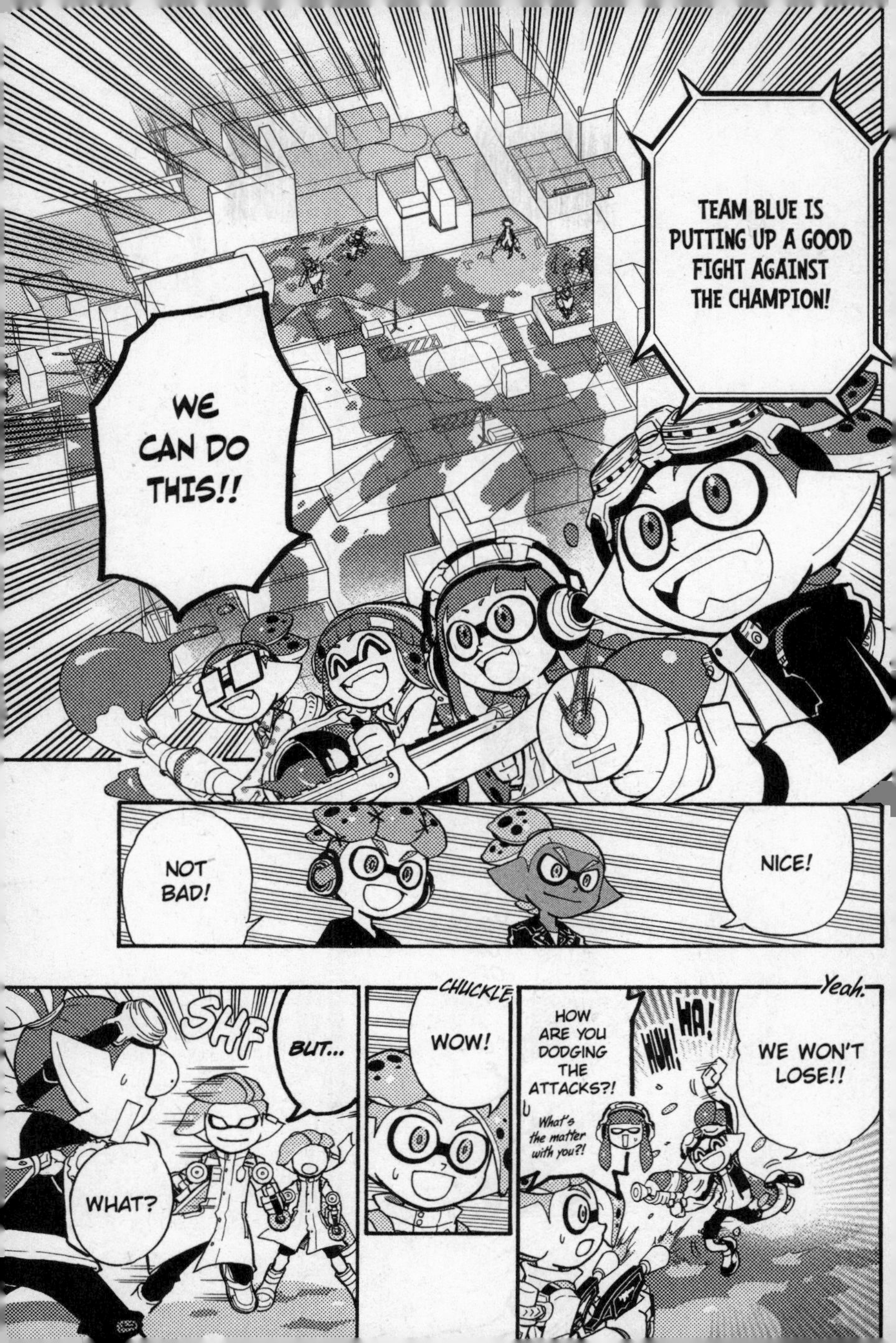
TEAM BLUE IS PUTTING UP A GOOD FIGHT AGAINST THE CHAMPION!
WE CAN DO THIS!!
NICE!
NOT BAD!
Yeah.
WE WON'T LOSE!!
HUH! HA!
HOW ARE YOU DODGING THE ATTACKS?!
What's the matter with you?!
CHUCKLE
WOW!
SHF
BUT...
WHAT?

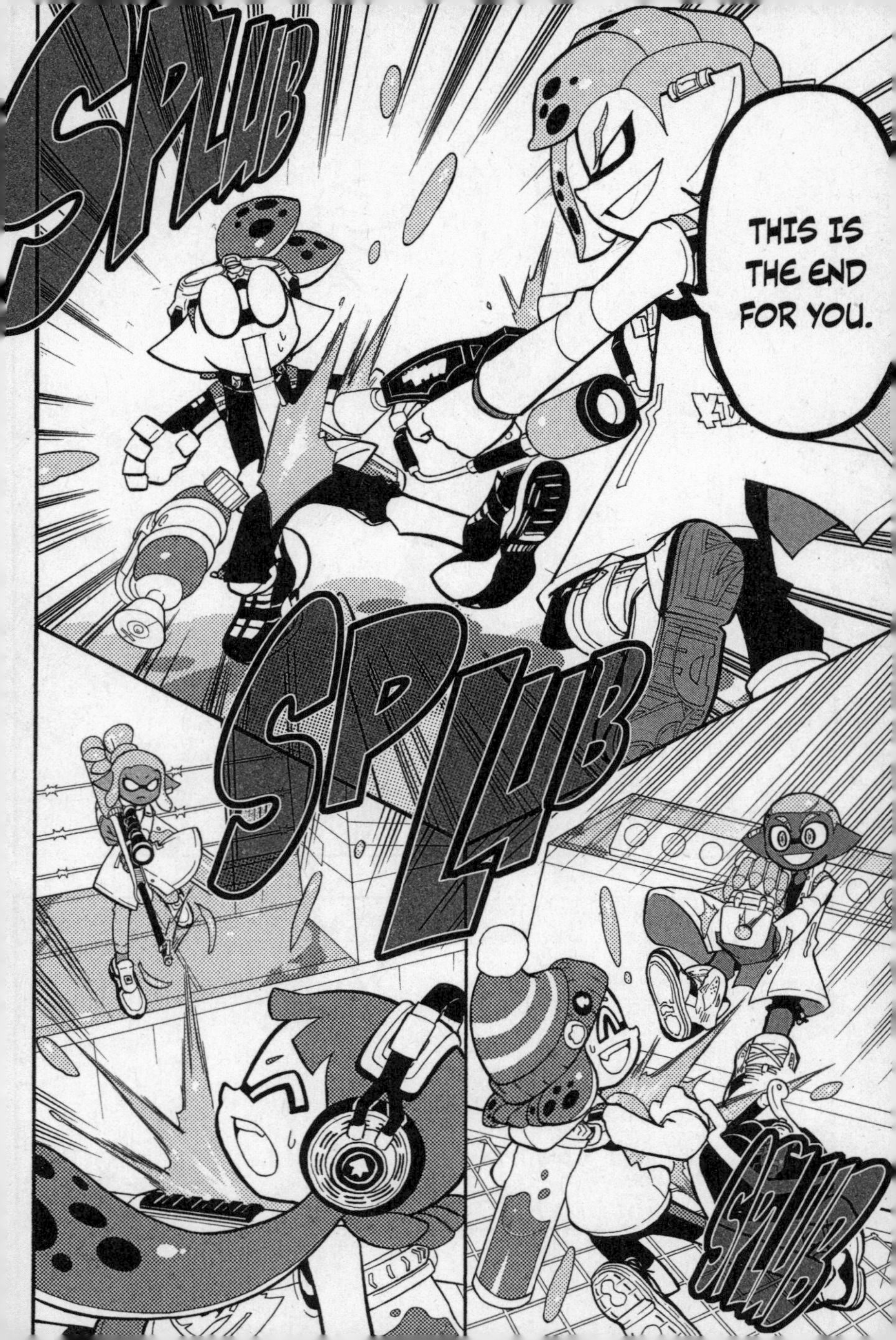
THIS IS THE END FOR YOU.
SPLUB
SPLUB
SPLUB

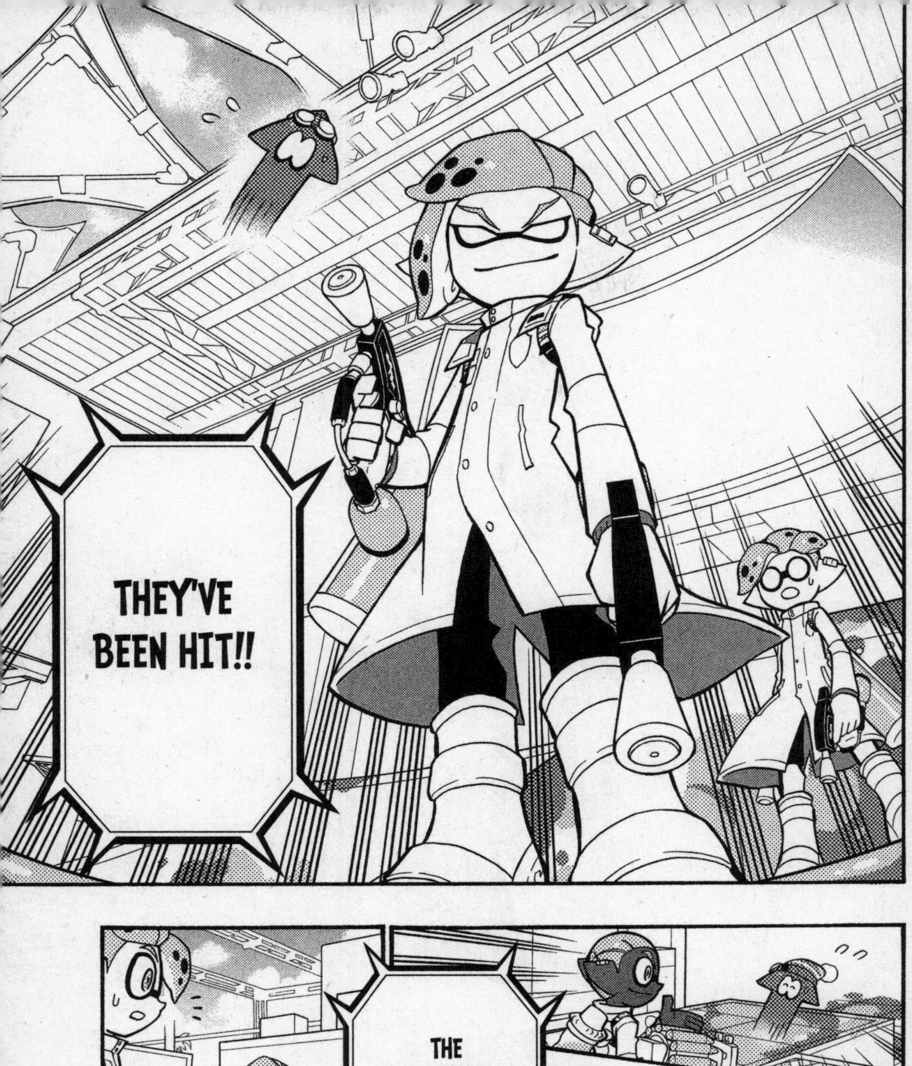
THEY'VE BEEN HIT!!

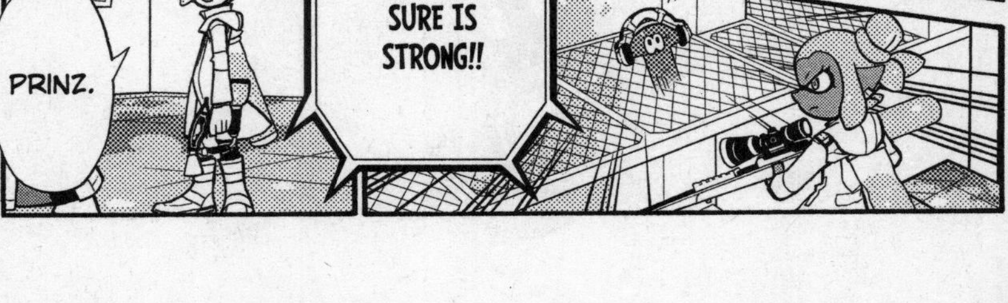
THE CHAMPION SURE IS STRONG!!
PRINZ.

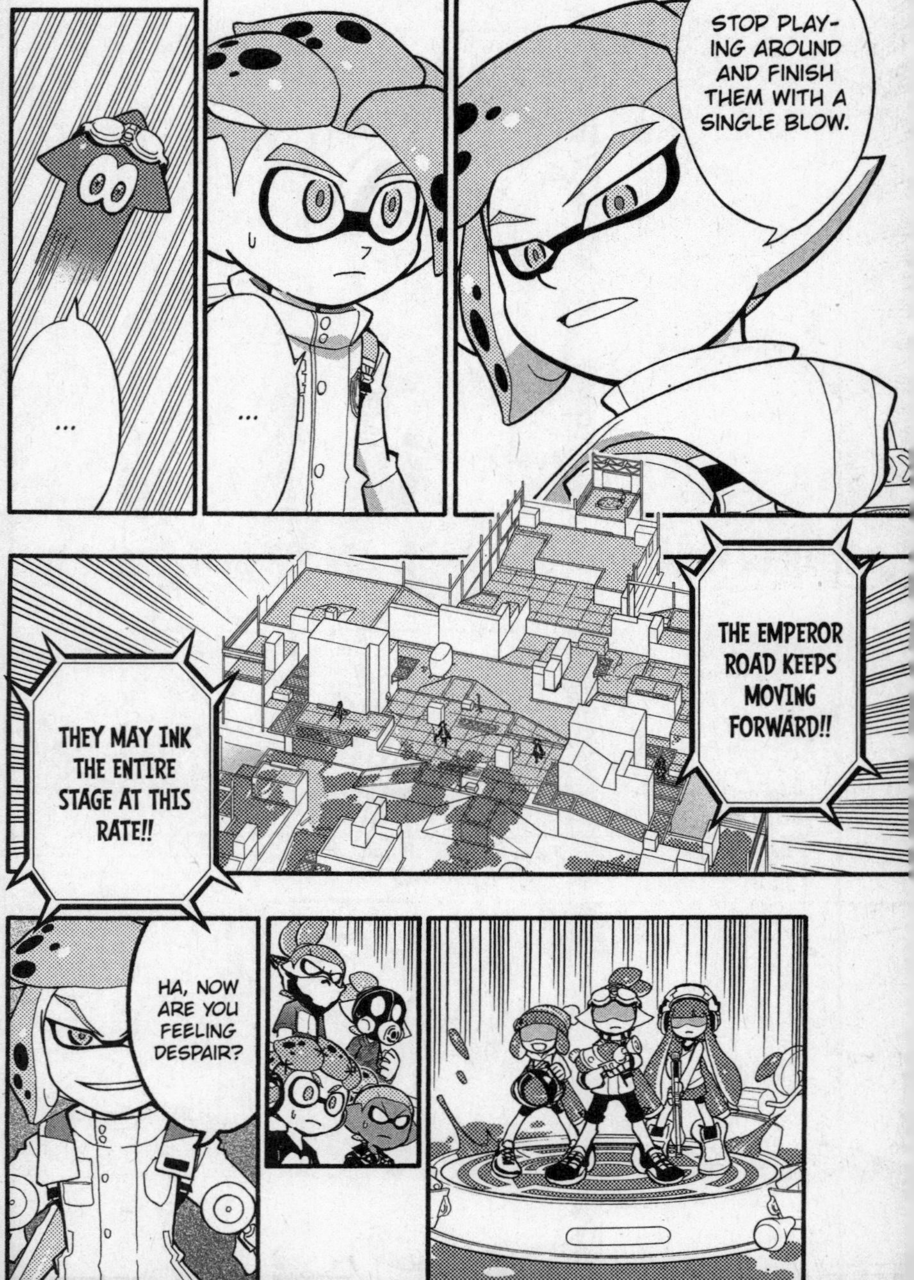
STOP PLAYING AROUND AND FINISH THEM WITH A SINGLE BLOW.
...
...
THE EMPEROR ROAD KEEPS MOVING FORWARD!!
THEY MAY INK THE ENTIRE STAGE AT THIS RATE!!
HA, NOW ARE YOU FEELING DESPAIR?

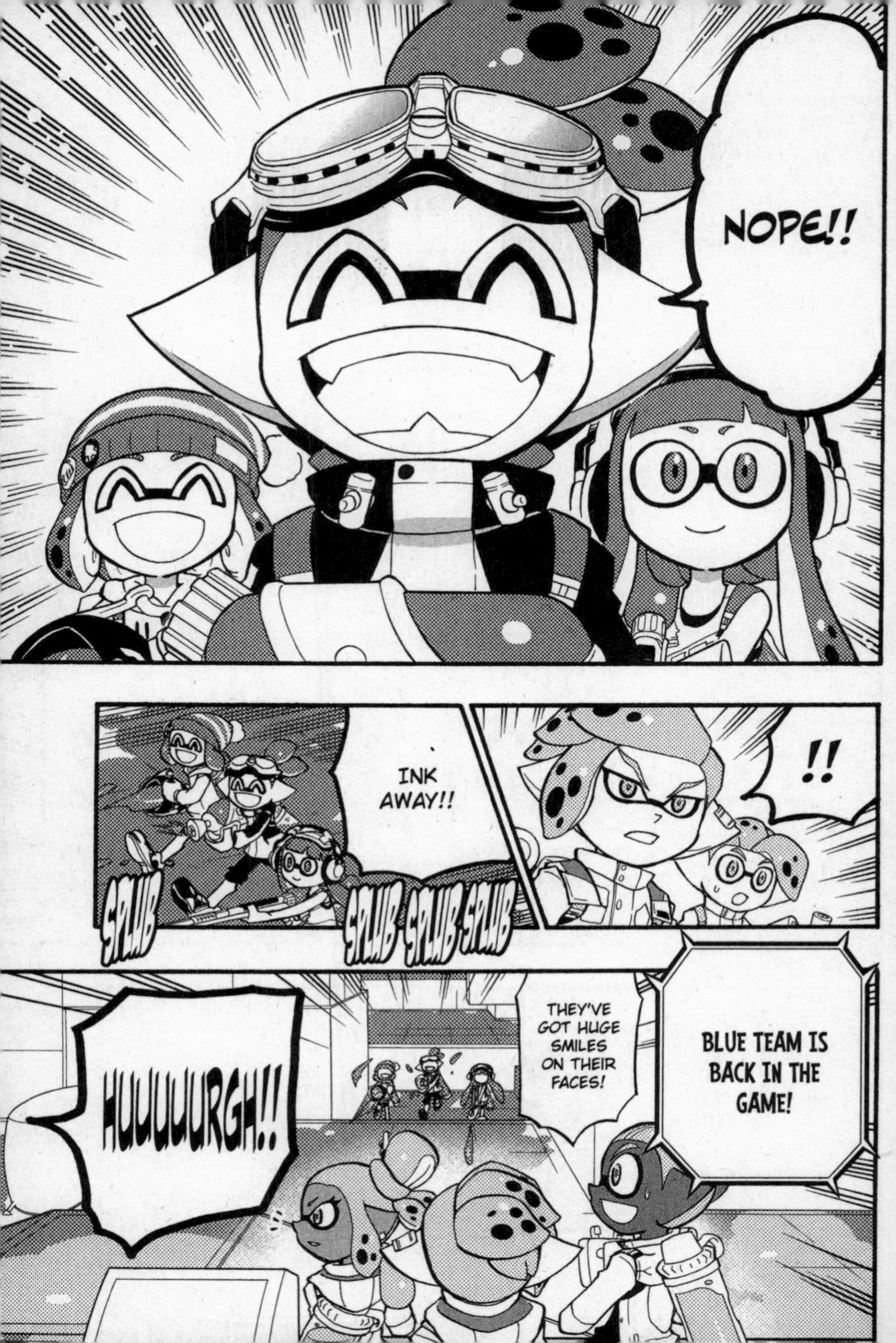
NOPE!!
!!
INK AWAY!!
SPLUB
SPLUB SPLUB SPLUB
BLUE TEAM IS BACK IN THE GAME!
THEY'VE GOT HUGE SMILES ON THEIR FACES!
HUUUUURGH!!

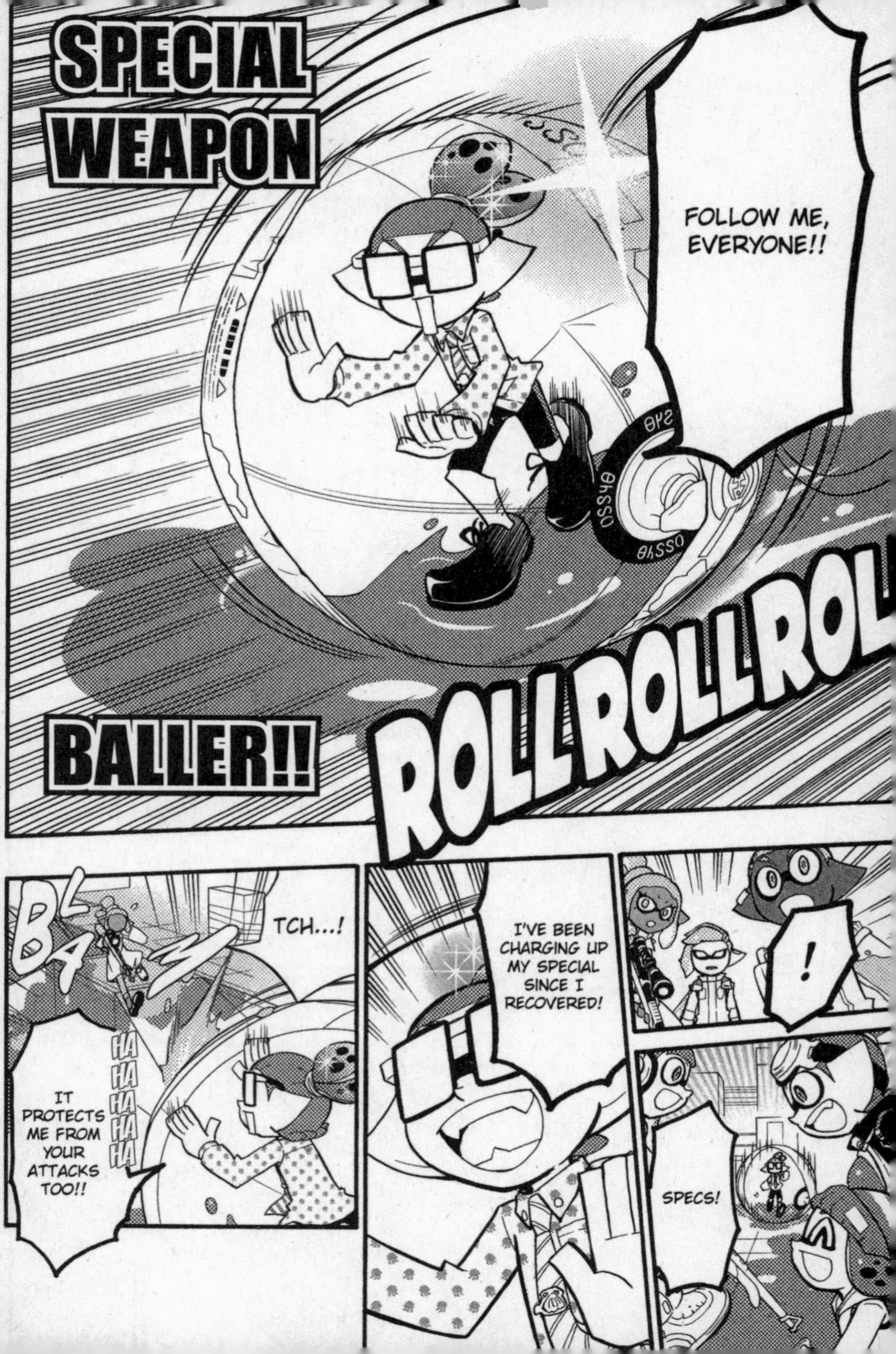
FOLLOW ME, EVERYONE!!
SPECIAL WEAPON
BALLER!!
ROLL ROLL ROL
!
SPECS!
I'VE BEEN CHARGING UP MY SPECIAL SINCE I RECOVERED!
TCH...!
BLAM
HA HA HA HA HA
IT PROTECTS ME FROM YOUR ATTACKS TOO!!

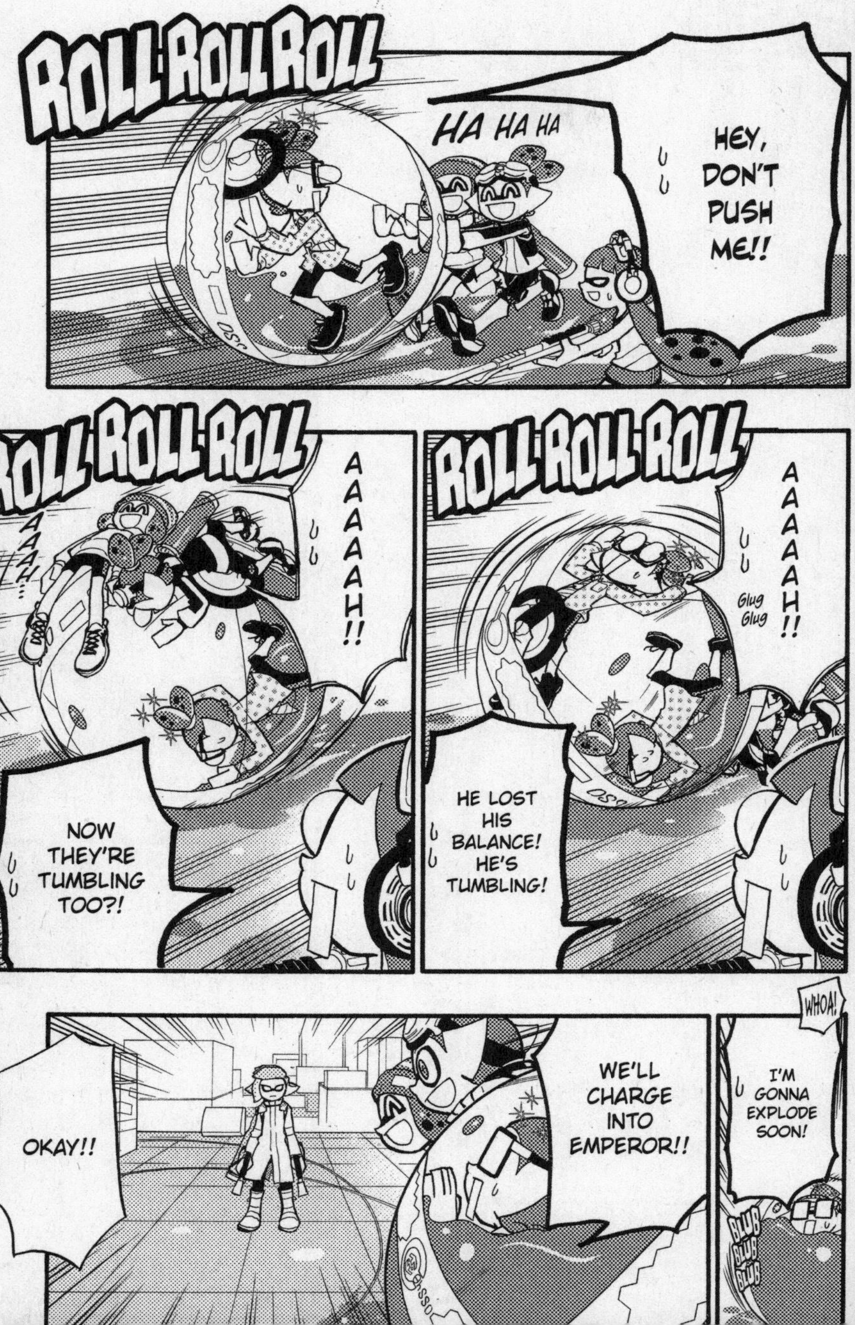

HEY, DON'T PUSH ME!!
HA HA HA
ROLL ROLL ROLL
ROLL ROLL ROLL
AAAAAAH!!
Glug Glug
HE LOST HIS BALANCE! HE'S TUMBLING!
ROLL ROLL ROLL
AAAAAH!!
AAAH...
NOW THEY'RE TUMBLING TOO?!
WHOA!
I'M GONNA EXPLODE SOON!
BLUB BLUB BLUB
WE'LL CHARGE INTO EMPEROR!!
OKAY!!

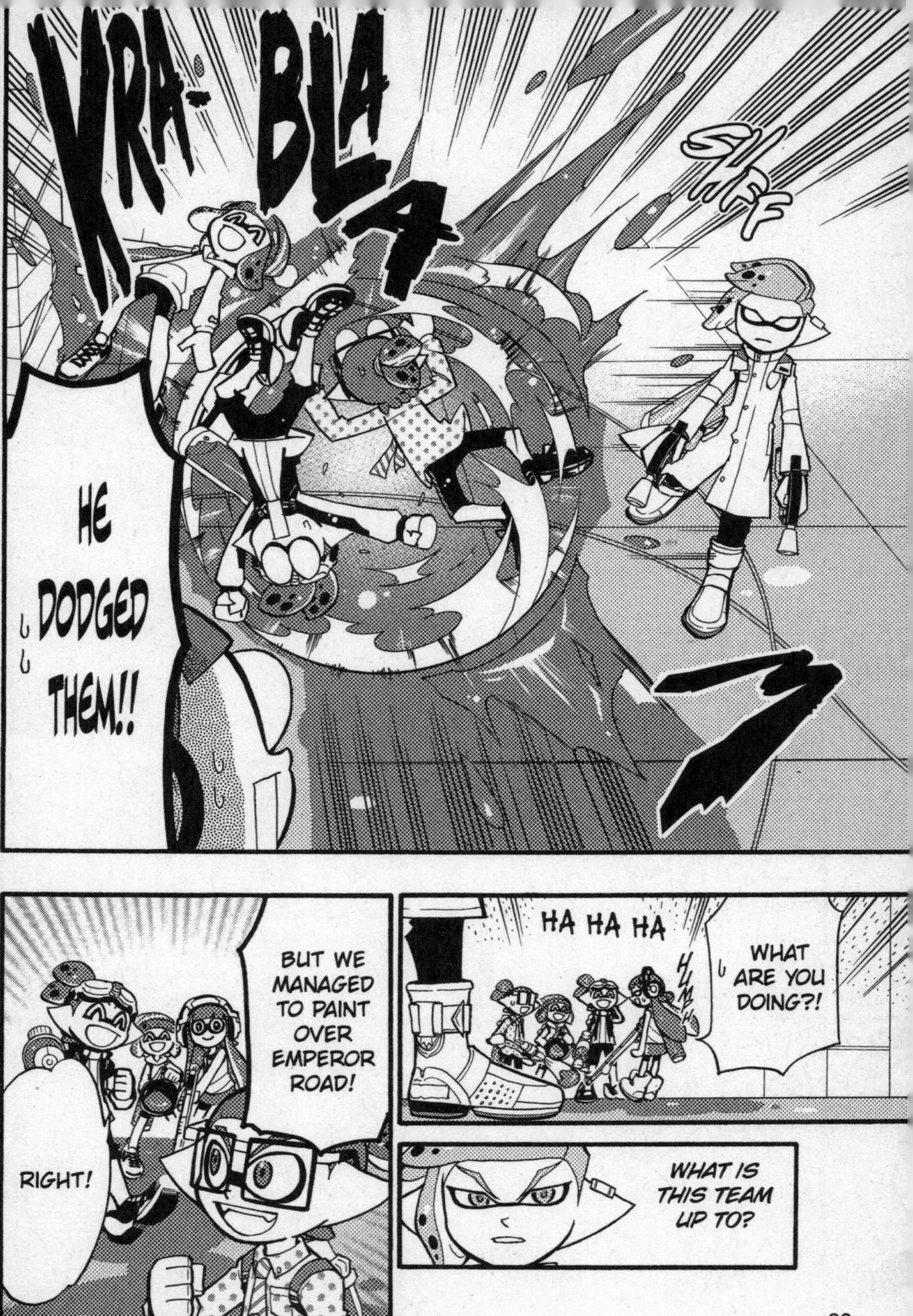
SHFF
KRA-BLA
HE DODGED THEM!!
WHAT ARE YOU DOING?!
HUMPH
HA HA HA
WHAT IS THIS TEAM UP TO?
BUT WE MANAGED TO PAINT OVER EMPEROR ROAD!
RIGHT!

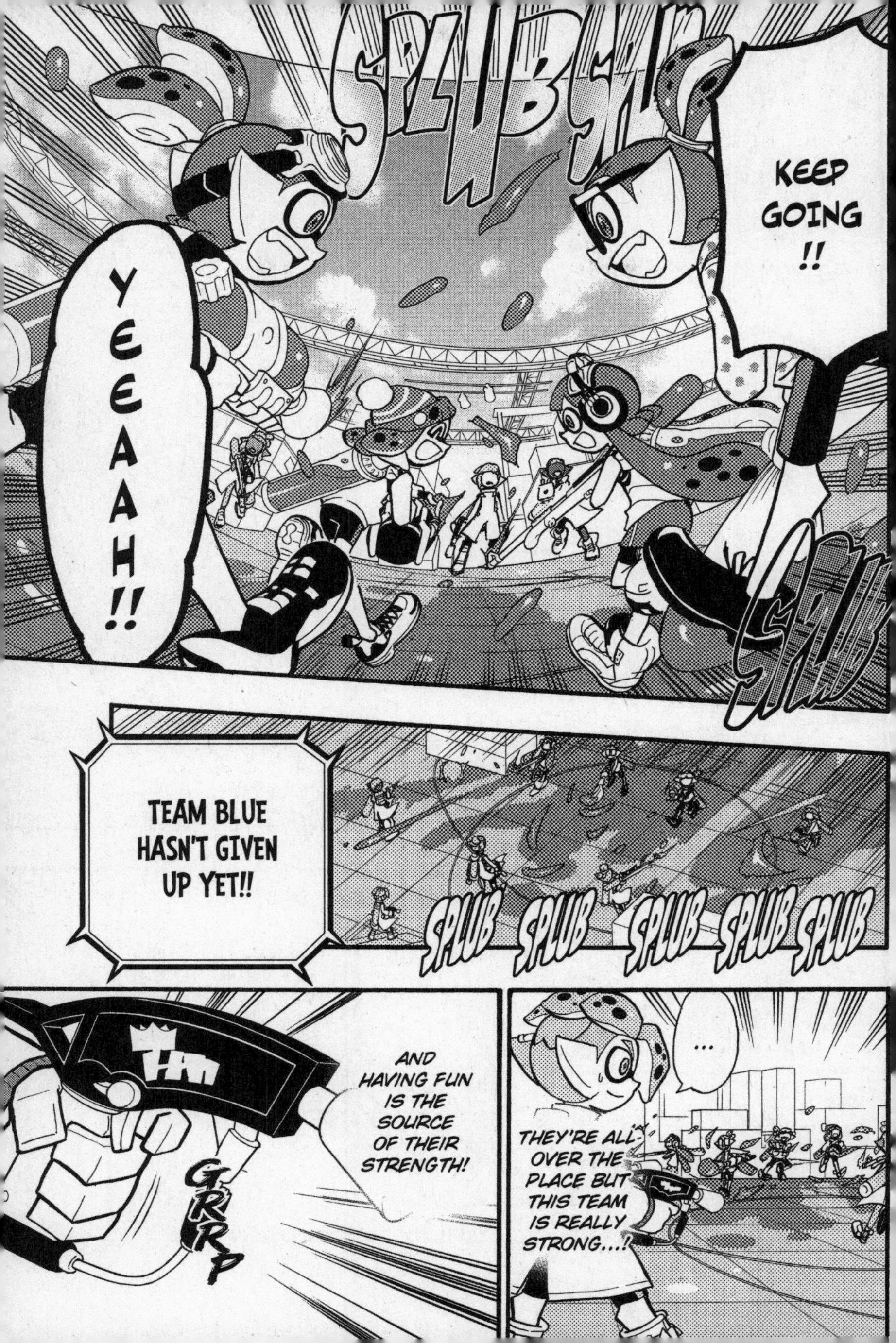
SPLUBGLUB
KEEP GOING!!
YEEAAH!!
TEAM BLUE HASN'T GIVEN UP YET!!
SPLUB SPLUB SPLUB SPLUB SPLUB
...
THEY'RE ALL OVER THE PLACE BUT THIS TEAM IS REALLY STRONG...!
AND HAVING FUN IS THE SOURCE OF THEIR STRENGTH!
GRRP

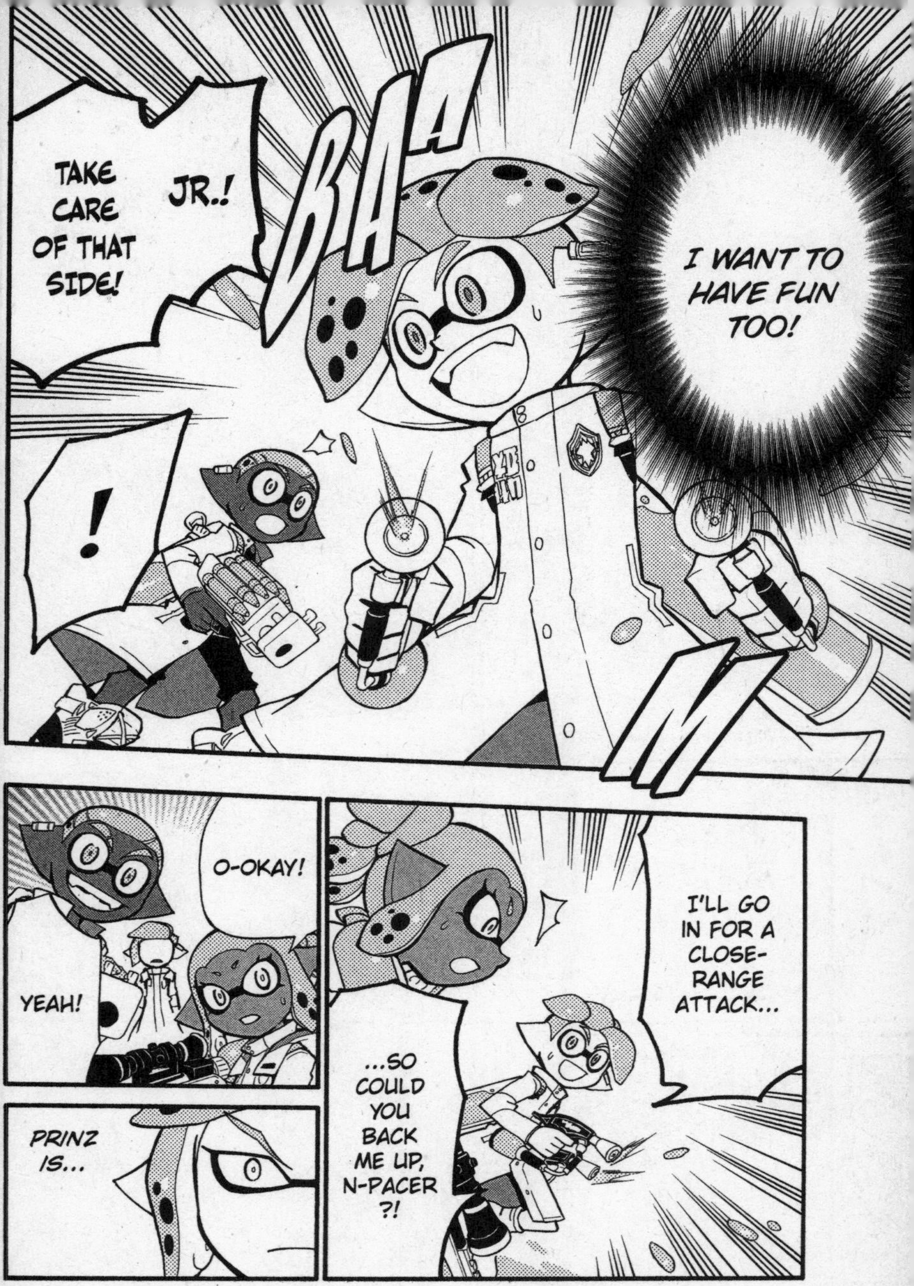
I WANT TO HAVE FUN TOO!
BAAM
JR.!
TAKE CARE OF THAT SIDE!
!
I'LL GO IN FOR A CLOSE-RANGE ATTACK...
...SO COULD YOU BACK ME UP, N-PACER?!
O-OKAY!
YEAH!
PRINZ IS...

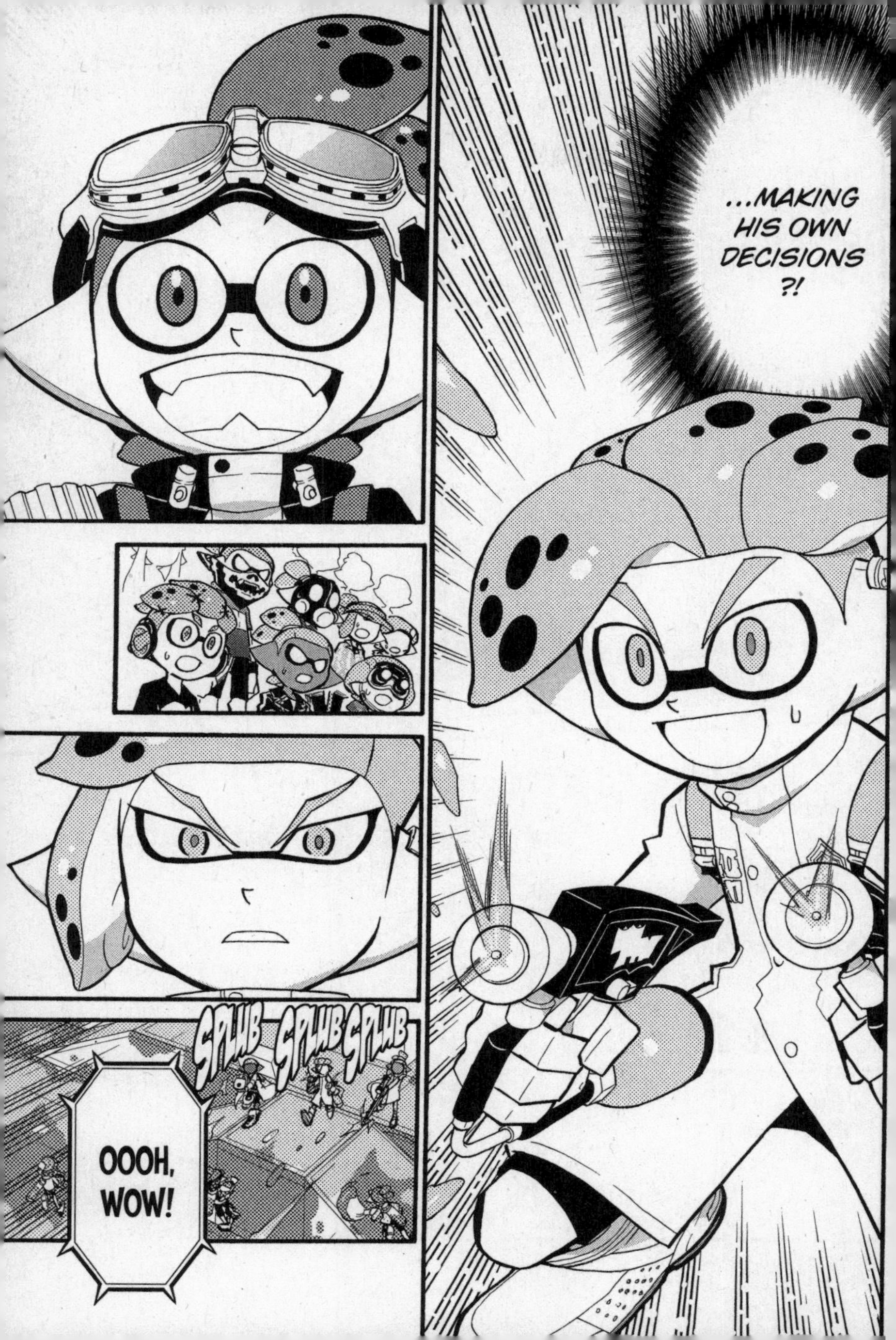
...MAKING HIS OWN DECISIONS ?!
SPLUB SPLUB SPLUB
OOOH, WOW!

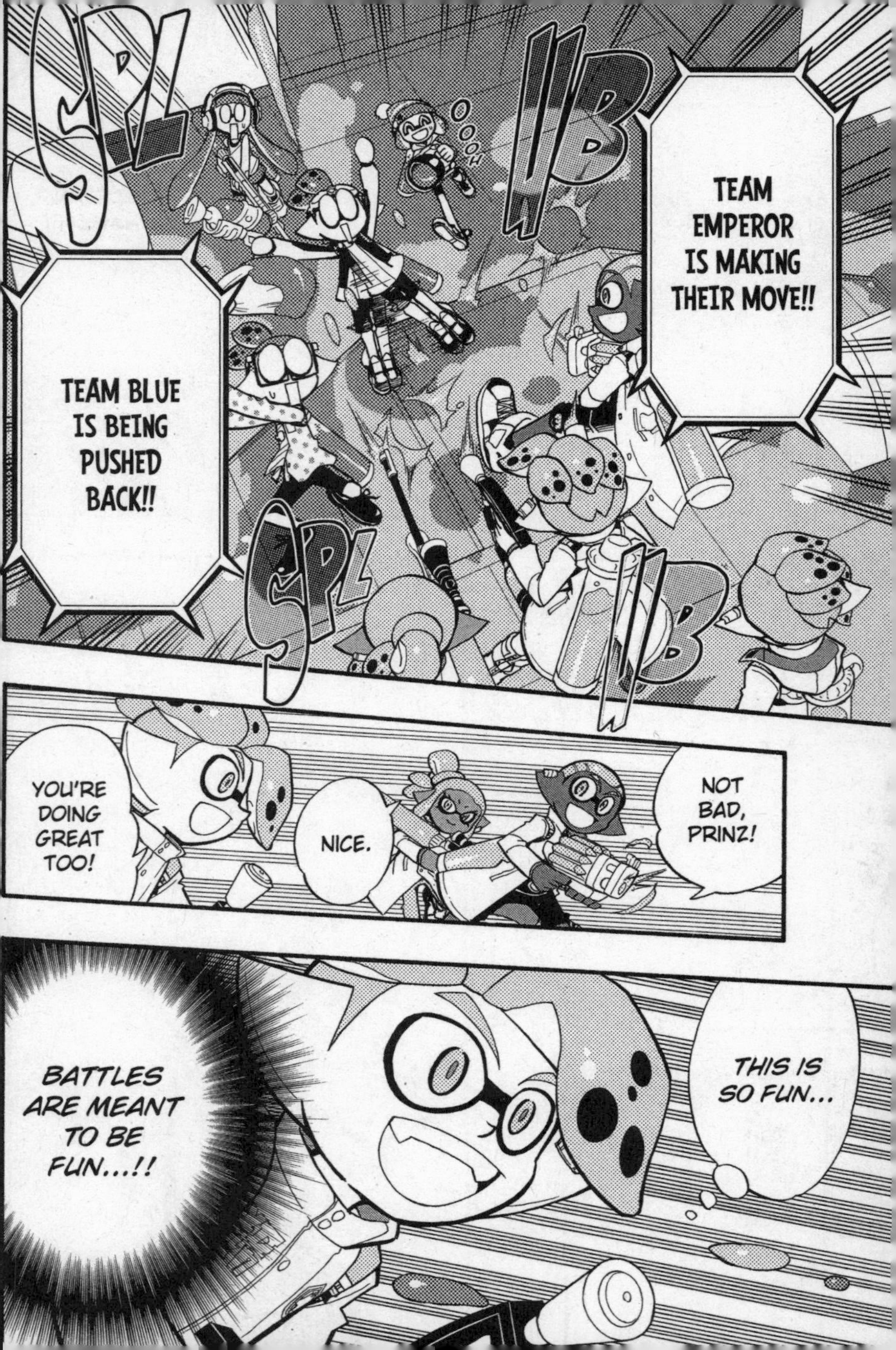
TEAM EMPEROR IS MAKING THEIR MOVE!!
TEAM BLUE IS BEING PUSHED BACK!!
NOT BAD, PRINZ!
NICE.
YOU'RE DOING GREAT TOO!
THIS IS SO FUN...
BATTLES ARE MEANT TO BE FUN...!!

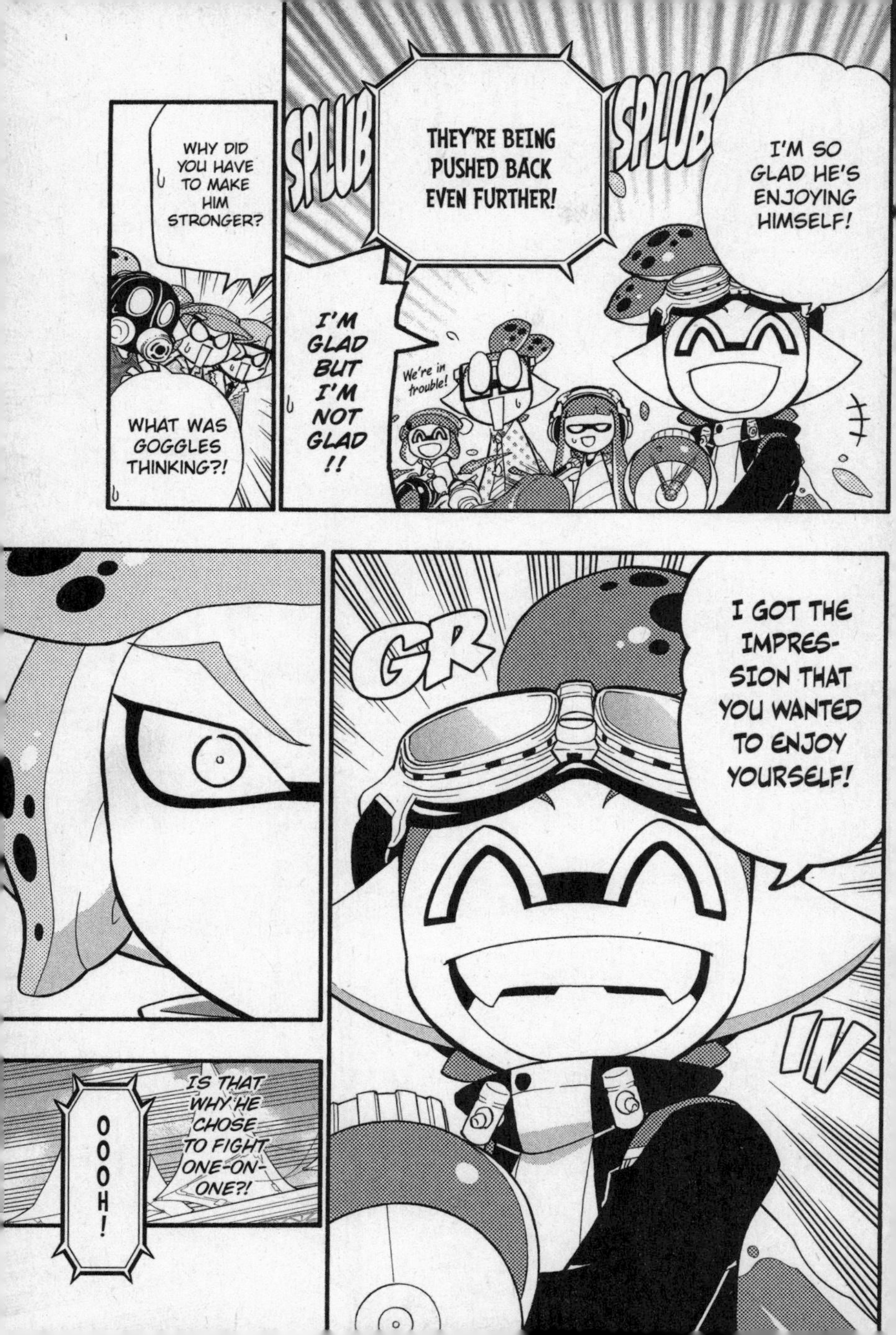
I'M SO GLAD HE'S ENJOYING HIMSELF!
SPLUB
THEY'RE BEING PUSHED BACK EVEN FURTHER!
SPLUB
I'M GLAD BUT I'M NOT GLAD!!
We're in trouble!
WHY DID YOU HAVE TO MAKE HIM STRONGER?
WHAT WAS GOGGLES THINKING?!
I GOT THE IMPRESSION THAT YOU WANTED TO ENJOY YOURSELF!
GR
IN
IS THAT WHY HE CHOSE TO FIGHT ONE-ON-ONE?!
OOOH!

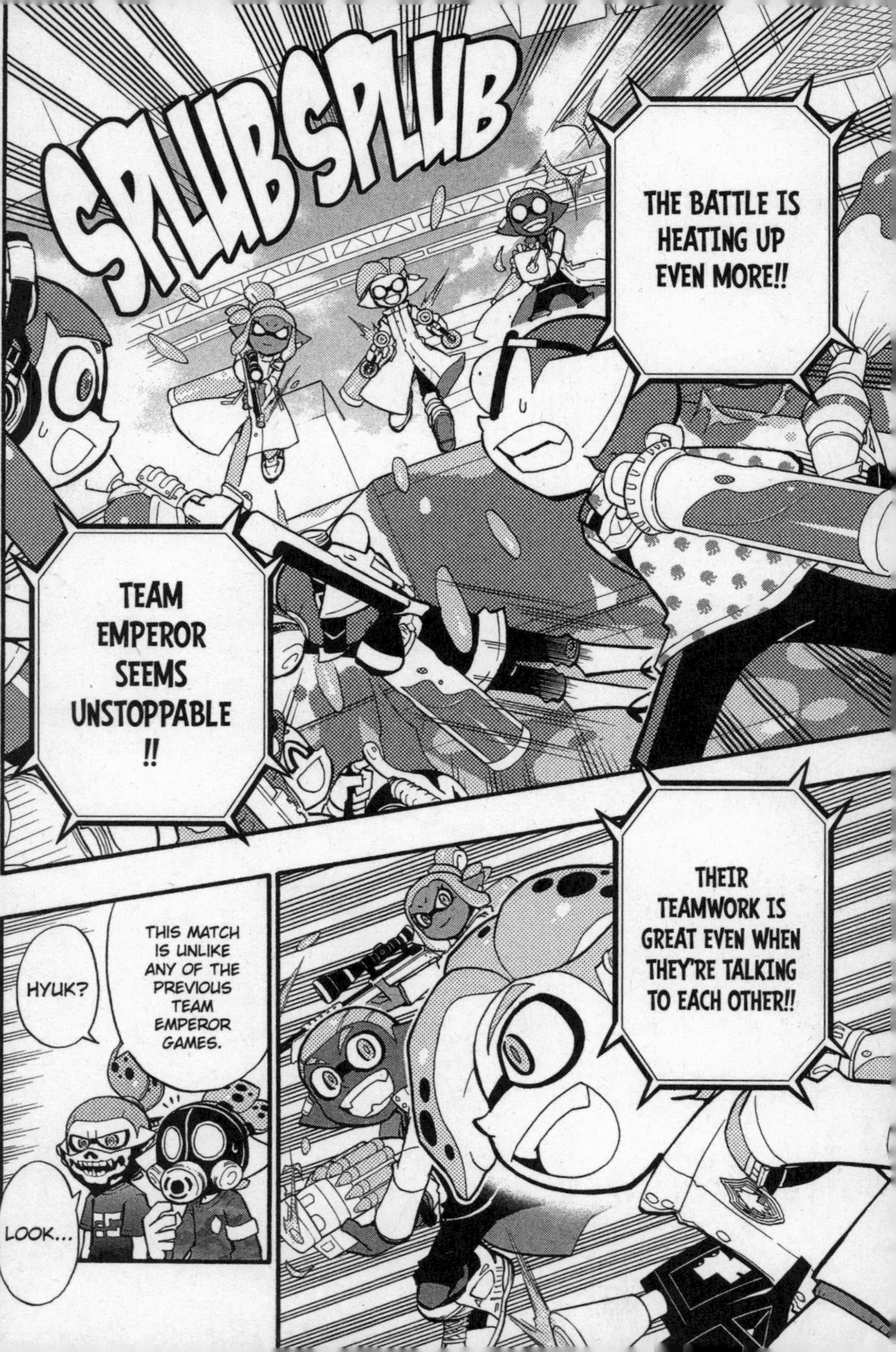
THE BATTLE IS HEATING UP EVEN MORE!!
SPLUB SPLUB
TEAM EMPEROR SEEMS UNSTOPPABLE!!
THEIR TEAMWORK IS GREAT EVEN WHEN THEY'RE TALKING TO EACH OTHER!!
THIS MATCH IS UNLIKE ANY OF THE PREVIOUS TEAM EMPEROR GAMES.
HYUK?
LOOK...

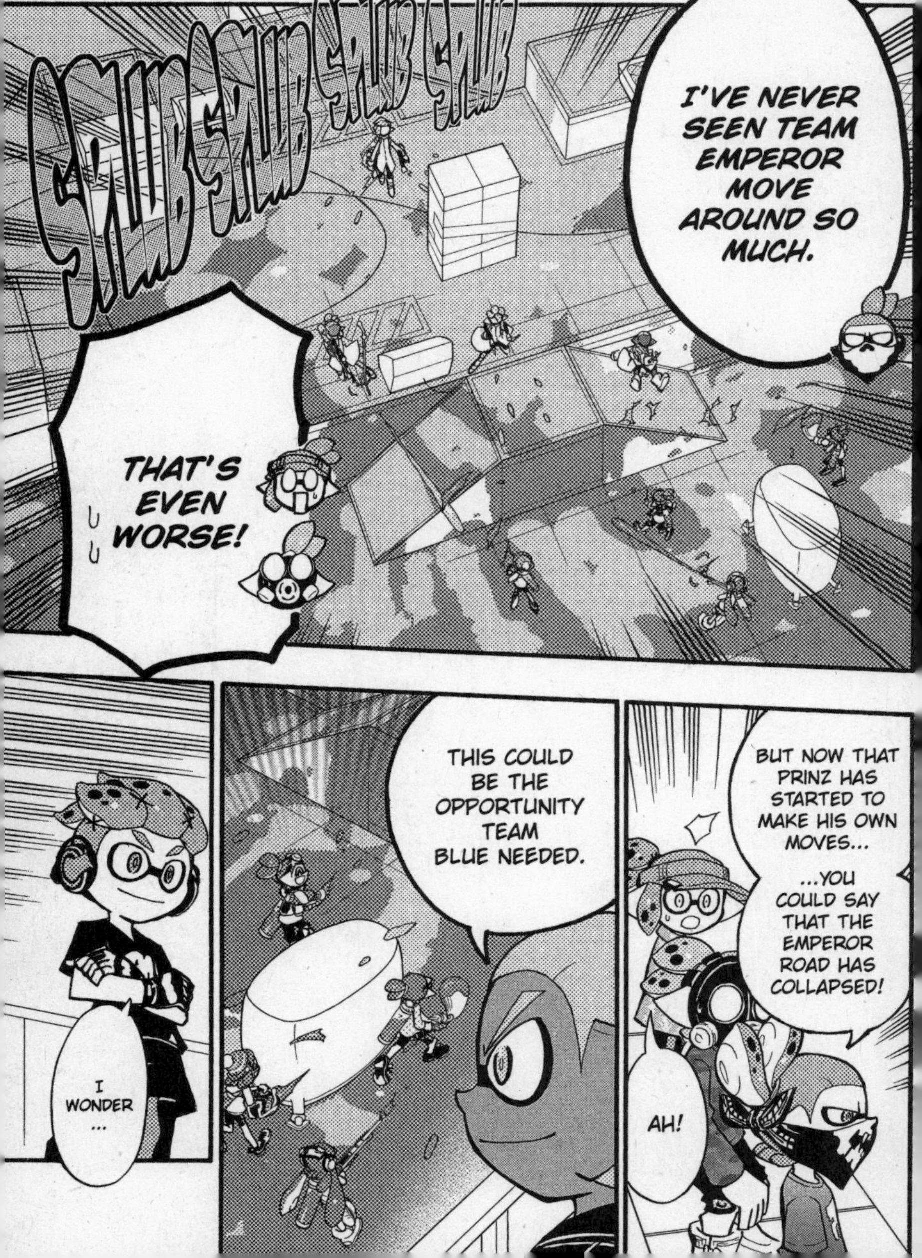
I'VE NEVER SEEN TEAM EMPEROR MOVE AROUND SO MUCH.
SPLUB SPLUB SPLUB SPLUB
THAT'S EVEN WORSE!
BUT NOW THAT PRINZ HAS STARTED TO MAKE HIS OWN MOVES...
...YOU COULD SAY THAT THE EMPEROR ROAD HAS COLLAPSED!
AH!
THIS COULD BE THE OPPORTUNITY TEAM BLUE NEEDED.
I WONDER...

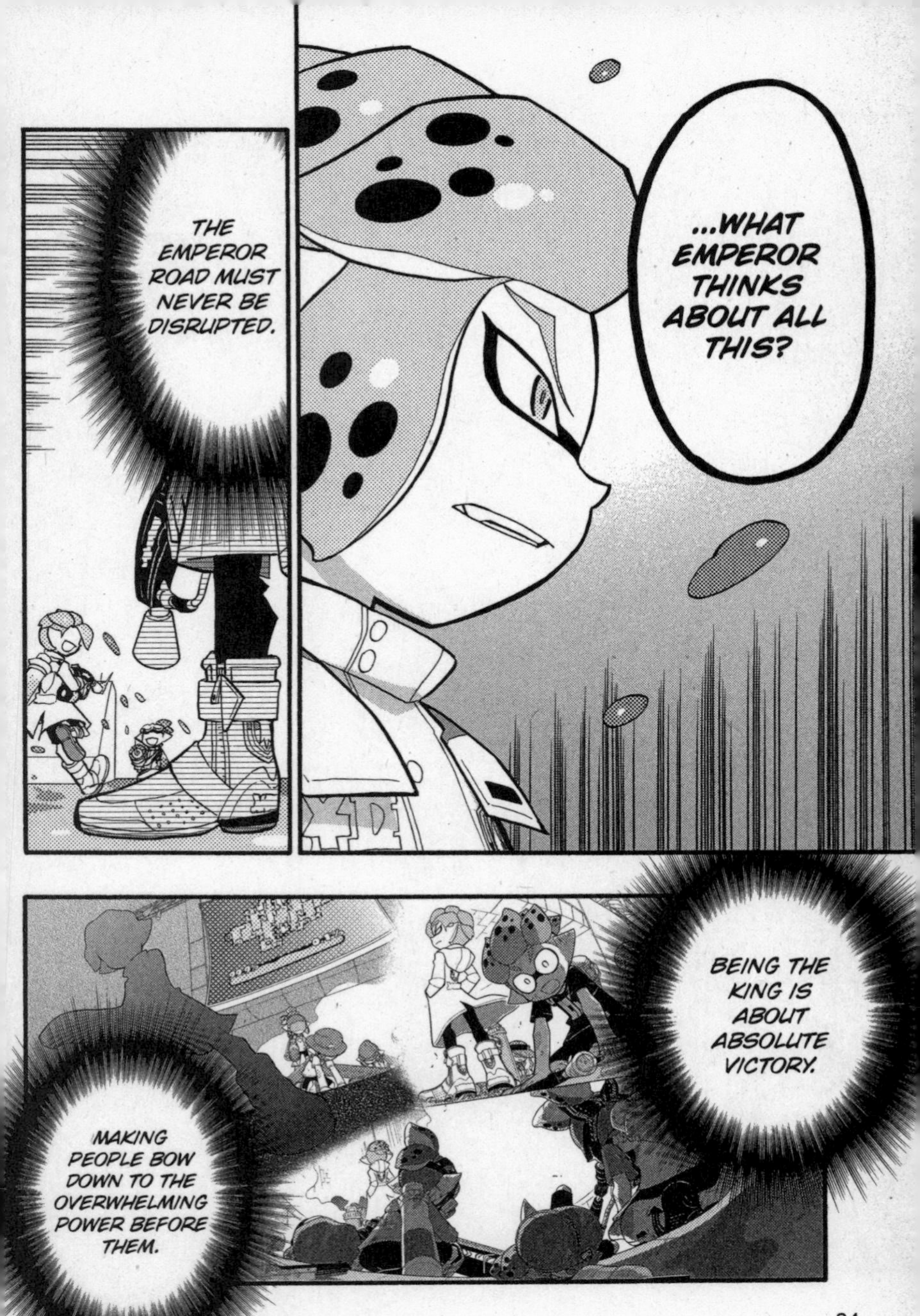
...WHAT EMPEROR THINKS ABOUT ALL THIS?
THE EMPEROR ROAD MUST NEVER BE DISRUPTED.
BEING THE KING IS ABOUT ABSOLUTE VICTORY.
MAKING PEOPLE BOW DOWN TO THE OVERWHELMING POWER BEFORE THEM.

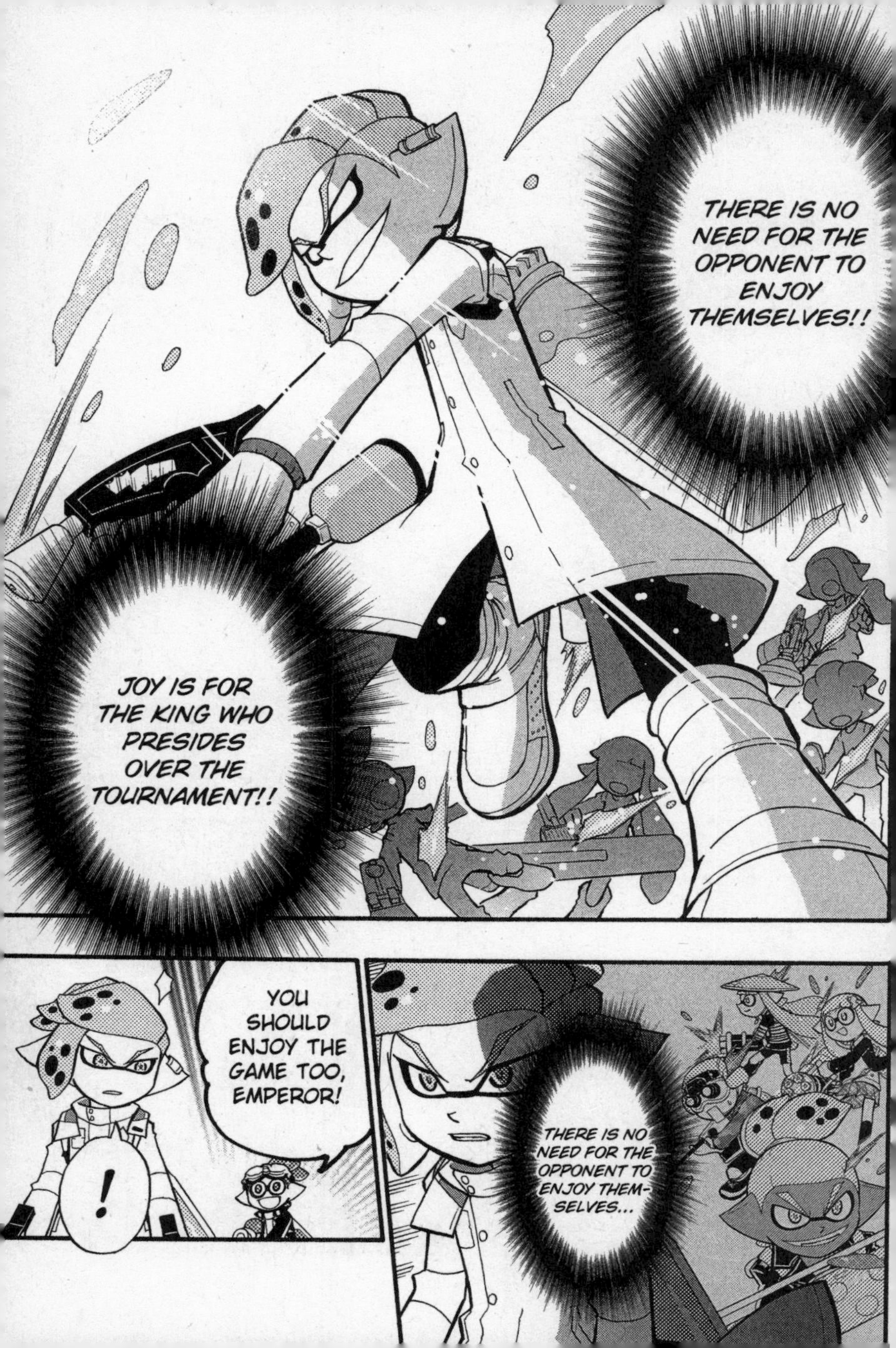
THERE IS NO NEED FOR THE OPPONENT TO ENJOY THEMSELVES!!
JOY IS FOR THE KING WHO PRESIDES OVER THE TOURNAMENT!!
THERE IS NO NEED FOR THE OPPONENT TO ENJOY THEM-SELVES...
YOU SHOULD ENJOY THE GAME TOO, EMPEROR!
!

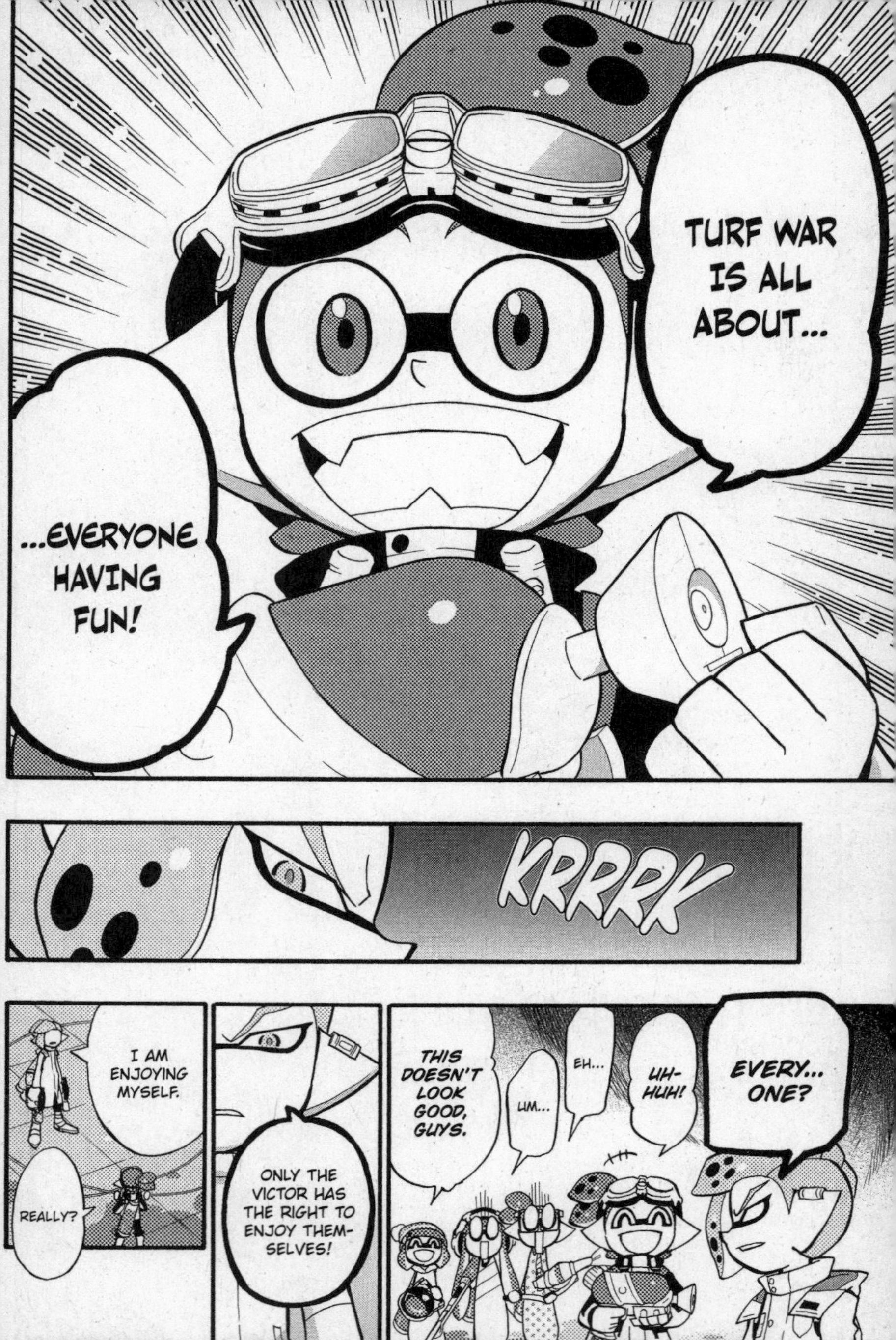
TURF WAR IS ALL ABOUT...
...EVERYONE HAVING FUN!
KRRRK
EVERY... ONE?
UH-HUH!
EH...
UM...
THIS DOESN'T LOOK GOOD, GUYS.
ONLY THE VICTOR HAS THE RIGHT TO ENJOY THEM-SELVES!
I AM ENJOYING MYSELF.
REALLY?

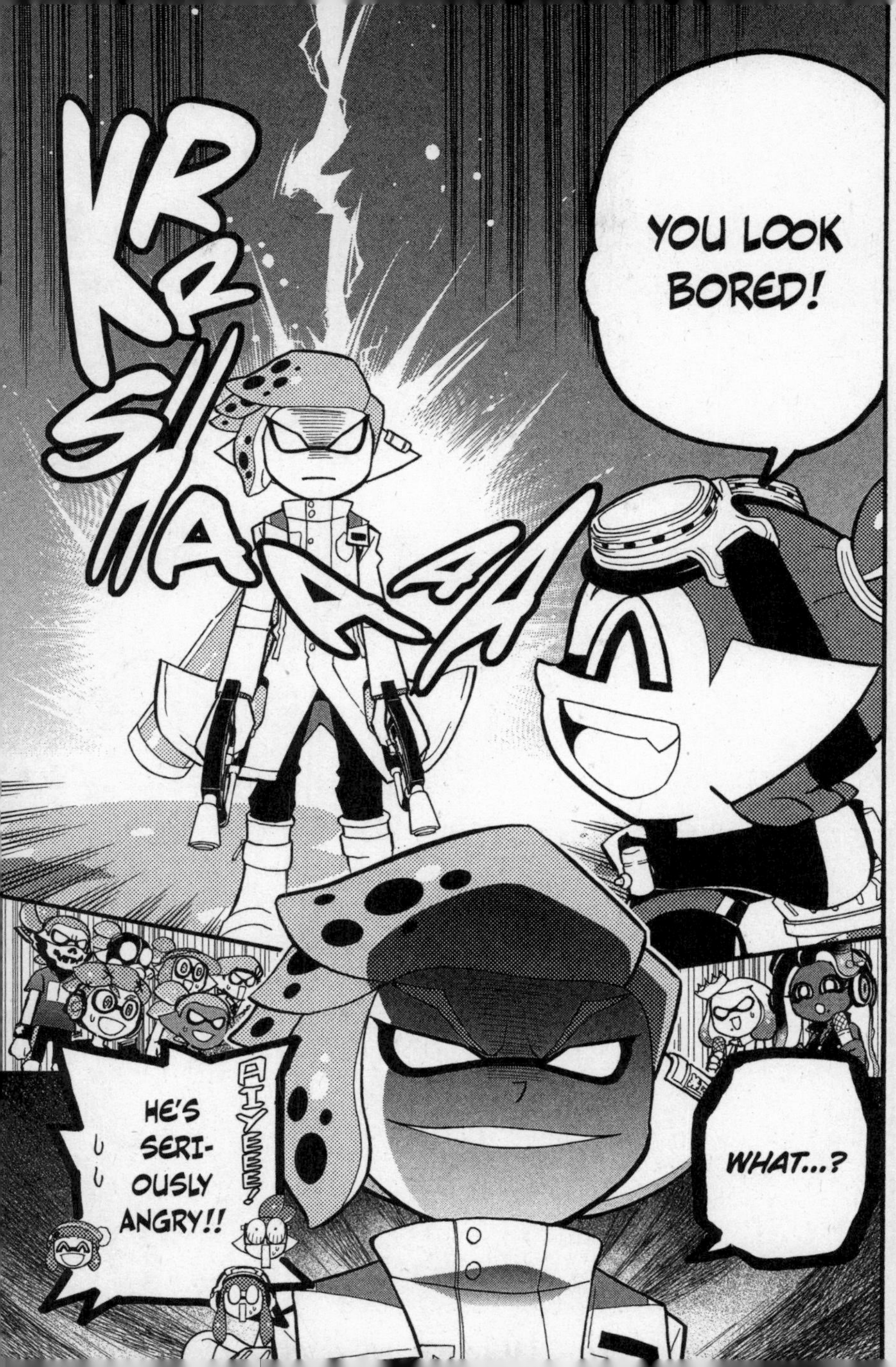
YOU LOOK BORED!
KRSHAAAA
WHAT...?
AIYEEEE!
HE'S SERI-OUSLY ANGRY!!

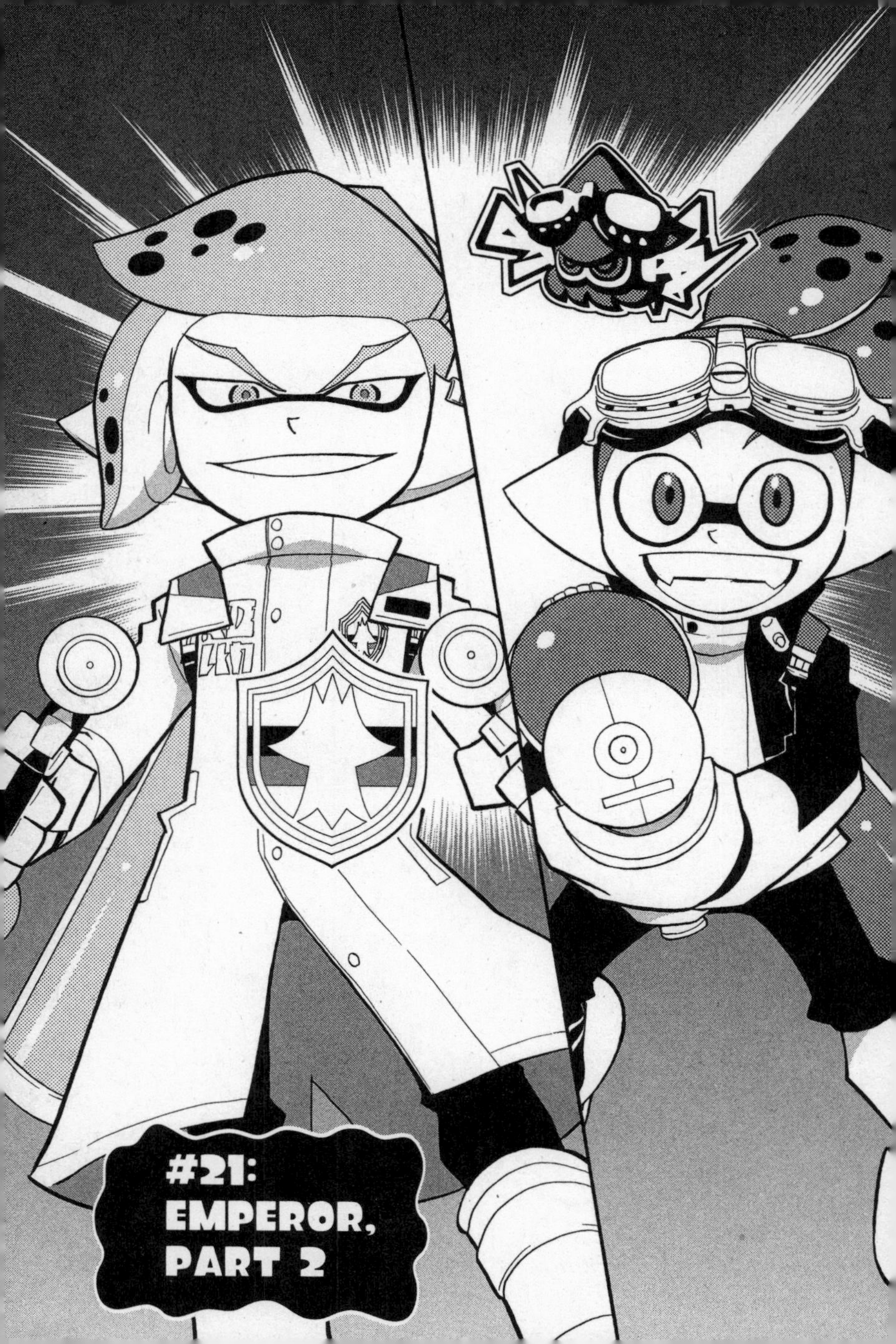
#21:
EMPEROR,
PART 2

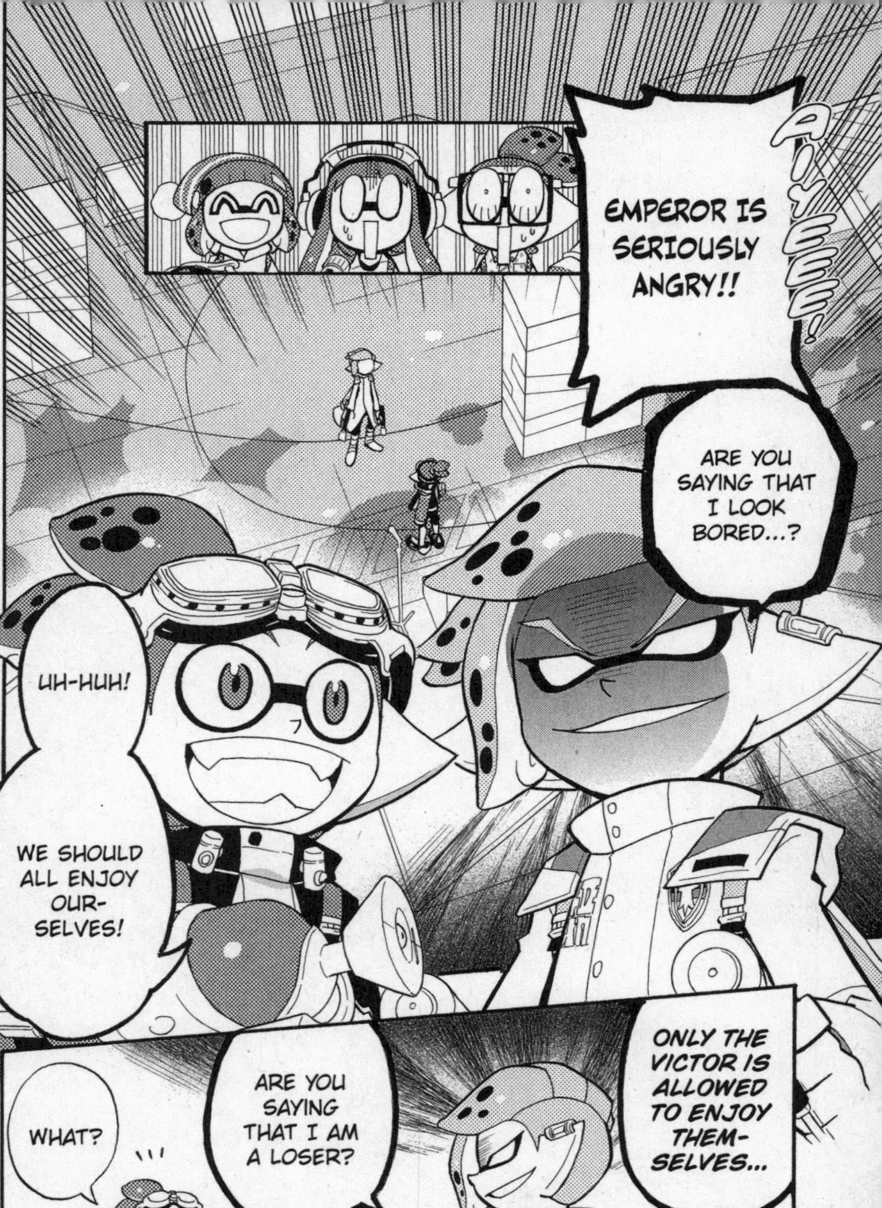
EMPEROR IS SERIOUSLY ANGRY!!
ARE YOU SAYING THAT I LOOK BORED...?
UH-HUH!
WE SHOULD ALL ENJOY OUR-SELVES!
ONLY THE VICTOR IS ALLOWED TO ENJOY THEM-SELVES...
ARE YOU SAYING THAT I AM A LOSER?
WHAT?

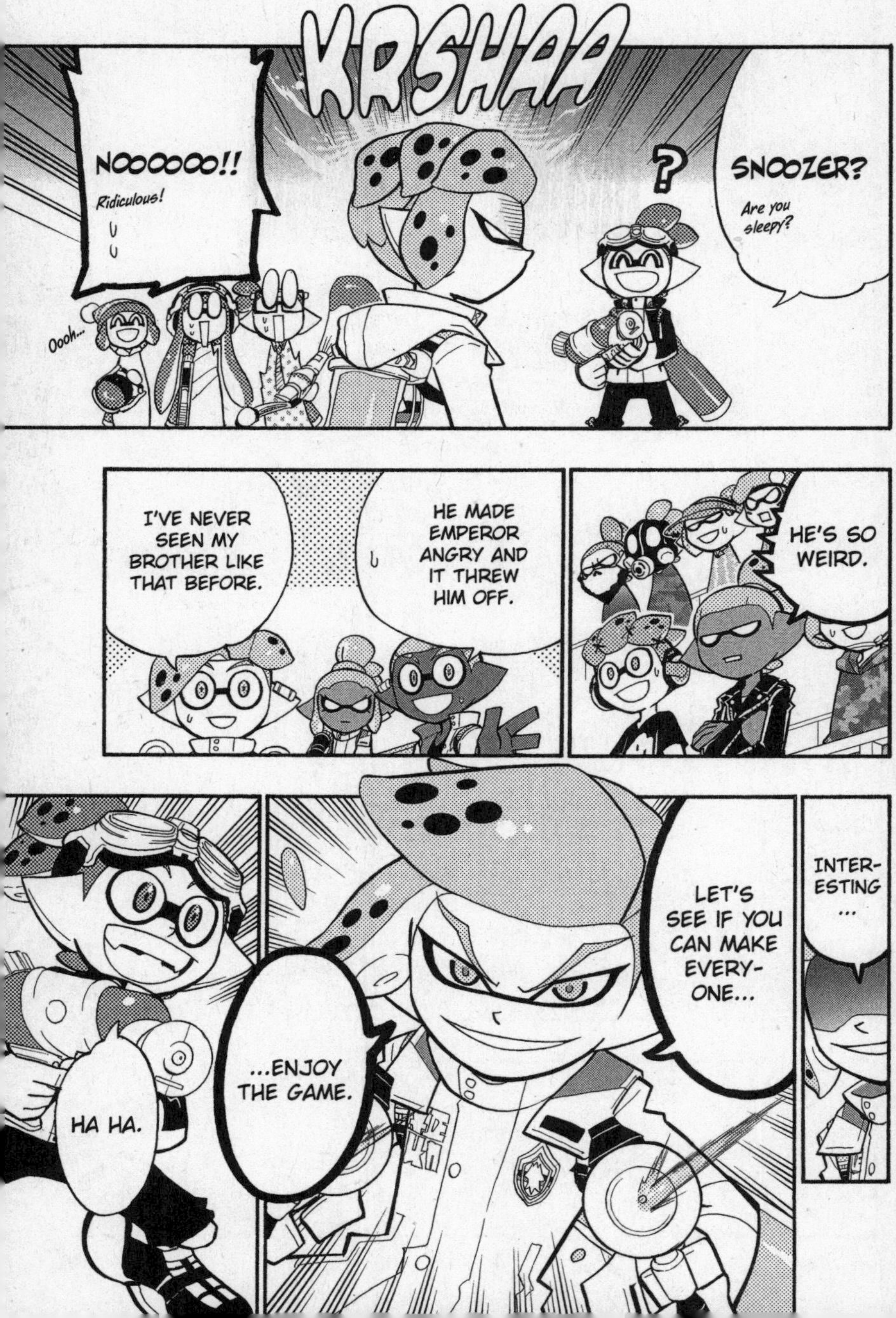
KRSHAA
SNOOZER?
Are you sleepy?
NOOOOOO!!
Ridiculous!
Oooh...
HE'S SO WEIRD.
HE MADE EMPEROR ANGRY AND IT THREW HIM OFF.
I'VE NEVER SEEN MY BROTHER LIKE THAT BEFORE.
INTER-ESTING...
LET'S SEE IF YOU CAN MAKE EVERY-ONE...
...ENJOY THE GAME.
HA HA.

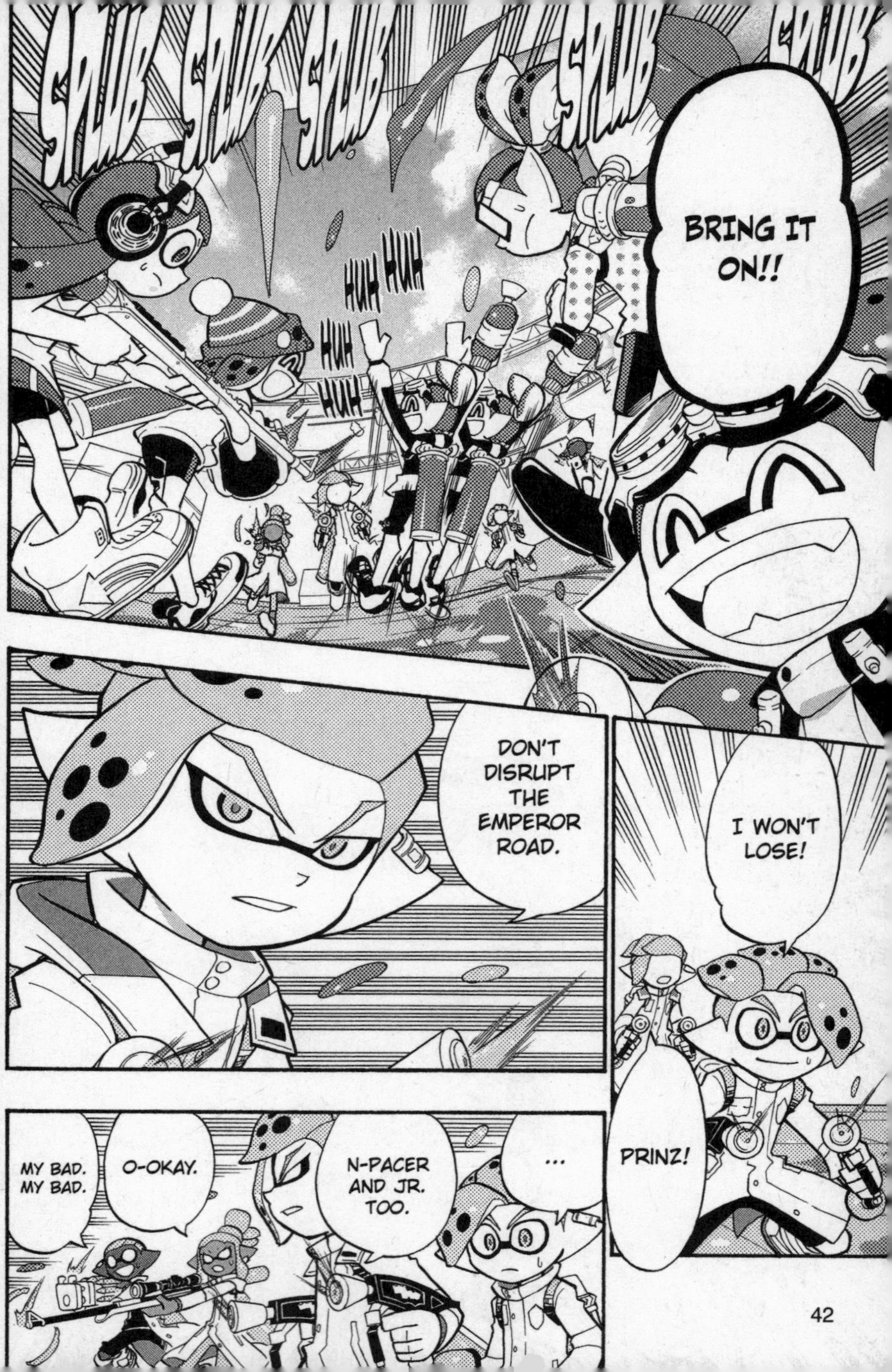
BRING IT ON!!
SPLUB SPLUB SPLUB SPLUB SPLUB
HUH HUH HUH HUH
I WON'T LOSE!
PRINZ!
DON'T DISRUPT THE EMPEROR ROAD.
...
N-PACER AND JR. TOO.
O-OKAY.
MY BAD. MY BAD.

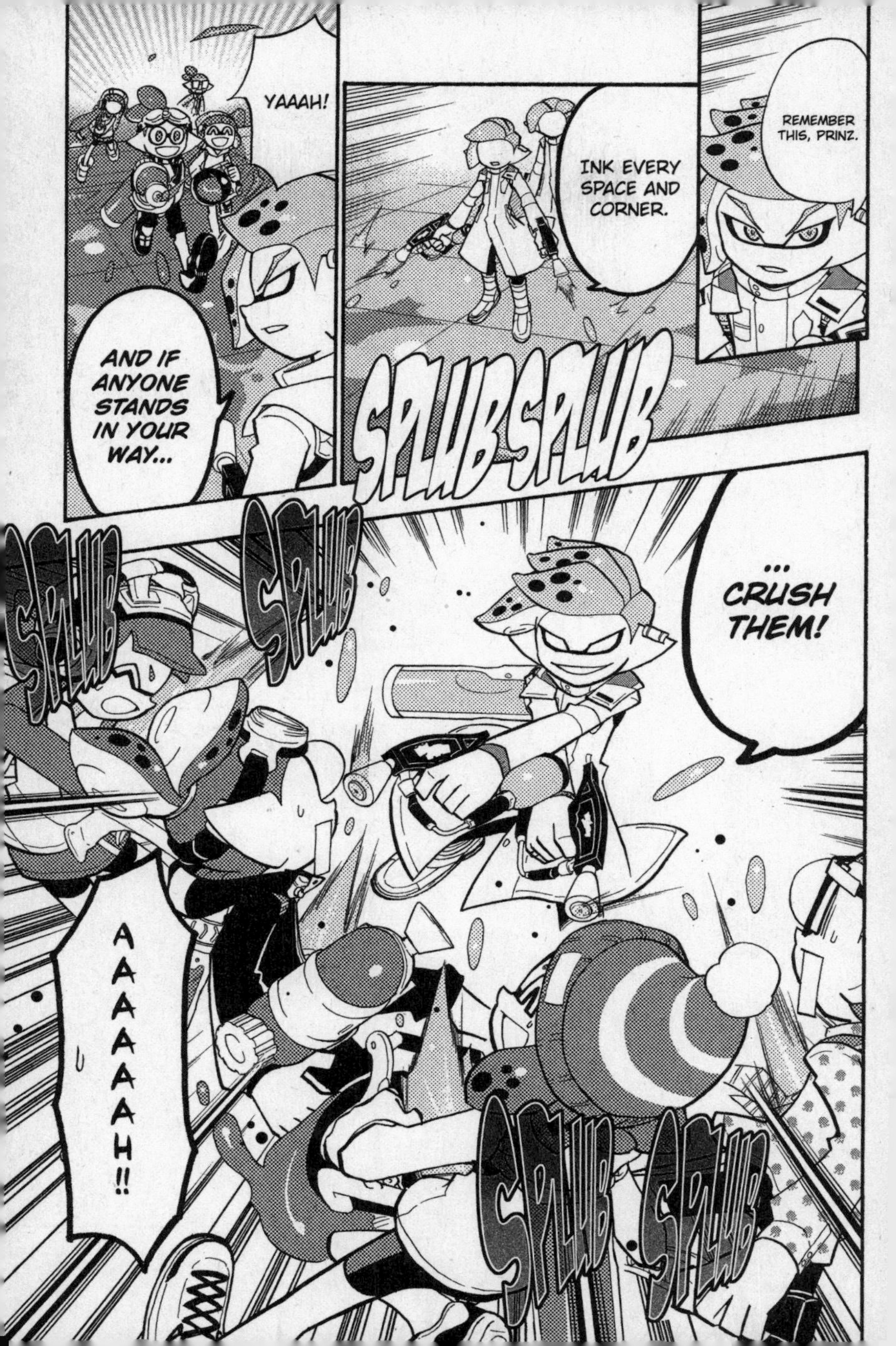
REMEMBER THIS, PRINZ.
INK EVERY SPACE AND CORNER.
SPLUB SPLUB
YAAAH!
AND IF ANYONE STANDS IN YOUR WAY...
... CRUSH THEM!
AAAAAAAH!!

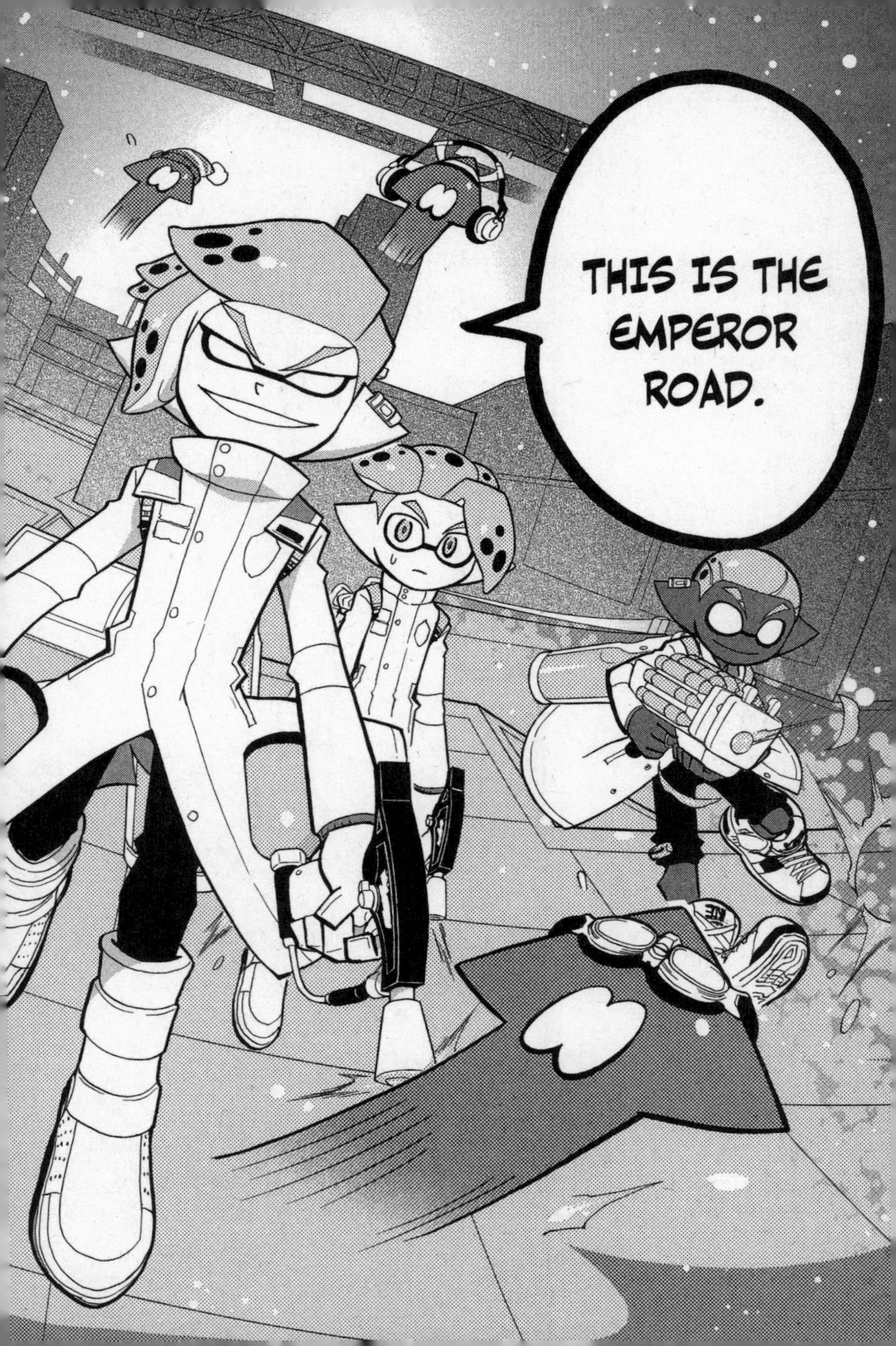
THIS IS THE EMPEROR ROAD.

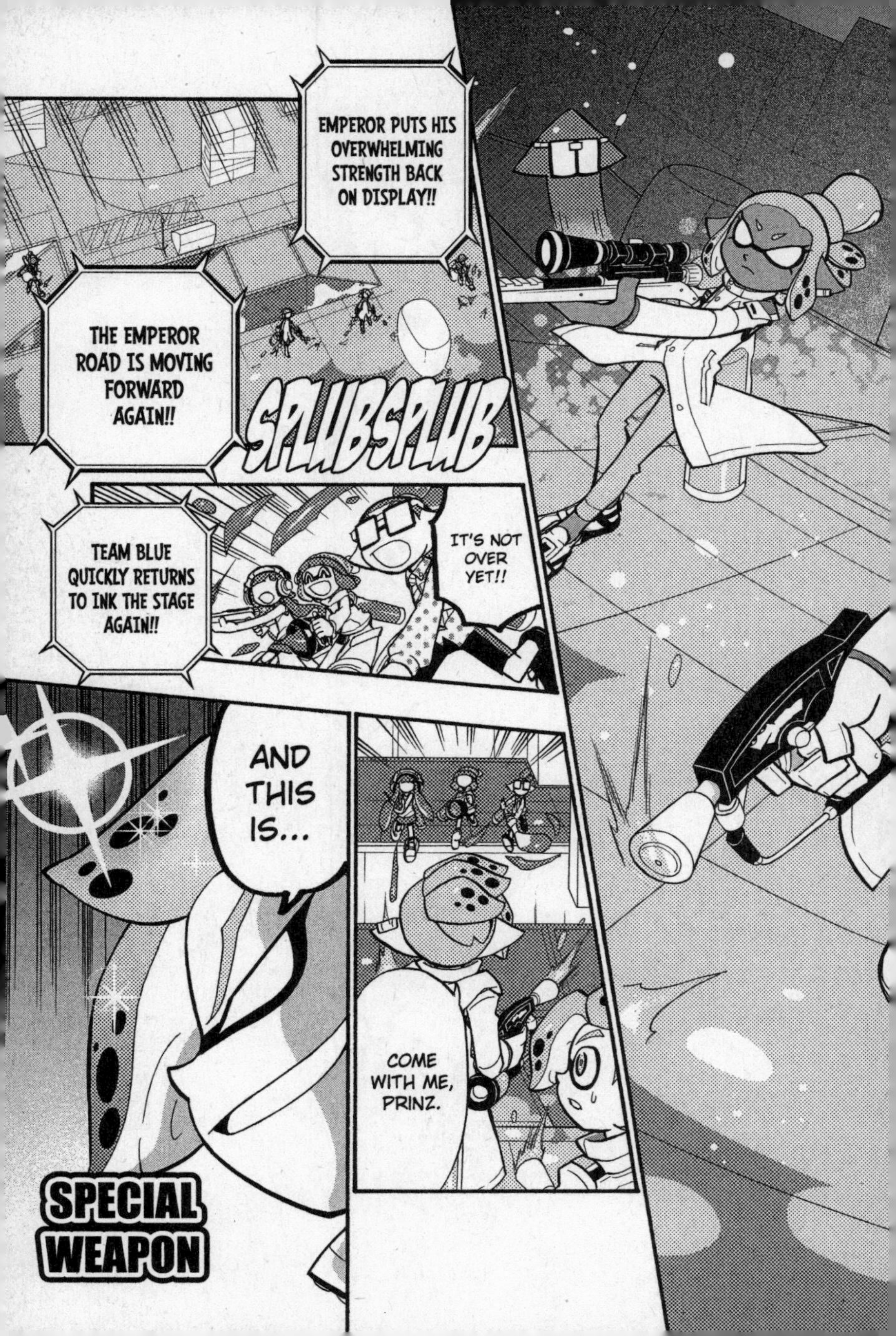
EMPEROR PUTS HIS OVERWHELMING STRENGTH BACK ON DISPLAY!!
THE EMPEROR ROAD IS MOVING FORWARD AGAIN!!
SPLUBSPLUB
IT'S NOT OVER YET!!
TEAM BLUE QUICKLY RETURNS TO INK THE STAGE AGAIN!!
COME WITH ME, PRINZ.
AND THIS IS...
SPECIAL WEAPON

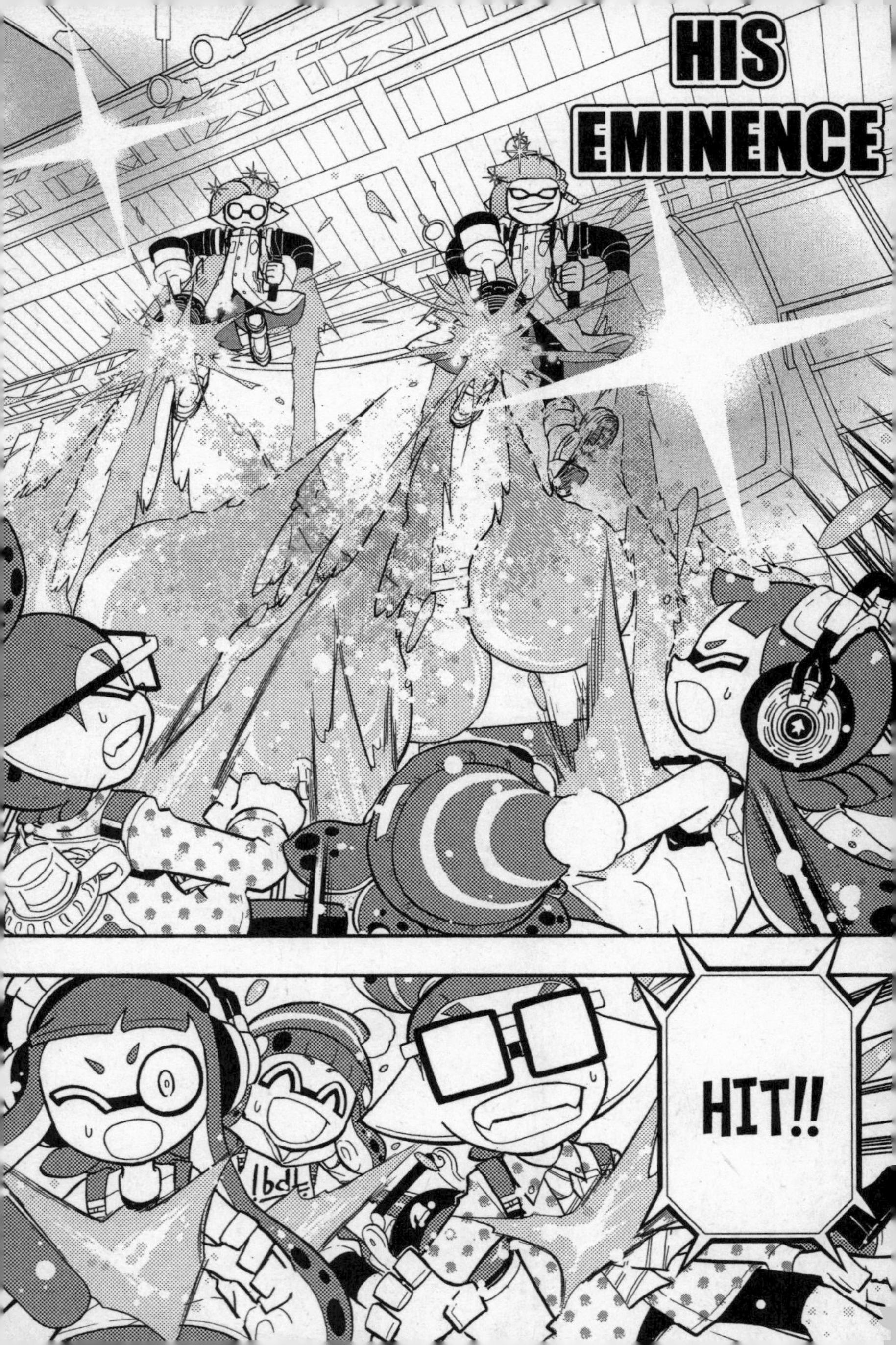
HIS EMINENCE
HIT!!

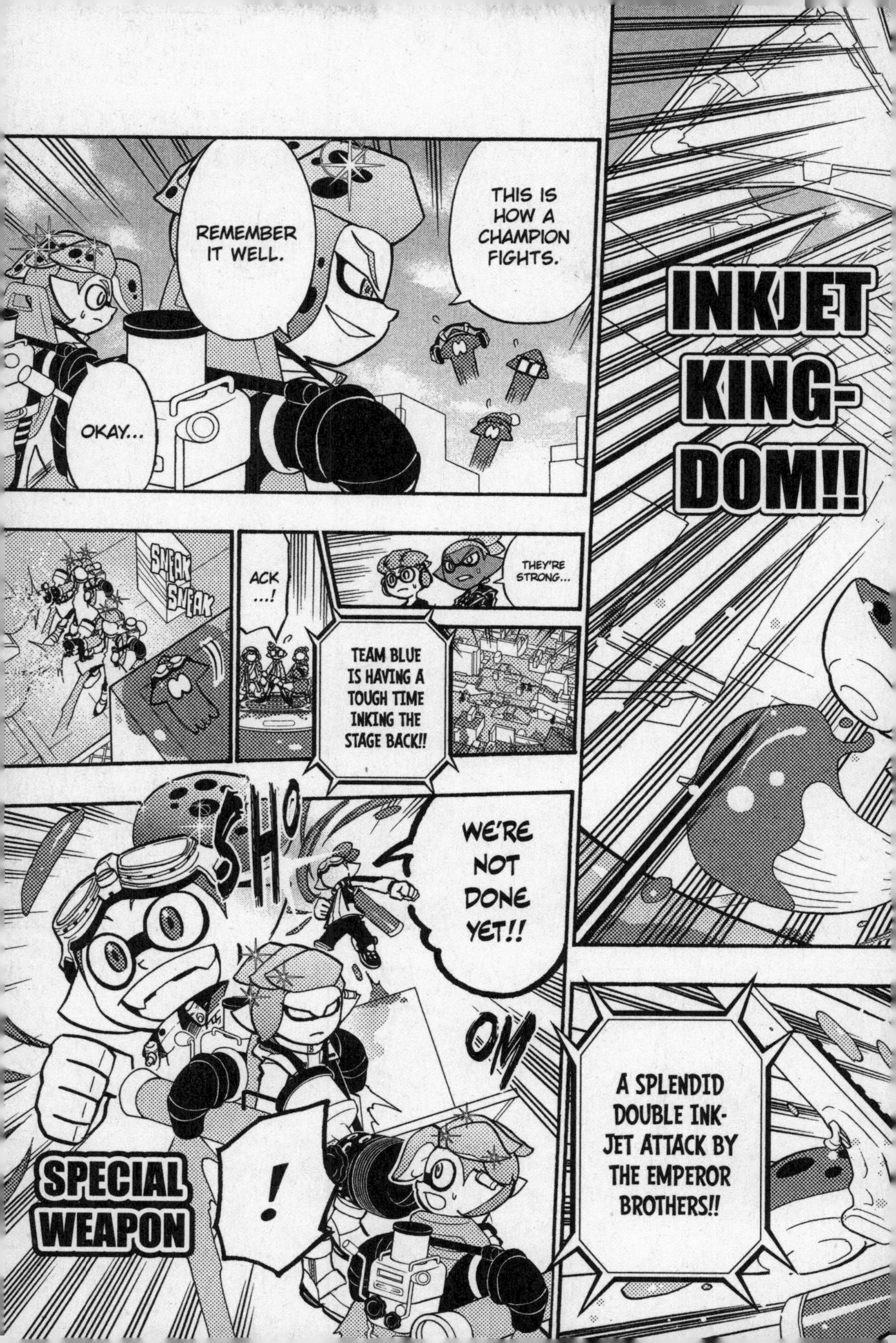
INKJET KING-DOM!!
THIS IS HOW A CHAMPION FIGHTS.
REMEMBER IT WELL.
OKAY...
THEY'RE STRONG...
ACK ...!
TEAM BLUE IS HAVING A TOUGH TIME INKING THE STAGE BACK!!
SNEAK SNEAK
A SPLENDID DOUBLE INK-JET ATTACK BY THE EMPEROR BROTHERS!!
WE'RE NOT DONE YET!!
SHOOM
SPECIAL WEAPON
!

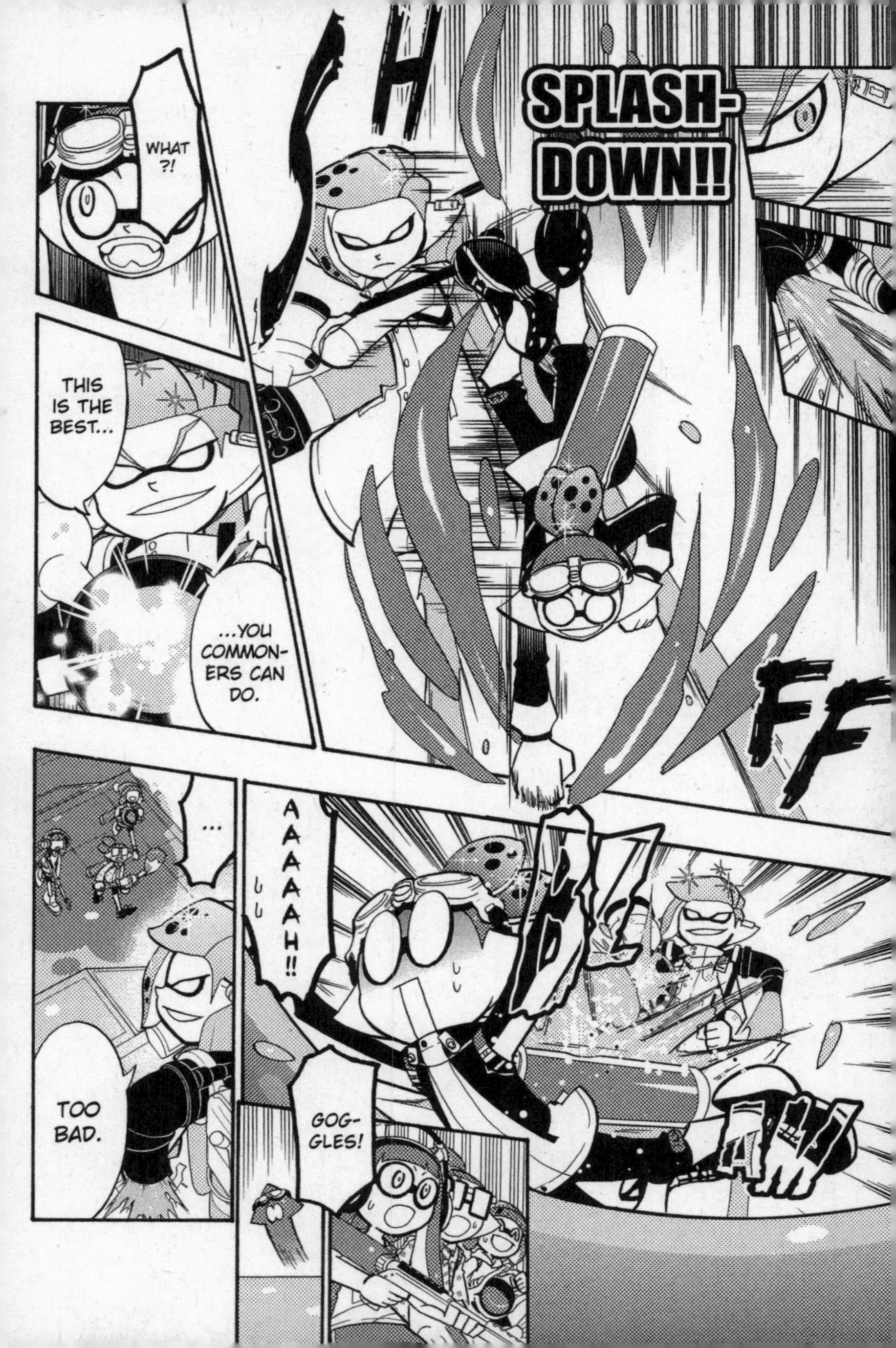
SPLASH-DOWN!!
WHAT ?!
THIS IS THE BEST...
...YOU COMMONERS CAN DO.
AAAAAH!!
GOG-GLES!
...
TOO BAD.

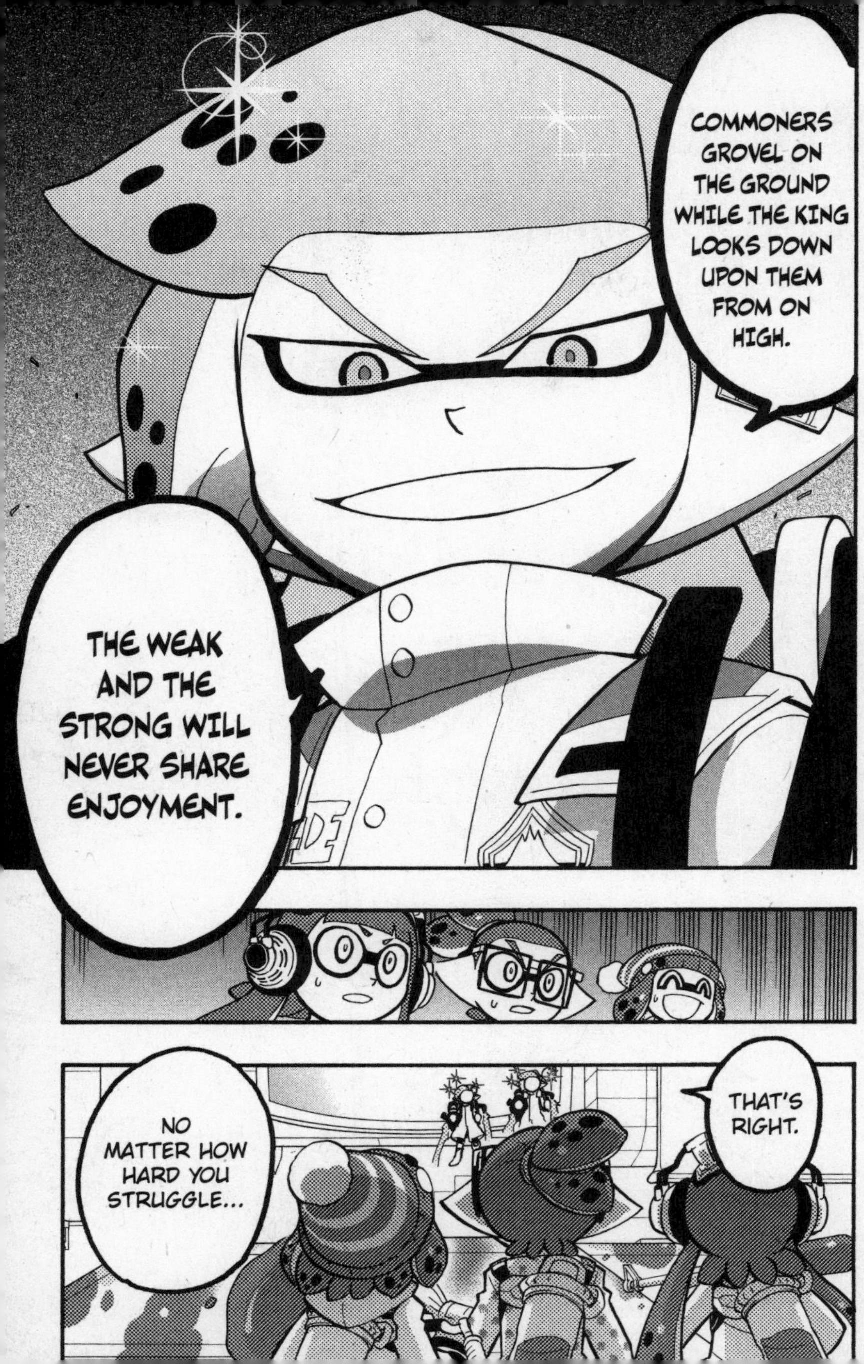
COMMONERS GROVEL ON THE GROUND WHILE THE KING LOOKS DOWN UPON THEM FROM ON HIGH.
THE WEAK AND THE STRONG WILL NEVER SHARE ENJOYMENT.
THAT'S RIGHT.
NO MATTER HOW HARD YOU STRUGGLE...

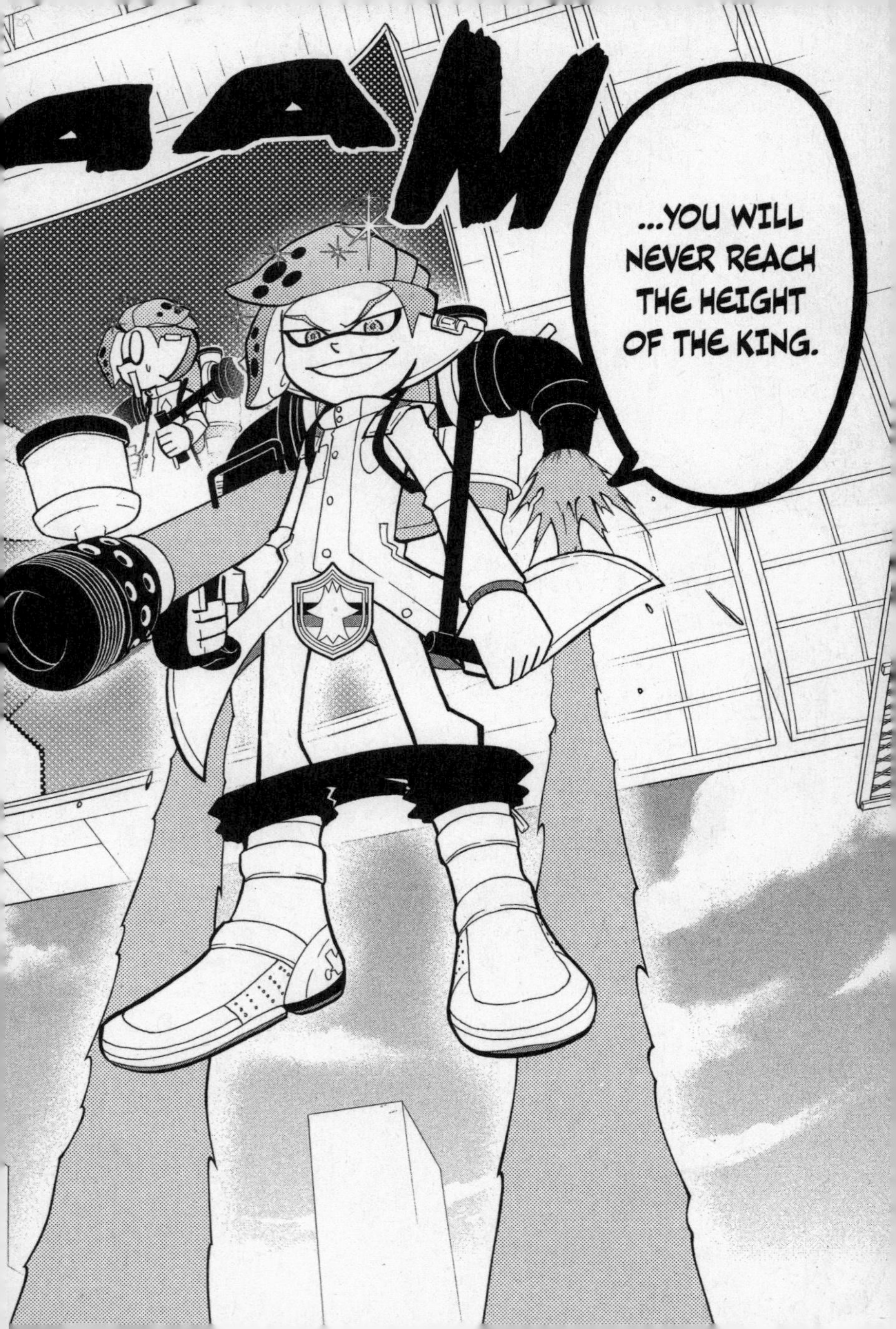
...YOU WILL NEVER REACH THE HEIGHT OF THE KING.

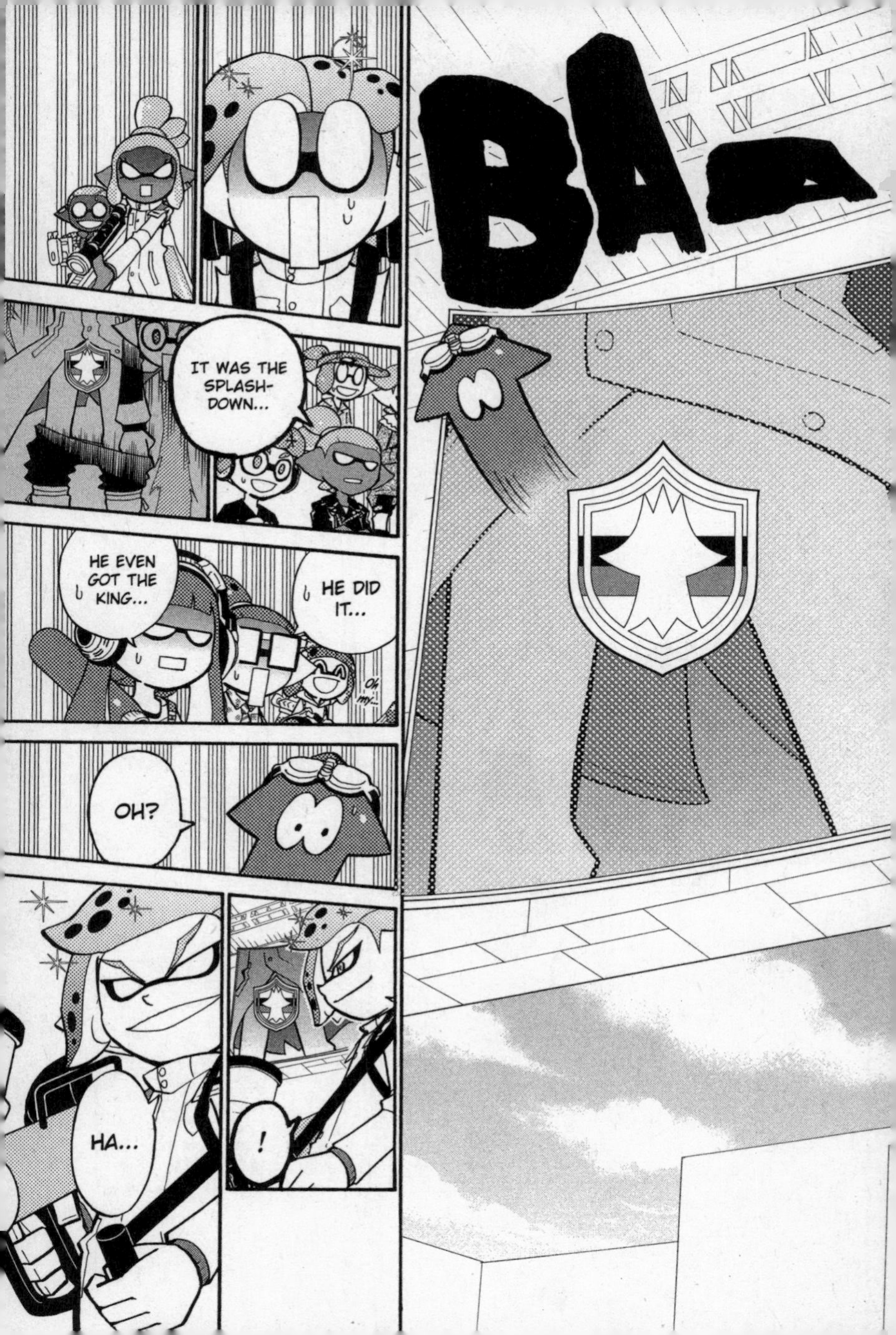
BA
IT WAS THE SPLASH-DOWN...
HE DID IT...
HE EVEN GOT THE KING...
Oh my...
OH?
!
HA...

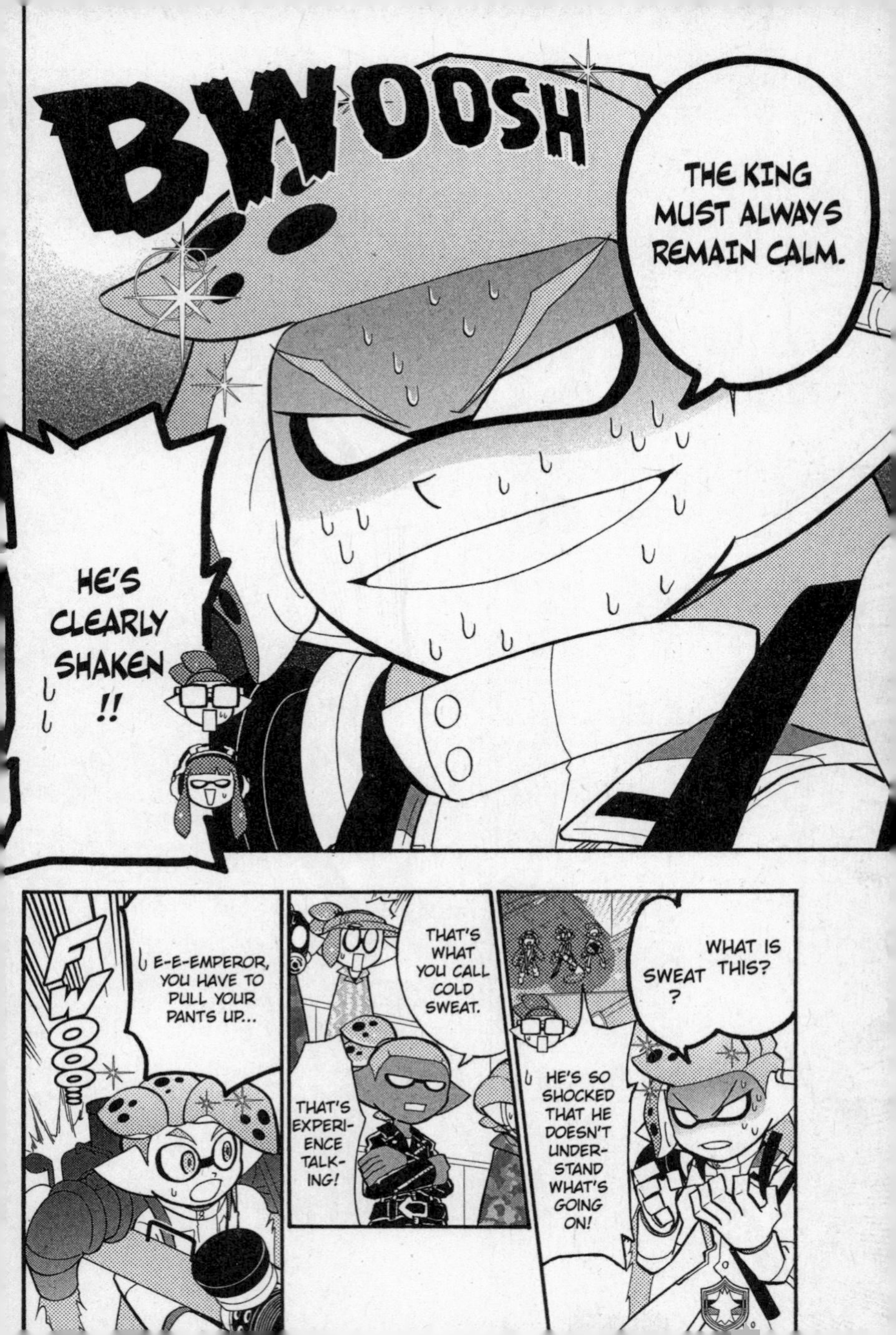
THE KING MUST ALWAYS REMAIN CALM.
BWOOSH
HE'S CLEARLY SHAKEN!!
WHAT IS THIS?
SWEAT?
HE'S SO SHOCKED THAT HE DOESN'T UNDER-STAND WHAT'S GOING ON!
THAT'S WHAT YOU CALL COLD SWEAT.
THAT'S EXPERI-ENCE TALK-ING!
E-E-EMPEROR, YOU HAVE TO PULL YOUR PANTS UP...
FWOOOOO

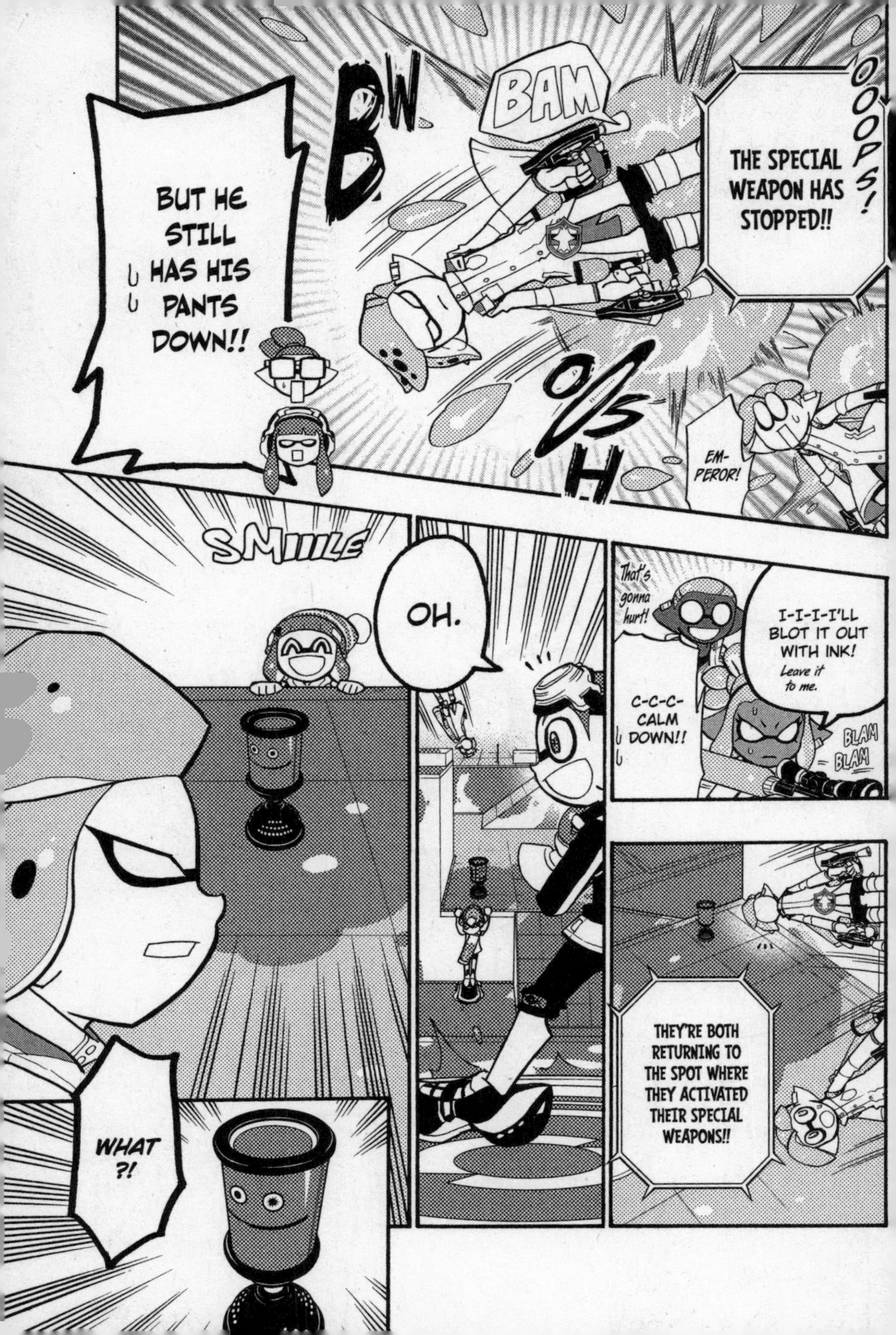
OOOOPS!
THE SPECIAL WEAPON HAS STOPPED!!
BAM
BW
EM-PEROR!
BUT HE STILL HAS HIS PANTS DOWN!!
I-I-I-I'LL BLOT IT OUT WITH INK! Leave it to me.
That's gonna hurt!
C-C-C-CALM DOWN!!
BLAM BLAM
THEY'RE BOTH RETURNING TO THE SPOT WHERE THEY ACTIVATED THEIR SPECIAL WEAPONS!!
OH.
SMIIIILE
WHAT?!

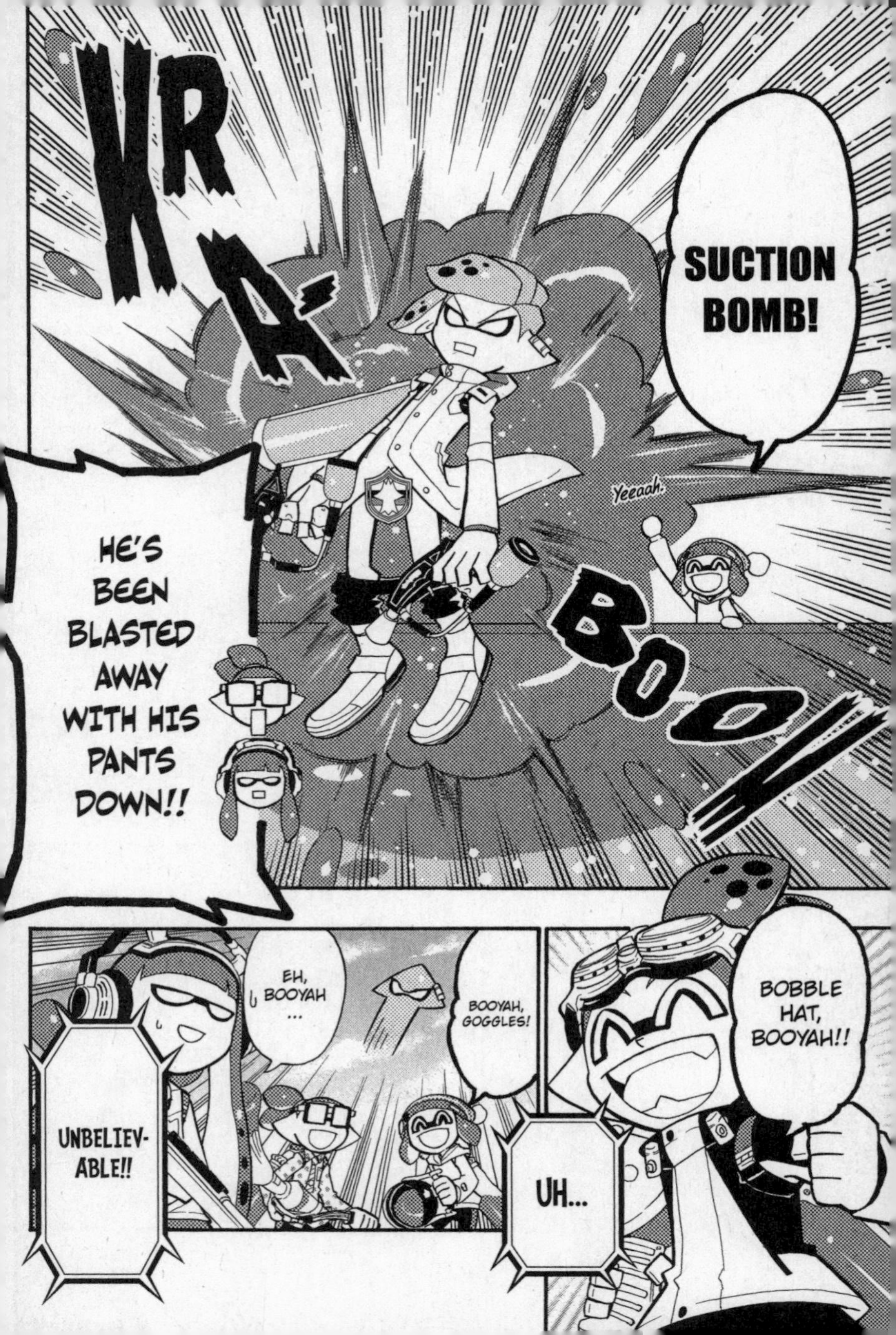
SUCTION BOMB!
KRA-
Yeeaah.
BOOM
HE'S BEEN BLASTED AWAY WITH HIS PANTS DOWN!!
BOBBLE HAT, BOOYAH!!
UH...
BOOYAH, GOGGLES!
EH, BOOYAH ...
UNBELIEV-ABLE!!

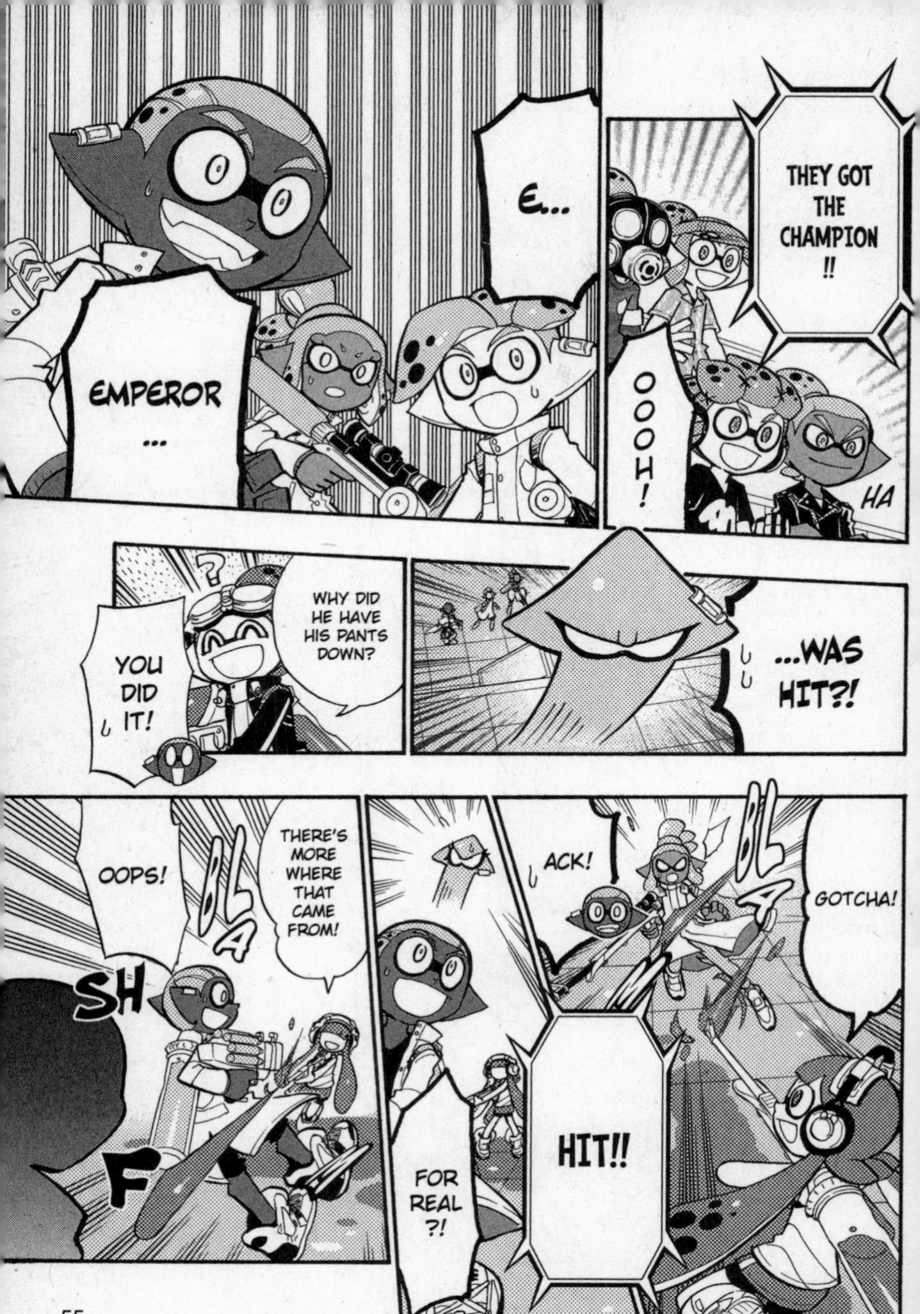

THEY GOT THE CHAMPION !!
OOOOH!
HA
E...
EMPEROR ...
...WAS HIT?!
WHY DID HE HAVE HIS PANTS DOWN?
YOU DID IT!
GOTCHA!
BLA
ACK!
HIT!!
FOR REAL ?!
THERE'S MORE WHERE THAT CAME FROM!
BLA
OOPS!
SH
F

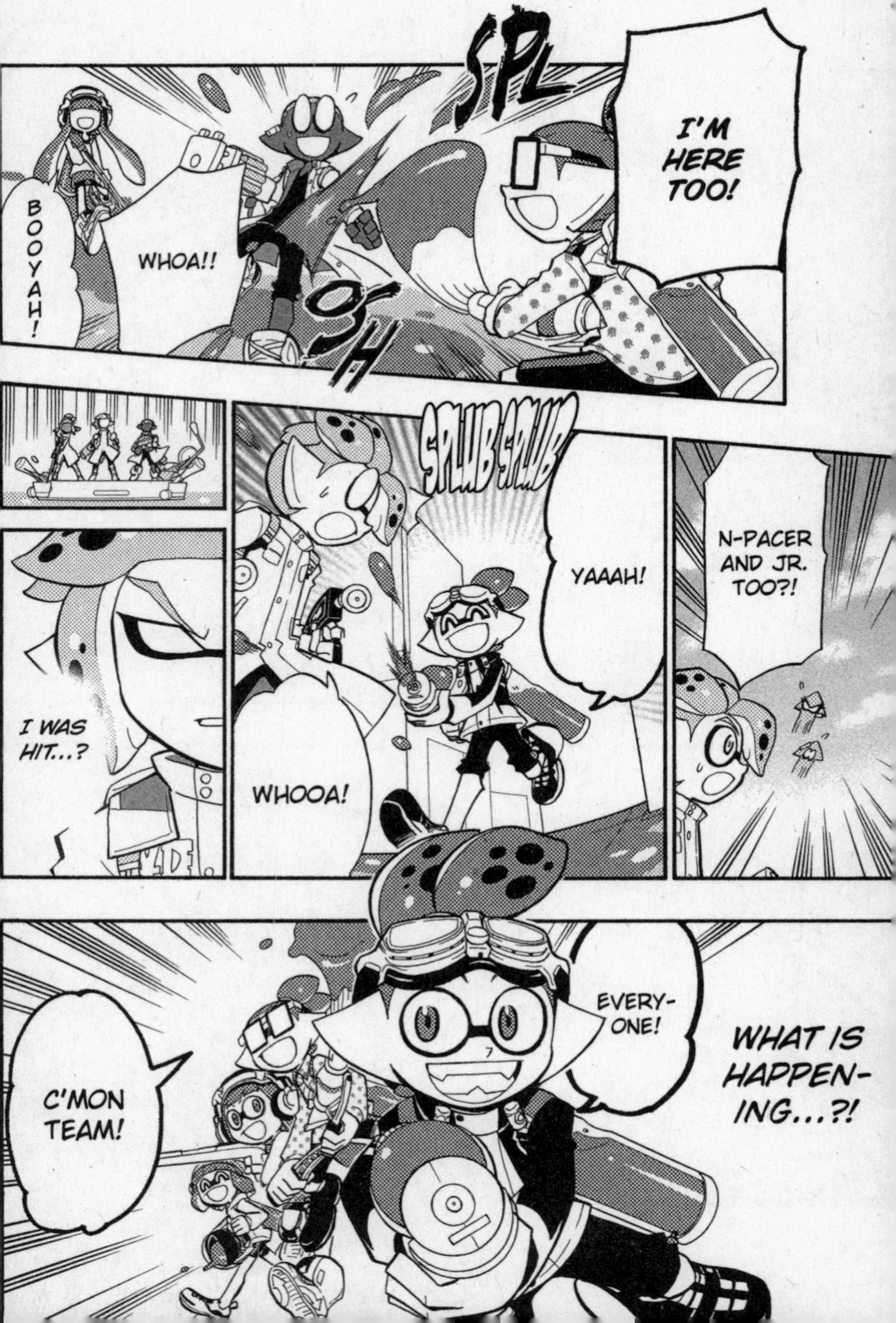
I'M HERE TOO!
SPL
WHOA!!
BOOYAH!
N-PACER AND JR. TOO?!
SPLUB SPLUB
YAAAH!
WHOOA!
I WAS HIT...?
WHAT IS HAPPEN-ING...?!
EVERY-ONE!
C'MON TEAM!

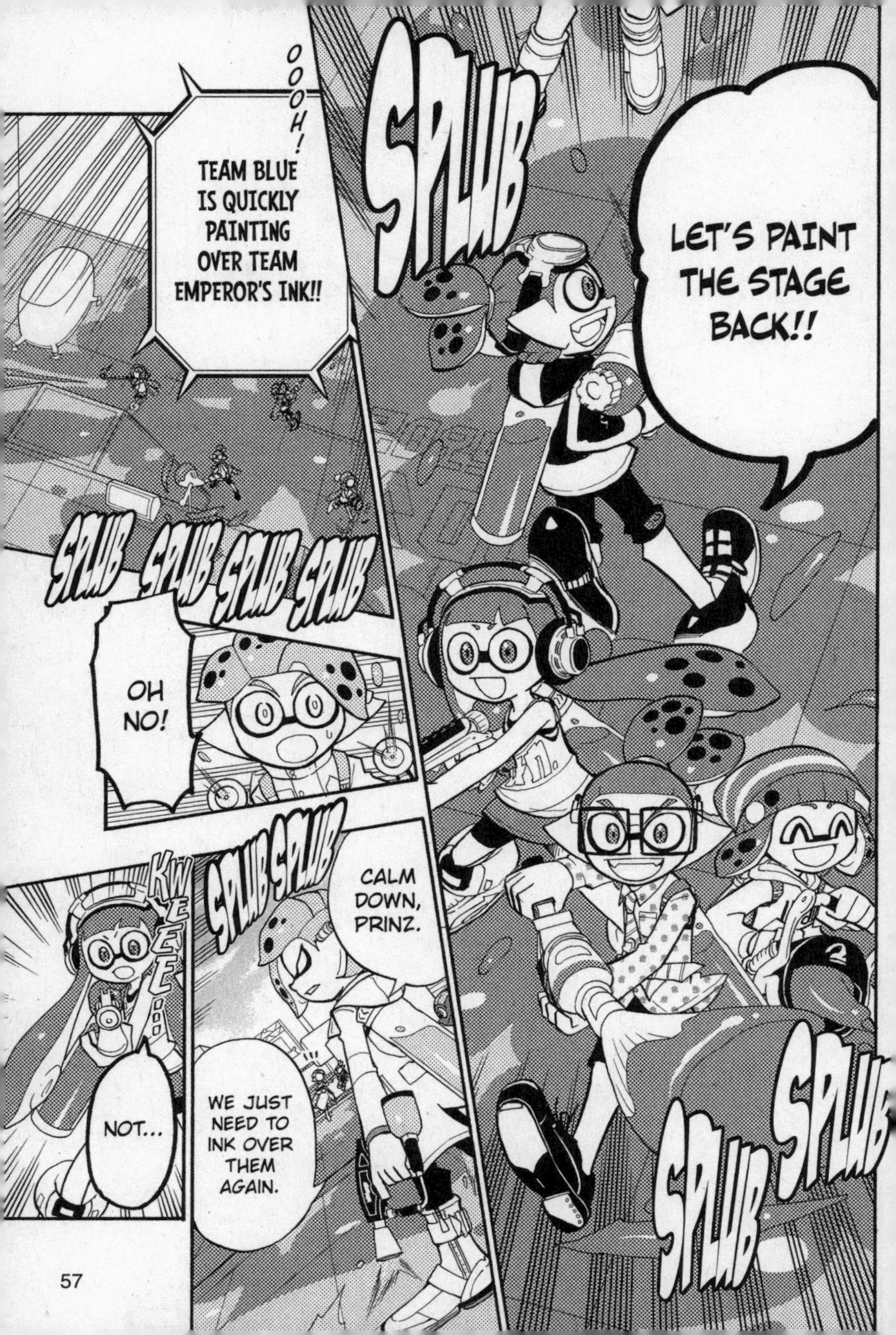
SPLUB
LET'S PAINT THE STAGE BACK!!
SPLUB
SPLUB
OOOOH!
TEAM BLUE IS QUICKLY PAINTING OVER TEAM EMPEROR'S INK!!
SPLUB SPLUB SPLUB SPLUB
OH NO!
SPLUB SPLUB
CALM DOWN, PRINZ.
WE JUST NEED TO INK OVER THEM AGAIN.
KWEEE...
NOT...

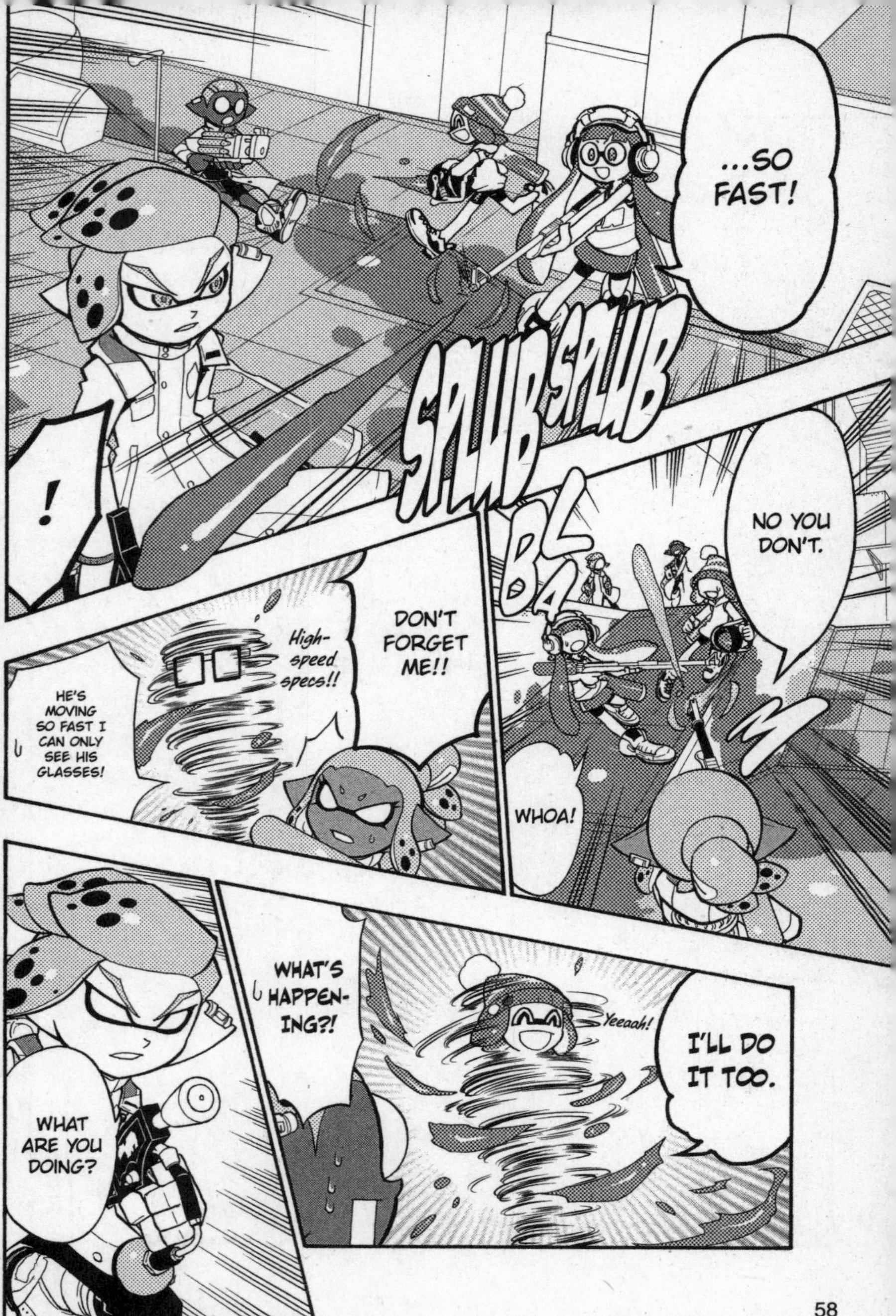
...SO FAST!
SPLUB SPLUB
!
NO YOU DON'T.
WHOA!
DON'T FORGET ME!!
High-speed specs!!
HE'S MOVING SO FAST I CAN ONLY SEE HIS GLASSES!
I'LL DO IT TOO.
Yeeaah!
WHAT'S HAPPEN-ING?!
WHAT ARE YOU DOING?

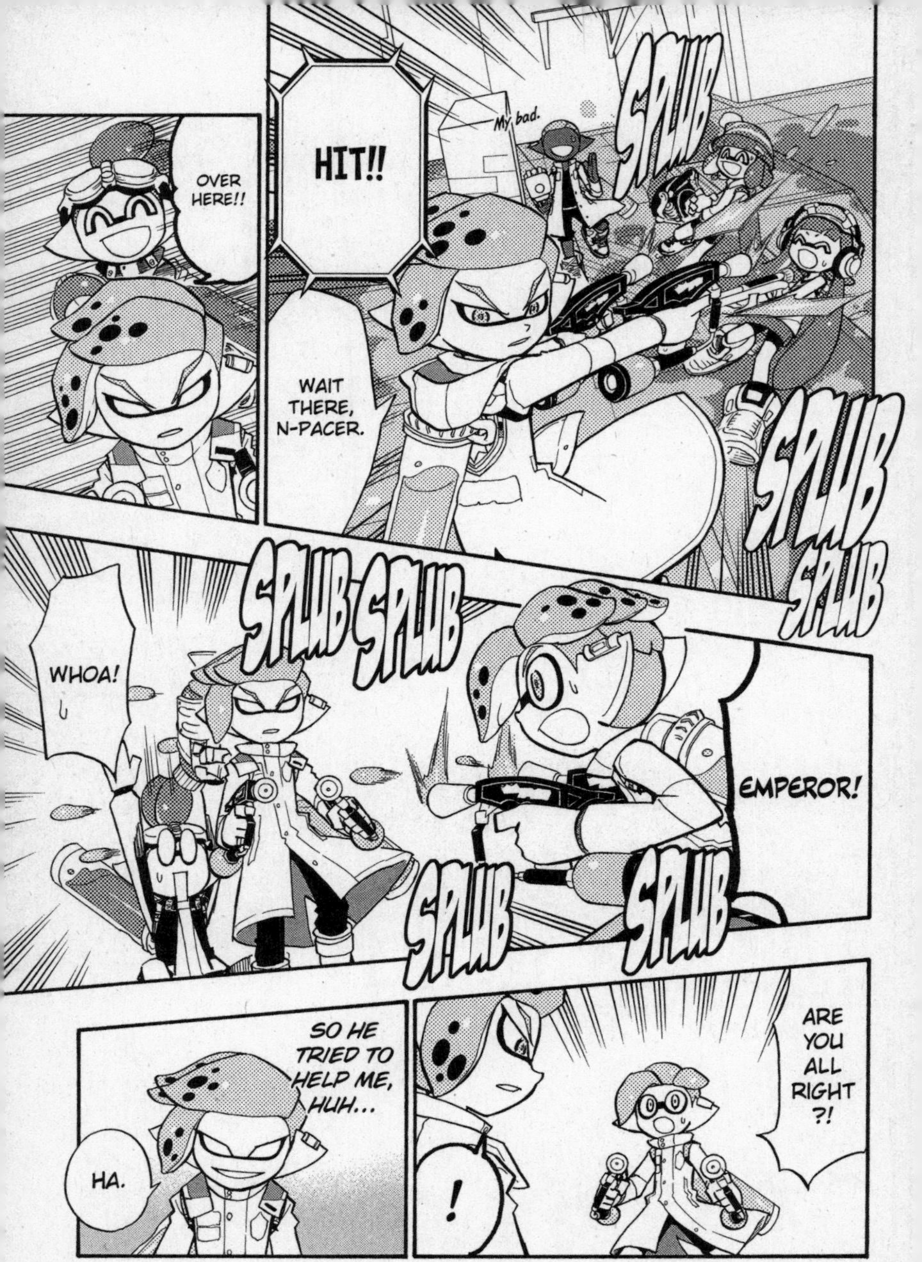
SPLUB
My bad.
HIT!!
SPLUB
SPLUB
WAIT THERE, N-PACER.
OVER HERE!!
SPLUB SPLUB
EMPEROR!
SPLUB
SPLUB
WHOA!
ARE YOU ALL RIGHT?!
!
SO HE TRIED TO HELP ME, HUH...
HA.

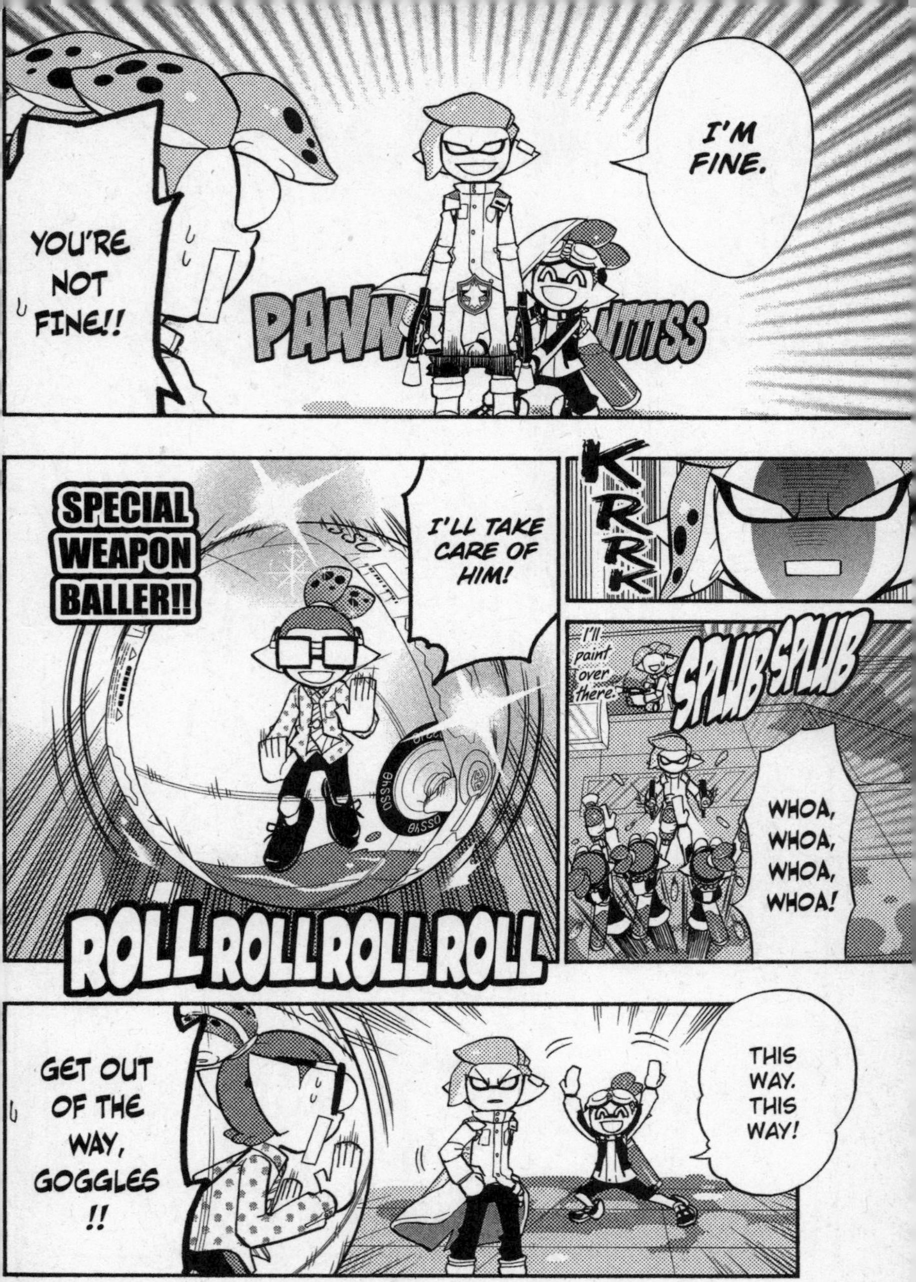
I'M FINE.
YOU'RE NOT FINE!!
KRRK
I'll paint over there.
SPLUB SPLUB
WHOA, WHOA, WHOA, WHOA!
I'LL TAKE CARE OF HIM!
SPECIAL WEAPON BALLER!!
ROLL ROLL ROLL ROLL
THIS WAY. THIS WAY!
GET OUT OF THE WAY, GOGGLES!!

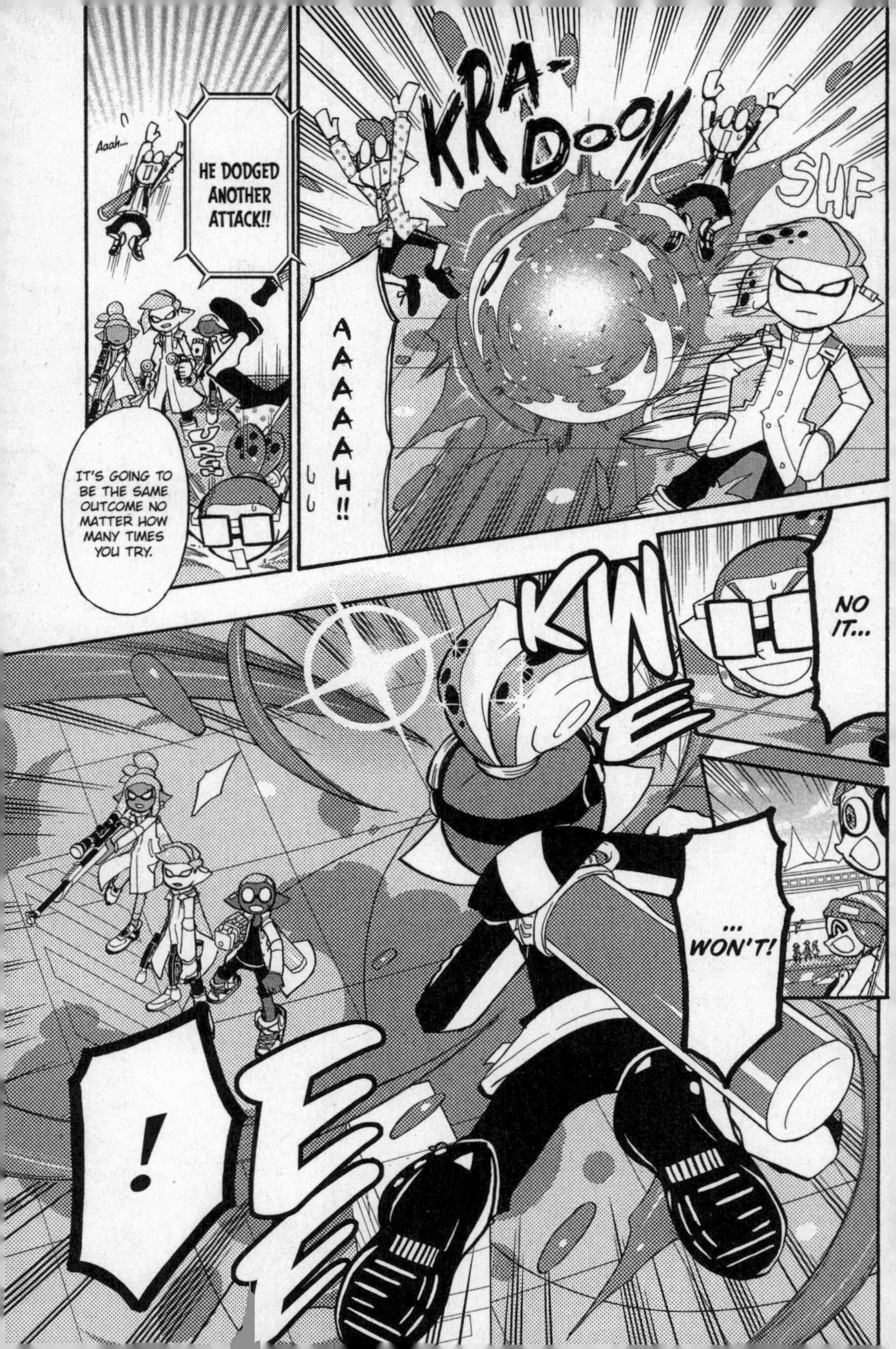
KRA-DOOM
SHF
AAAAAAH!!
Aaah...
HE DODGED ANOTHER ATTACK!!
URG!
IT'S GOING TO BE THE SAME OUTCOME NO MATTER HOW MANY TIMES YOU TRY.
NO IT...
...WON'T!
KWEEE
!

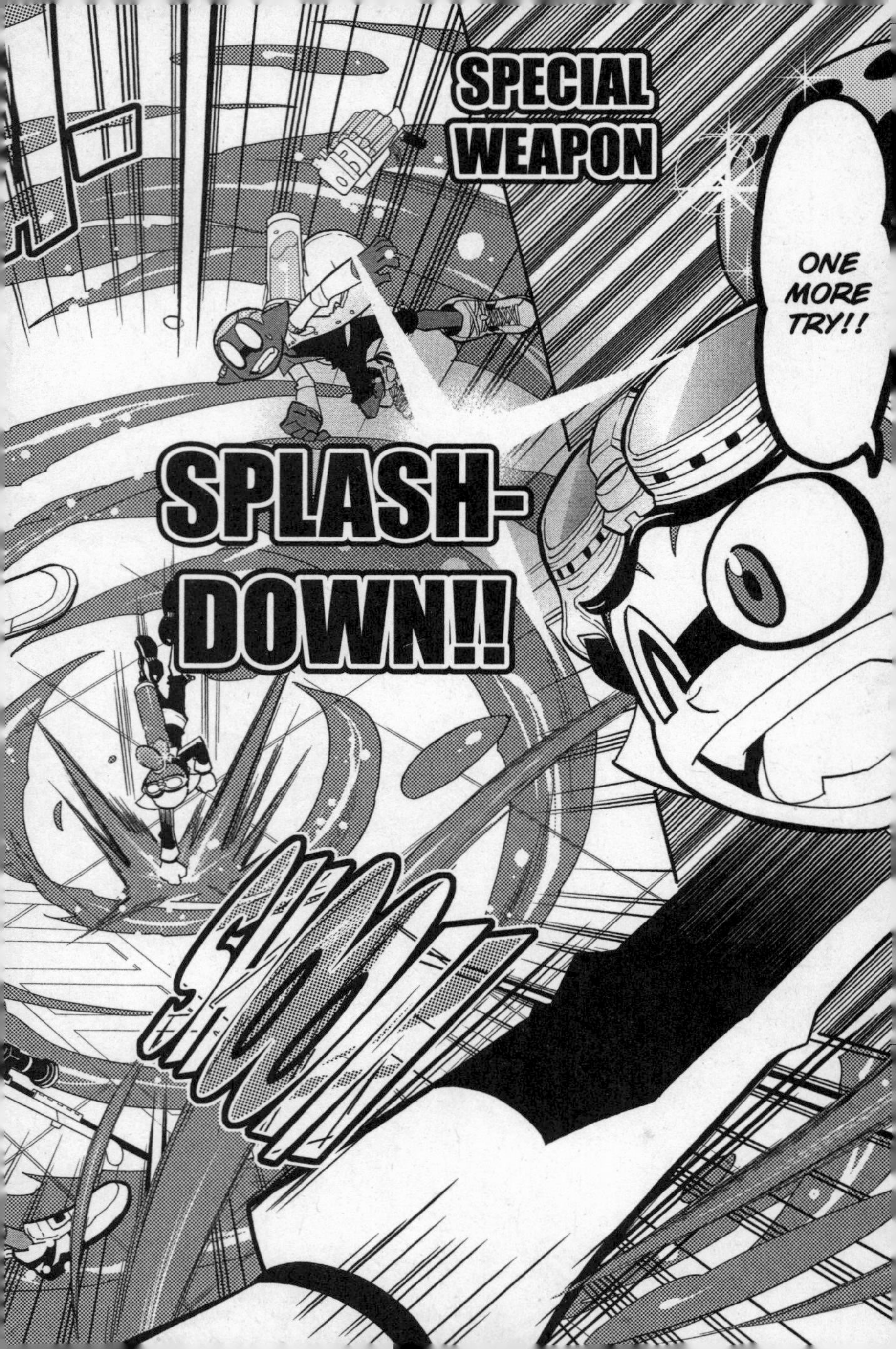
ONE MORE TRY!!
SPECIAL WEAPON
SPLASH-DOWN!!

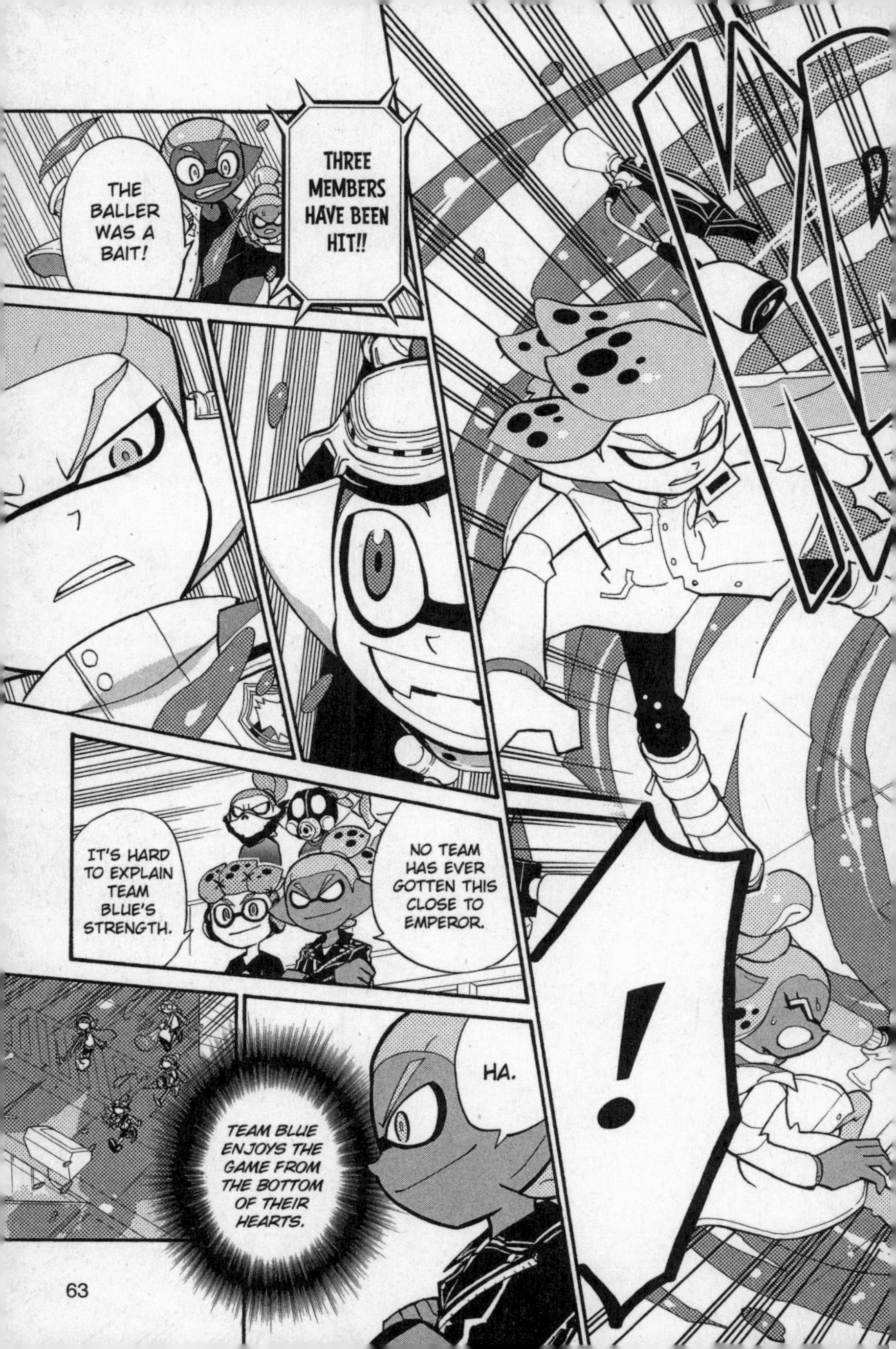
THREE MEMBERS HAVE BEEN HIT!!
THE BALLER WAS A BAIT!
NO TEAM HAS EVER GOTTEN THIS CLOSE TO EMPEROR.
IT'S HARD TO EXPLAIN TEAM BLUE'S STRENGTH.
!
HA.
TEAM BLUE ENJOYS THE GAME FROM THE BOTTOM OF THEIR HEARTS.

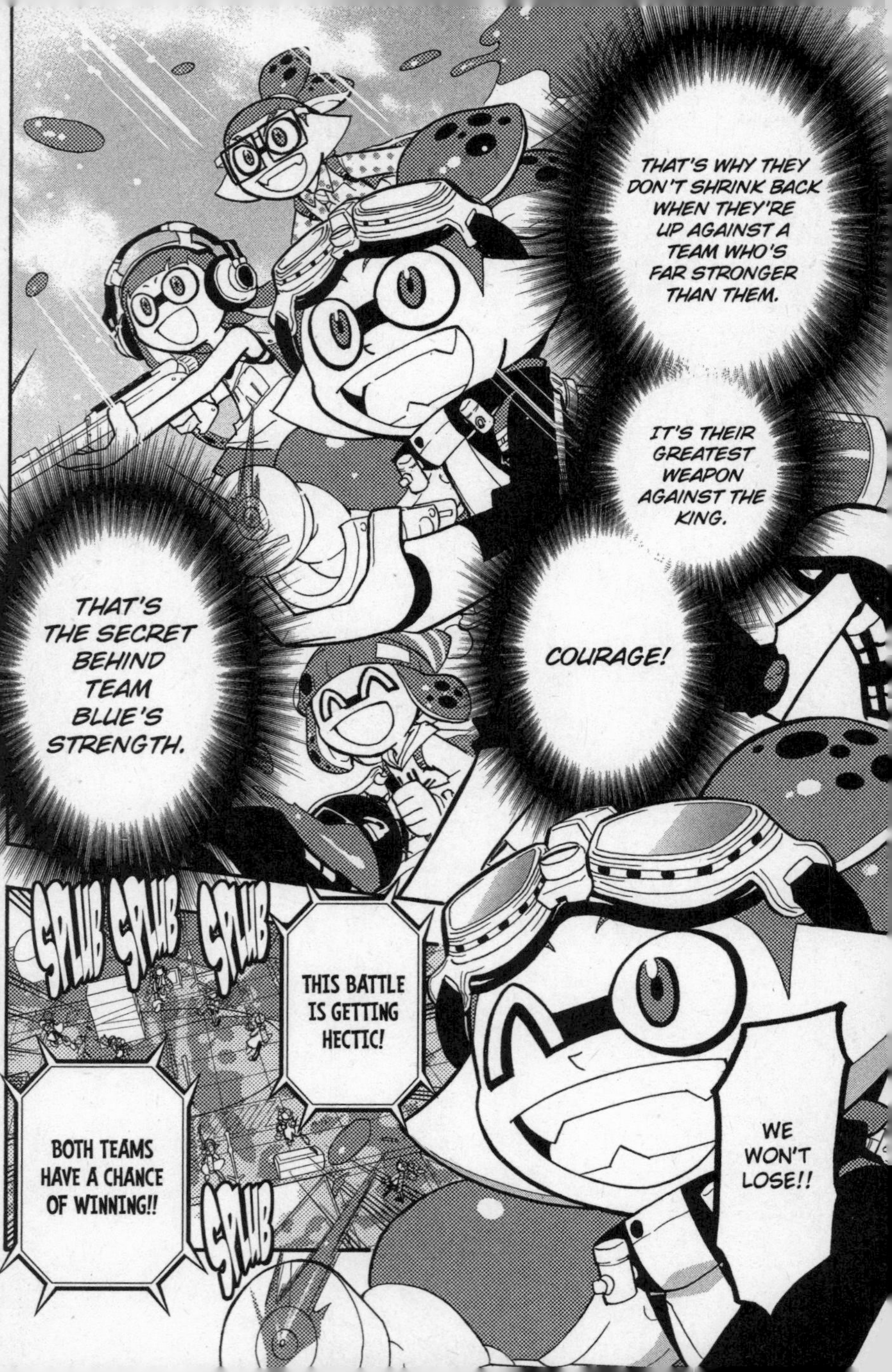
THAT'S WHY THEY DON'T SHRINK BACK WHEN THEY'RE UP AGAINST A TEAM WHO'S FAR STRONGER THAN THEM.
IT'S THEIR GREATEST WEAPON AGAINST THE KING.
COURAGE!
THAT'S THE SECRET BEHIND TEAM BLUE'S STRENGTH.
WE WON'T LOSE!!
SPLUB SPLUB SPLUB
THIS BATTLE IS GETTING HECTIC!
BOTH TEAMS HAVE A CHANCE OF WINNING!!
SPLUB

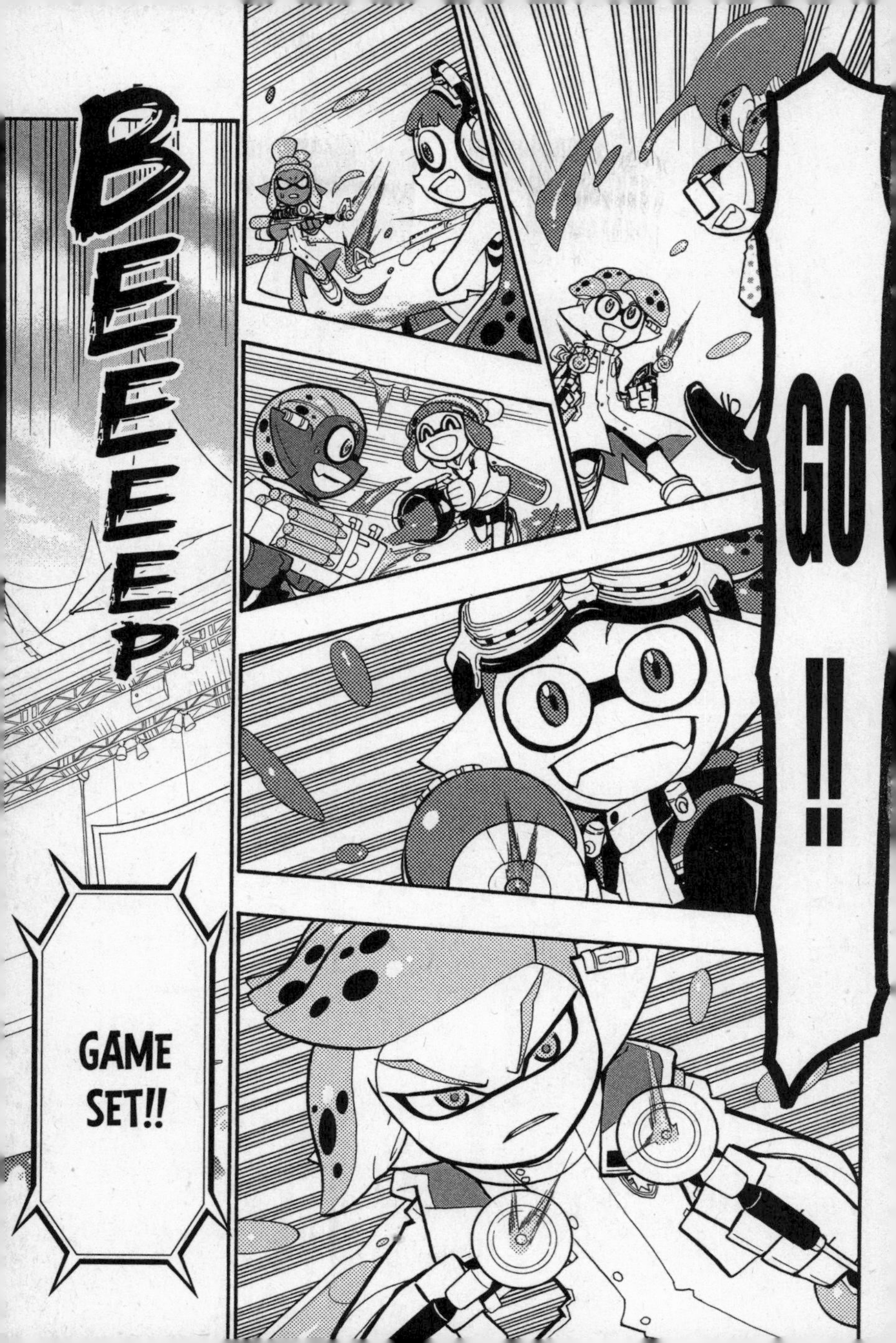
GO!!
BEEEEEP
GAME SET!!

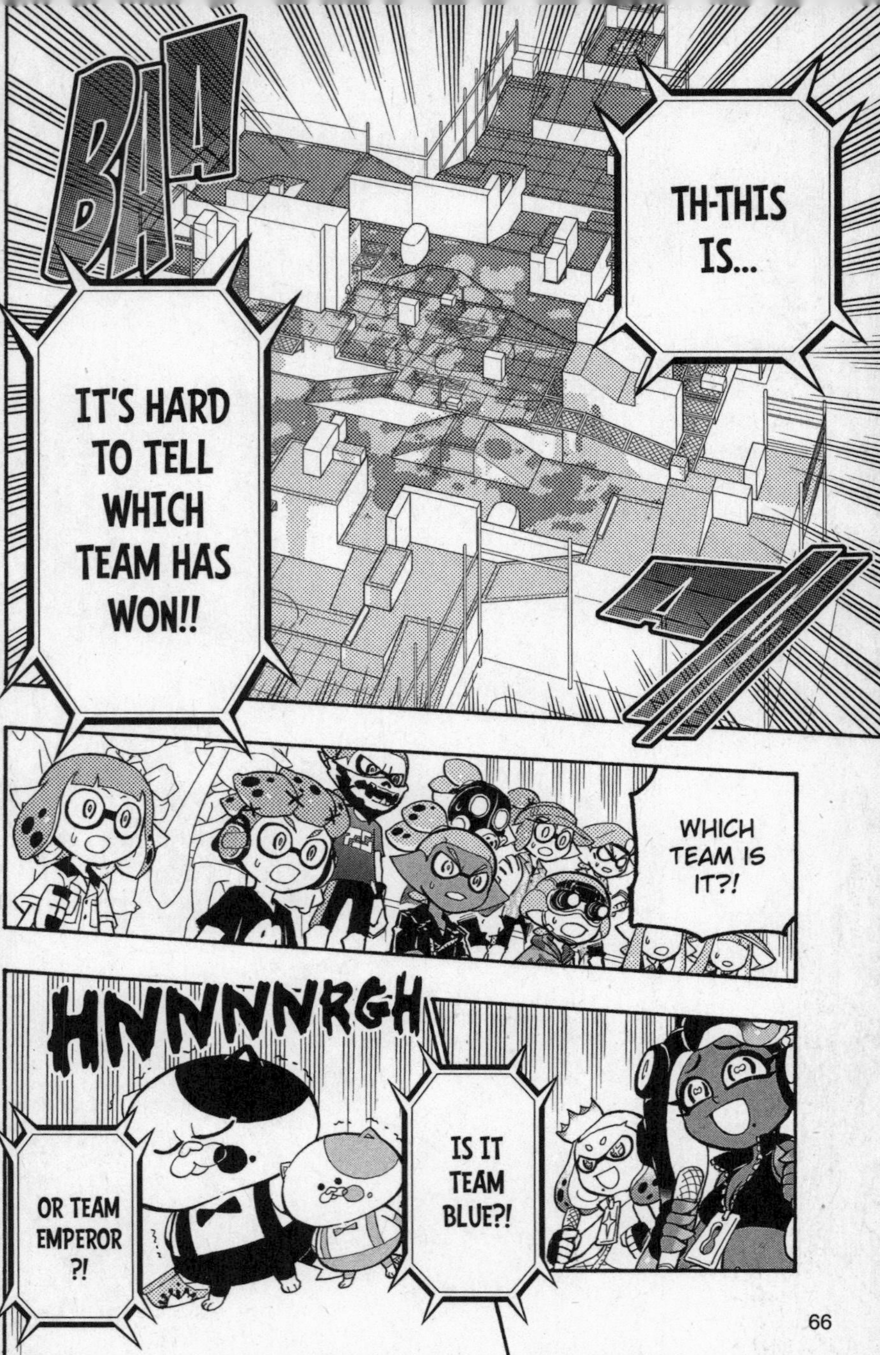
TH-THIS IS...
BAA
IT'S HARD TO TELL WHICH TEAM HAS WON!!
WHICH TEAM IS IT?!
HNNNNRGH
IS IT TEAM BLUE?!
OR TEAM EMPEROR ?!

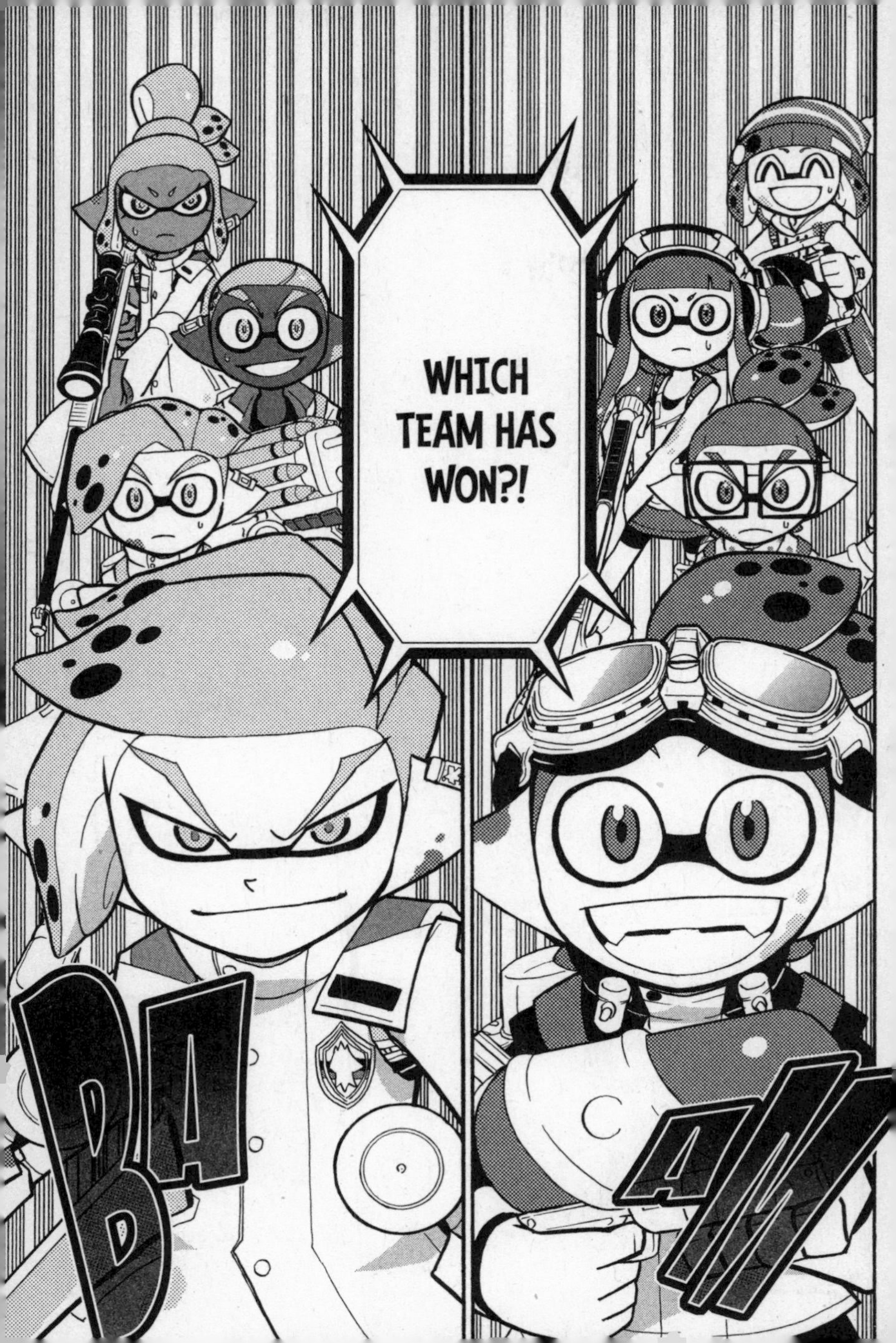
WHICH TEAM HAS WON?!
BA
DA
AN

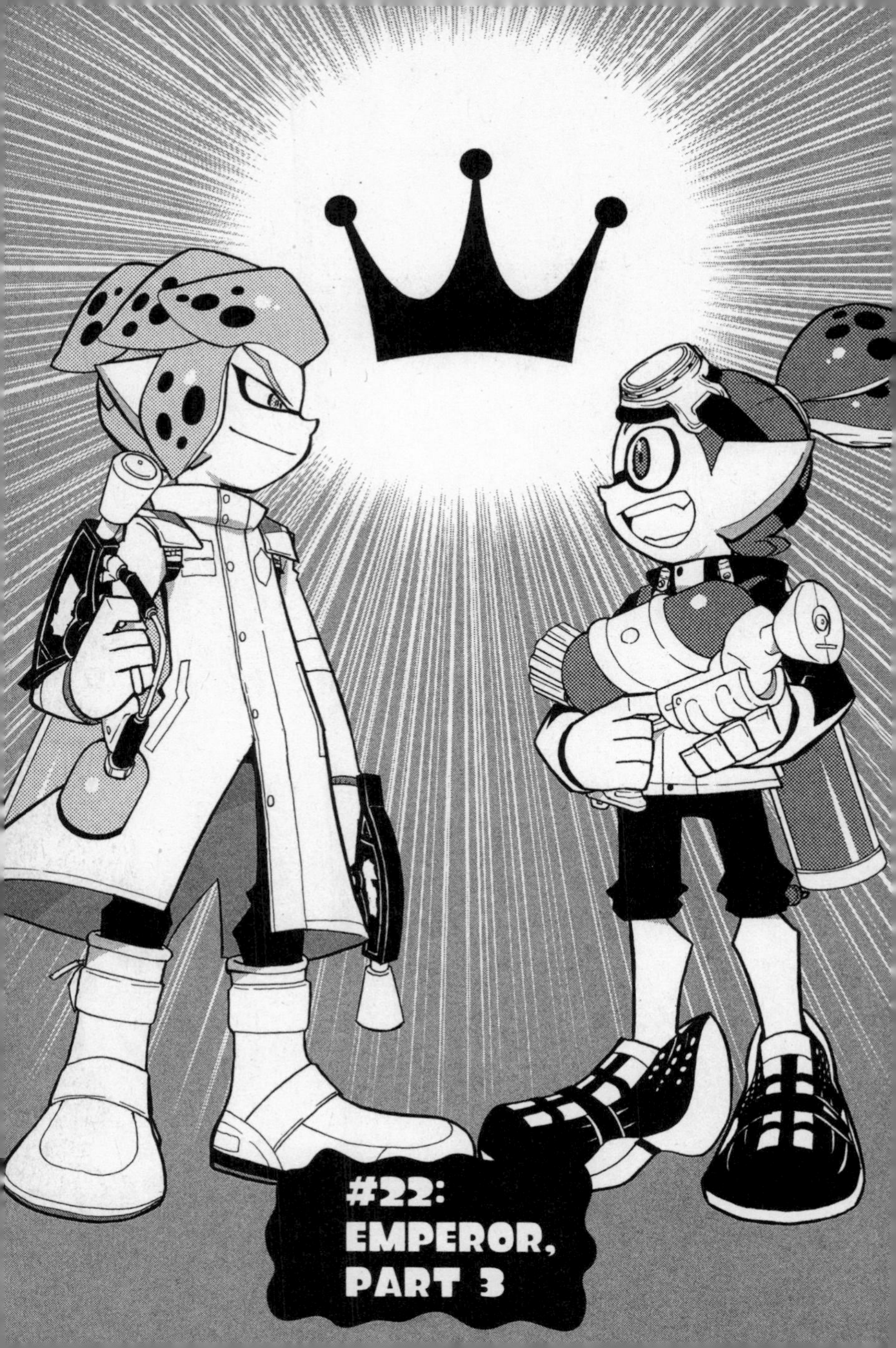
#22:
EMPEROR,
PART 3

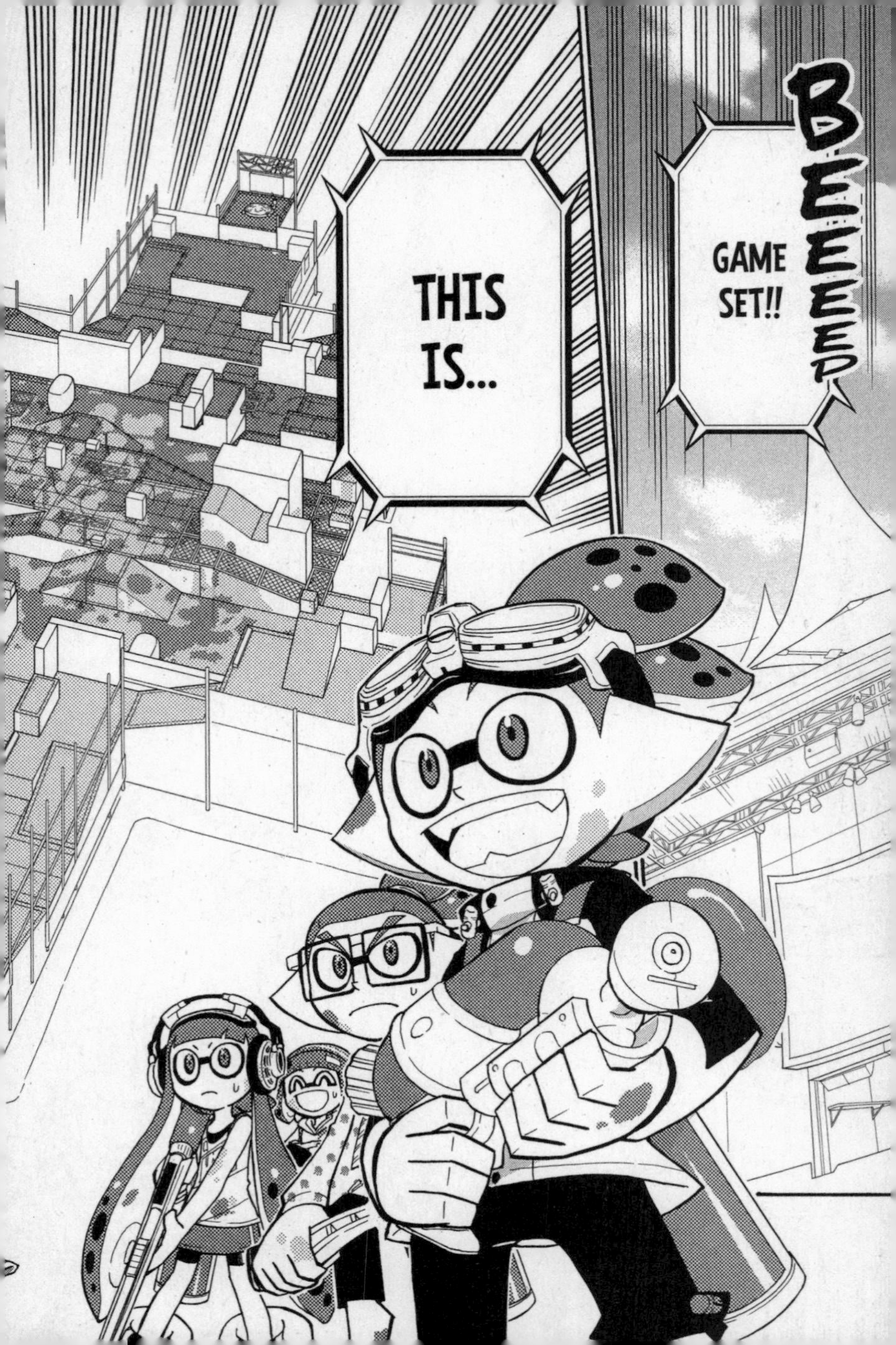
BEEEEP
GAME SET!!
THIS IS...

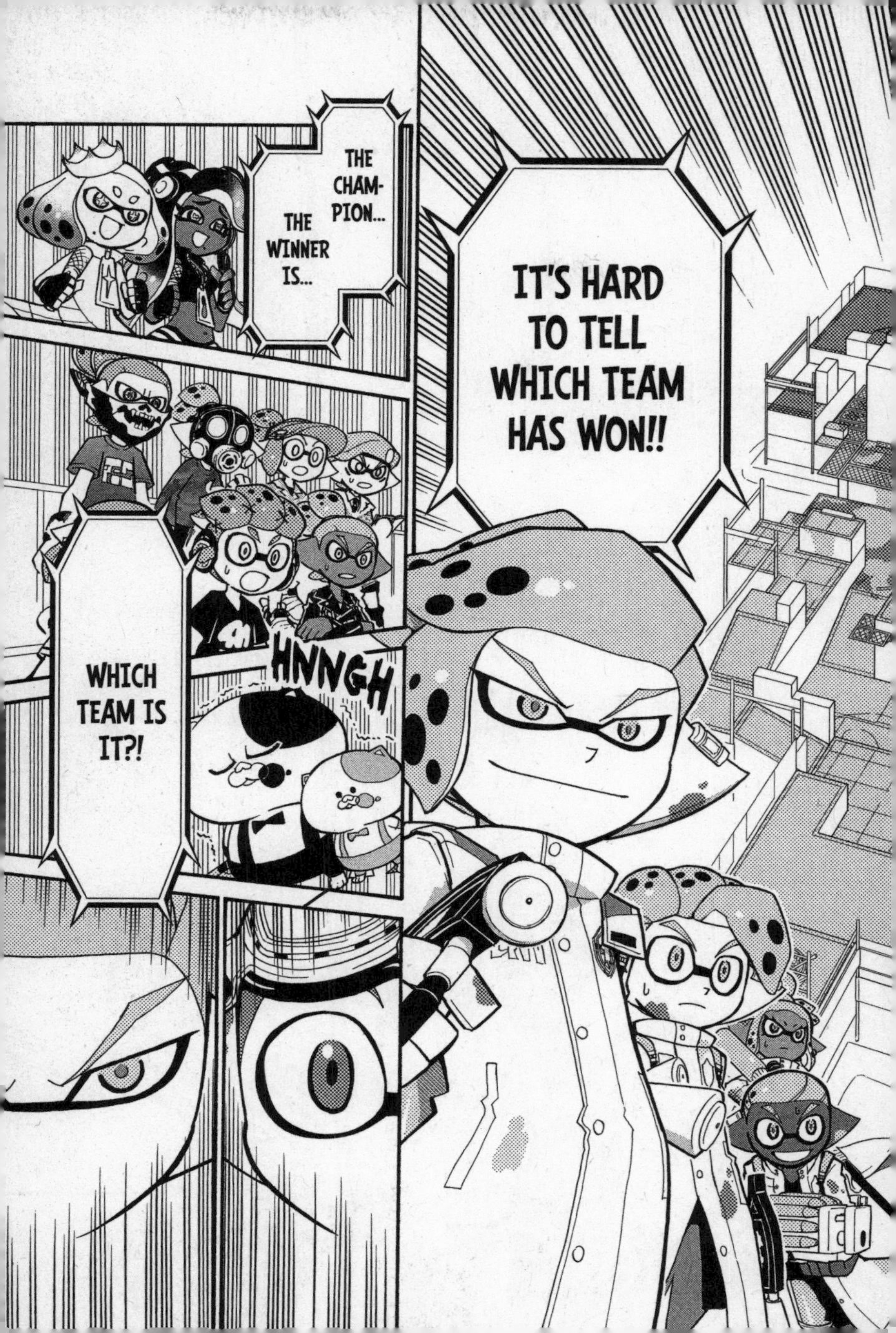
IT'S HARD TO TELL WHICH TEAM HAS WON!!
THE CHAMPION...
THE WINNER IS...
WHICH TEAM IS IT?!
HNNGH

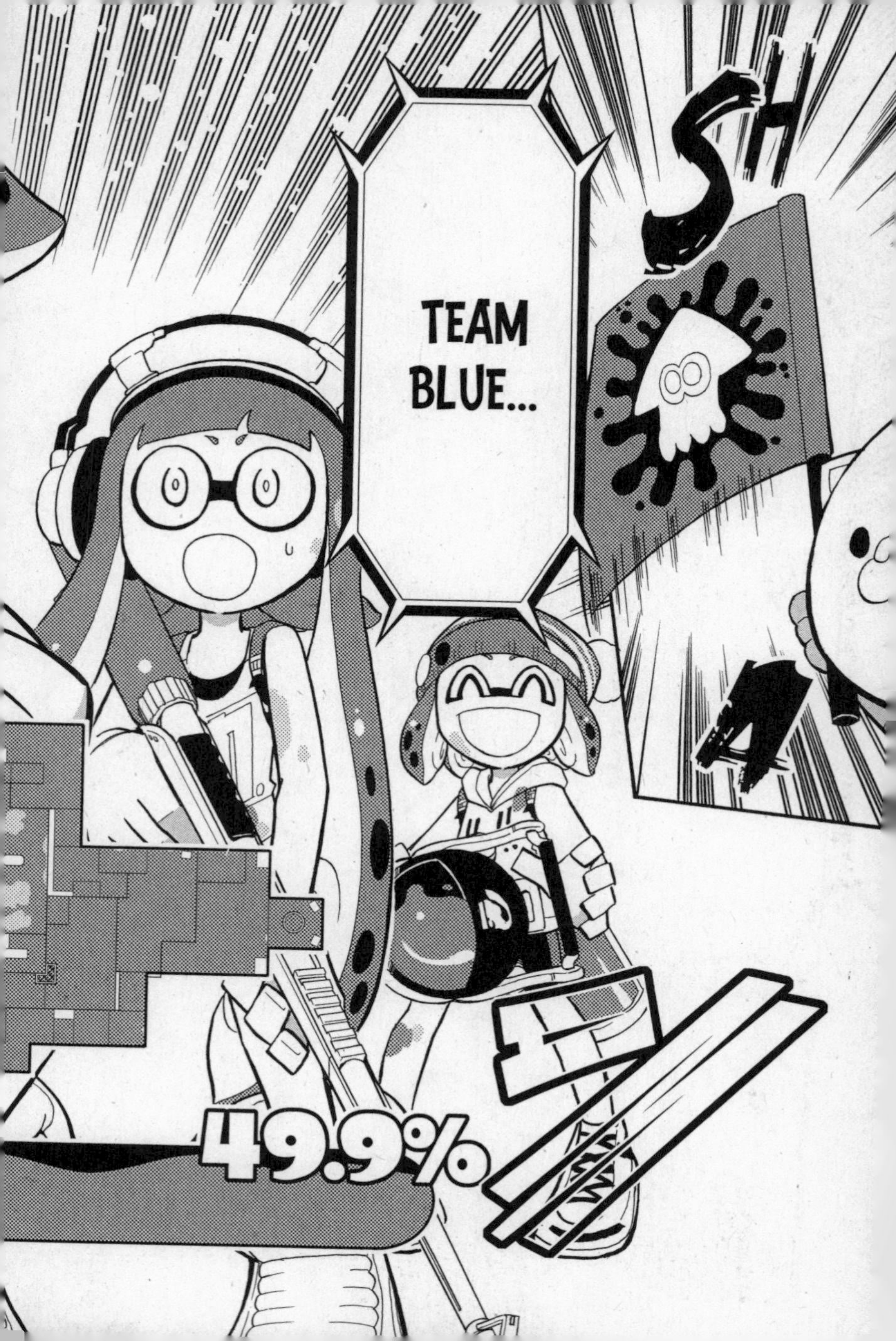
SH
TEAM BLUE...
49.9%

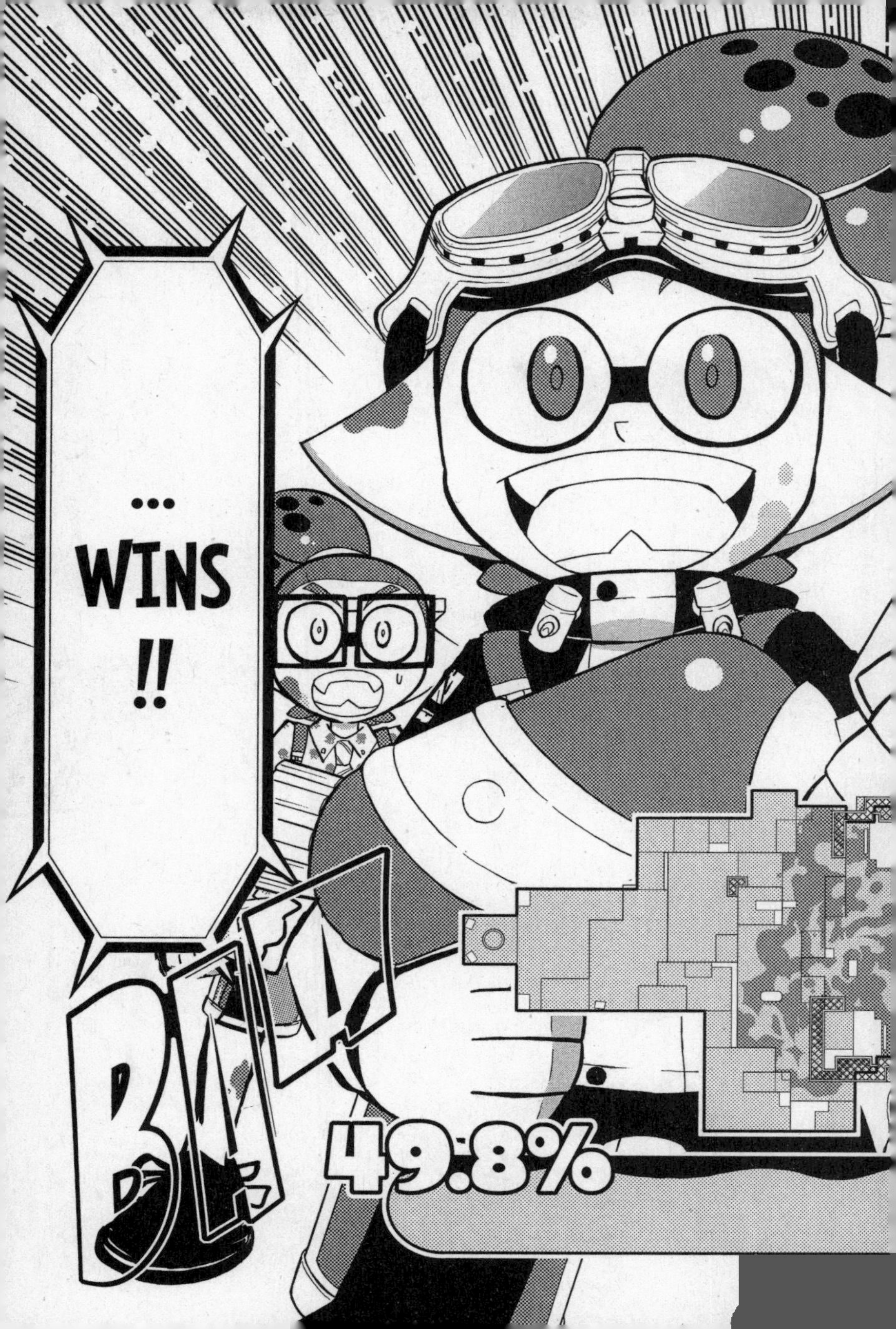
... WINS !!
49.8%

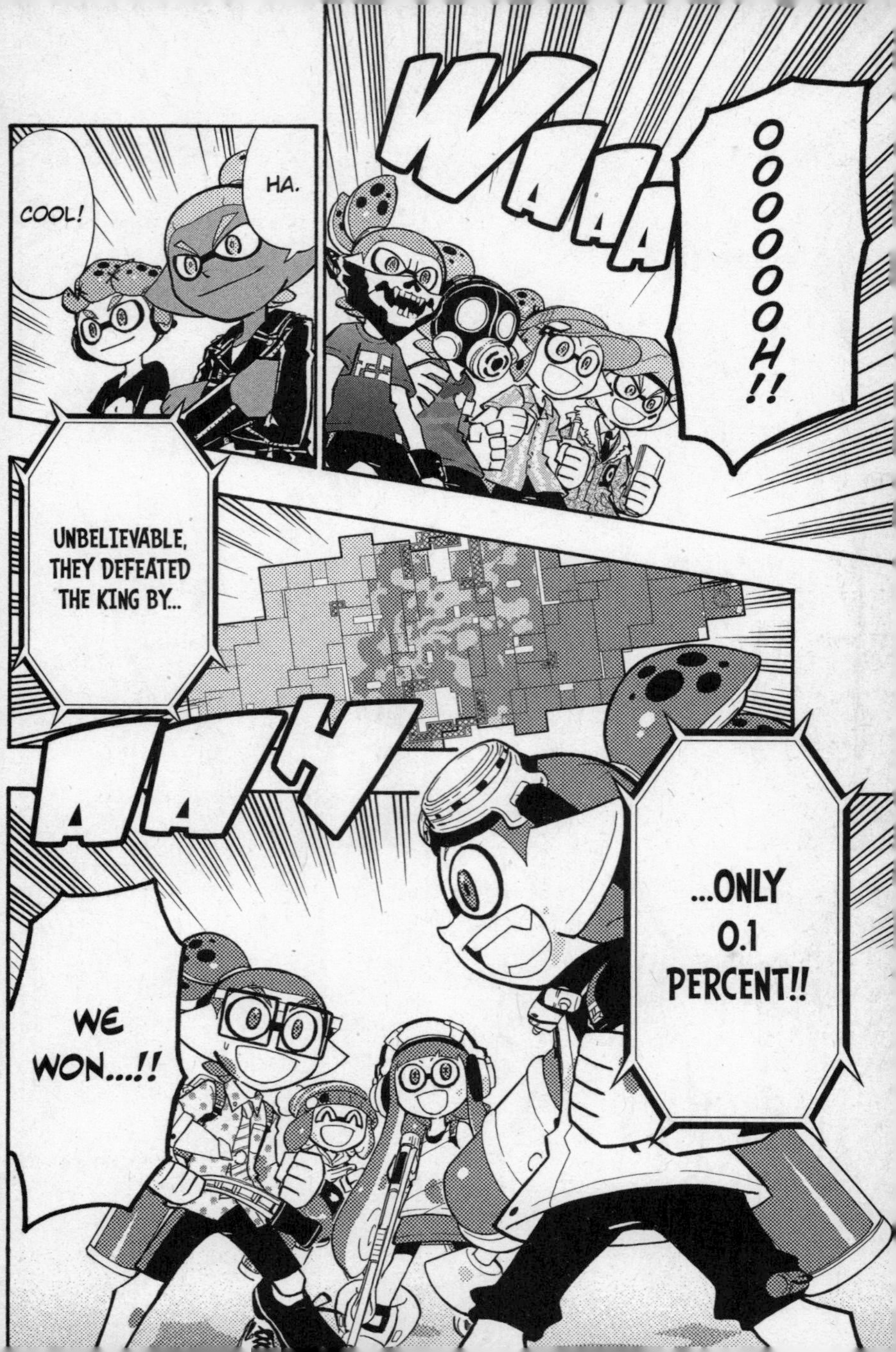
WAAAA
OOOOOOOH!!
HA.
COOL!
UNBELIEVABLE, THEY DEFEATED THE KING BY...
AAH
...ONLY 0.1 PERCENT!!
WE WON...!!

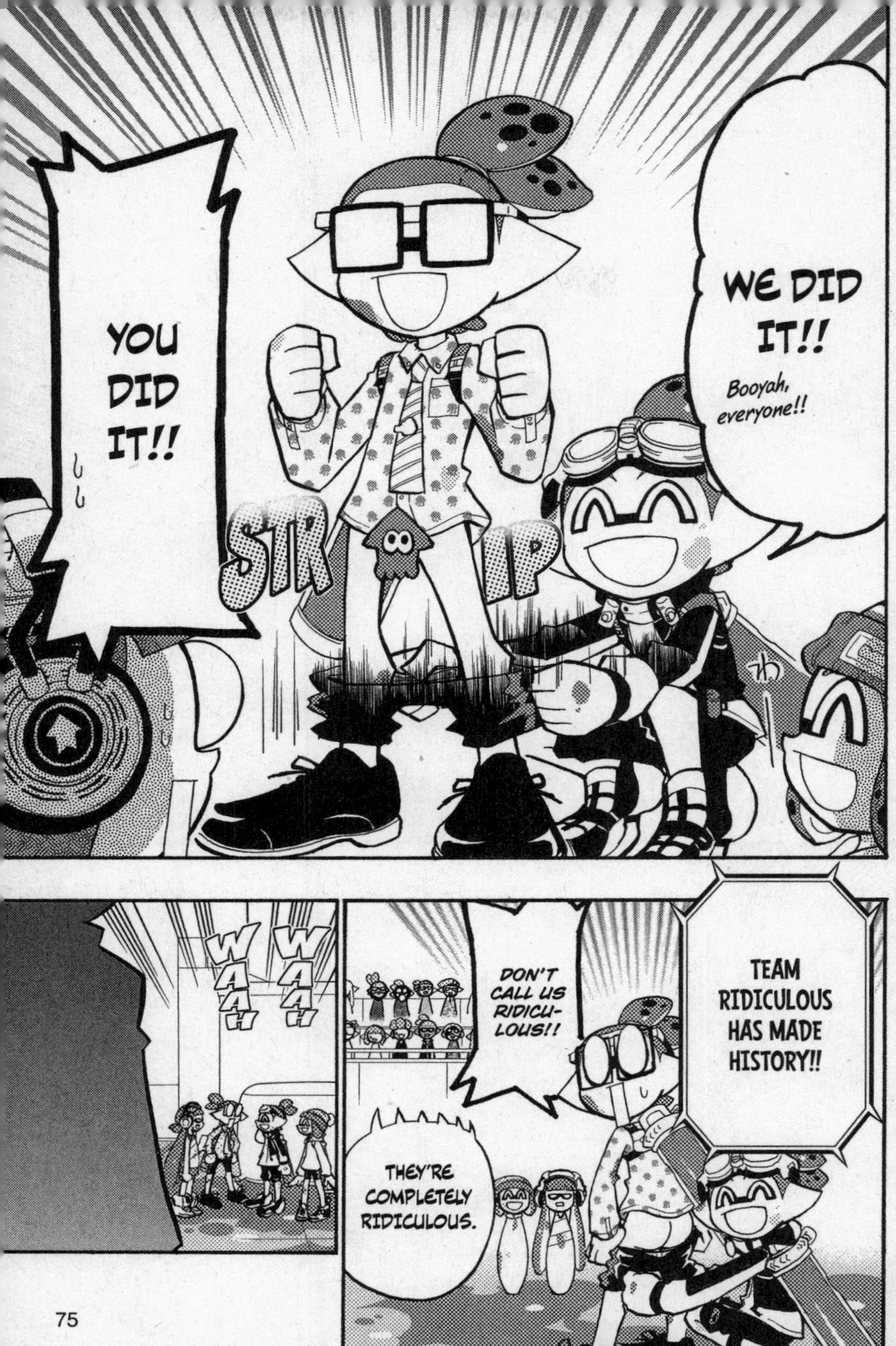
WE DID IT!!
Booyah, everyone!!
YOU DID IT!!
STRIP
TEAM RIDICULOUS HAS MADE HISTORY!!
DON'T CALL US RIDICULOUS!!
THEY'RE COMPLETELY RIDICULOUS.
WAAH
WAAH

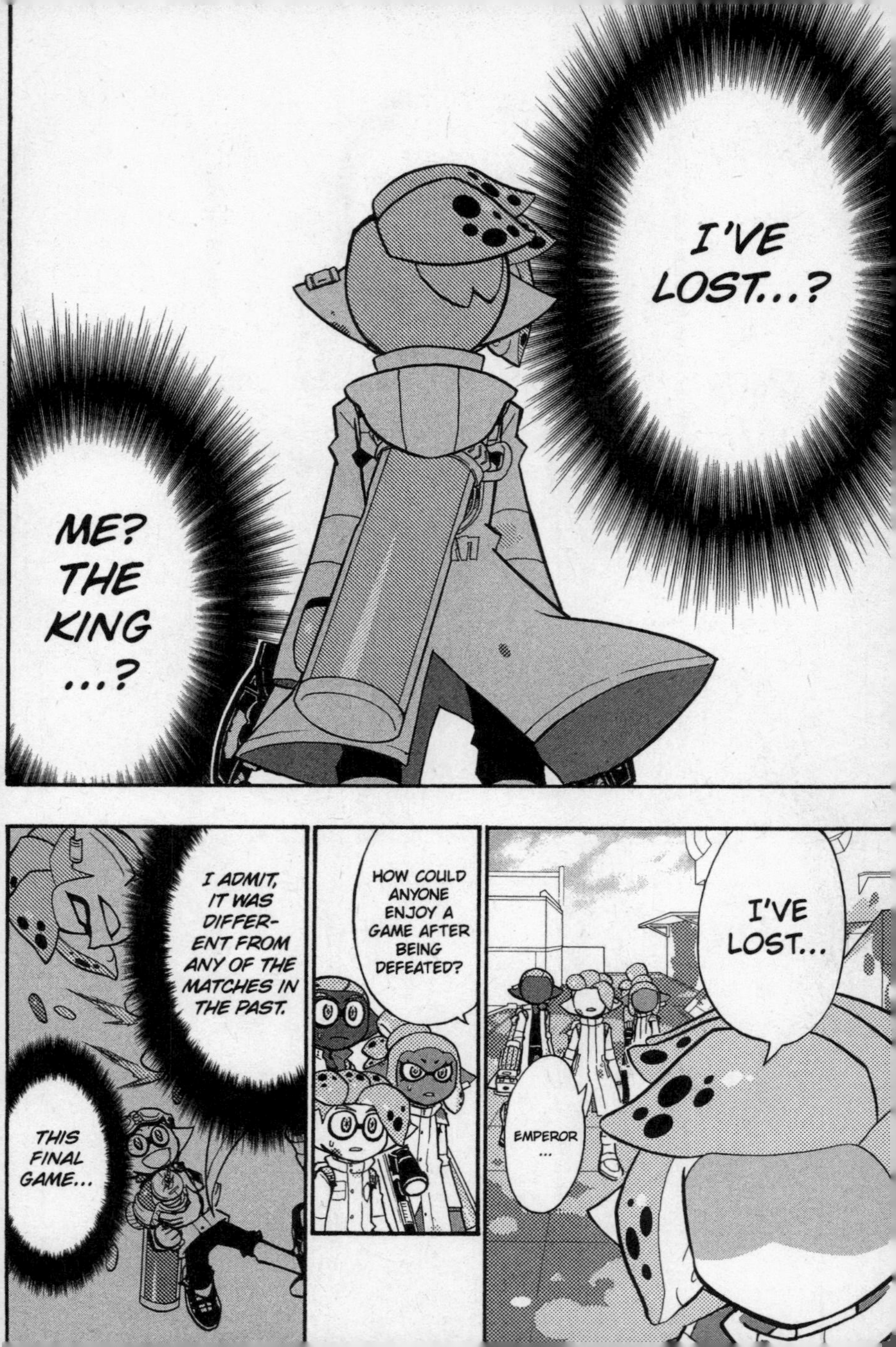
I'VE LOST...?
ME? THE KING ...?
I'VE LOST...
EMPEROR ...
HOW COULD ANYONE ENJOY A GAME AFTER BEING DEFEATED?
I ADMIT, IT WAS DIFFER-ENT FROM ANY OF THE MATCHES IN THE PAST.
THIS FINAL GAME...

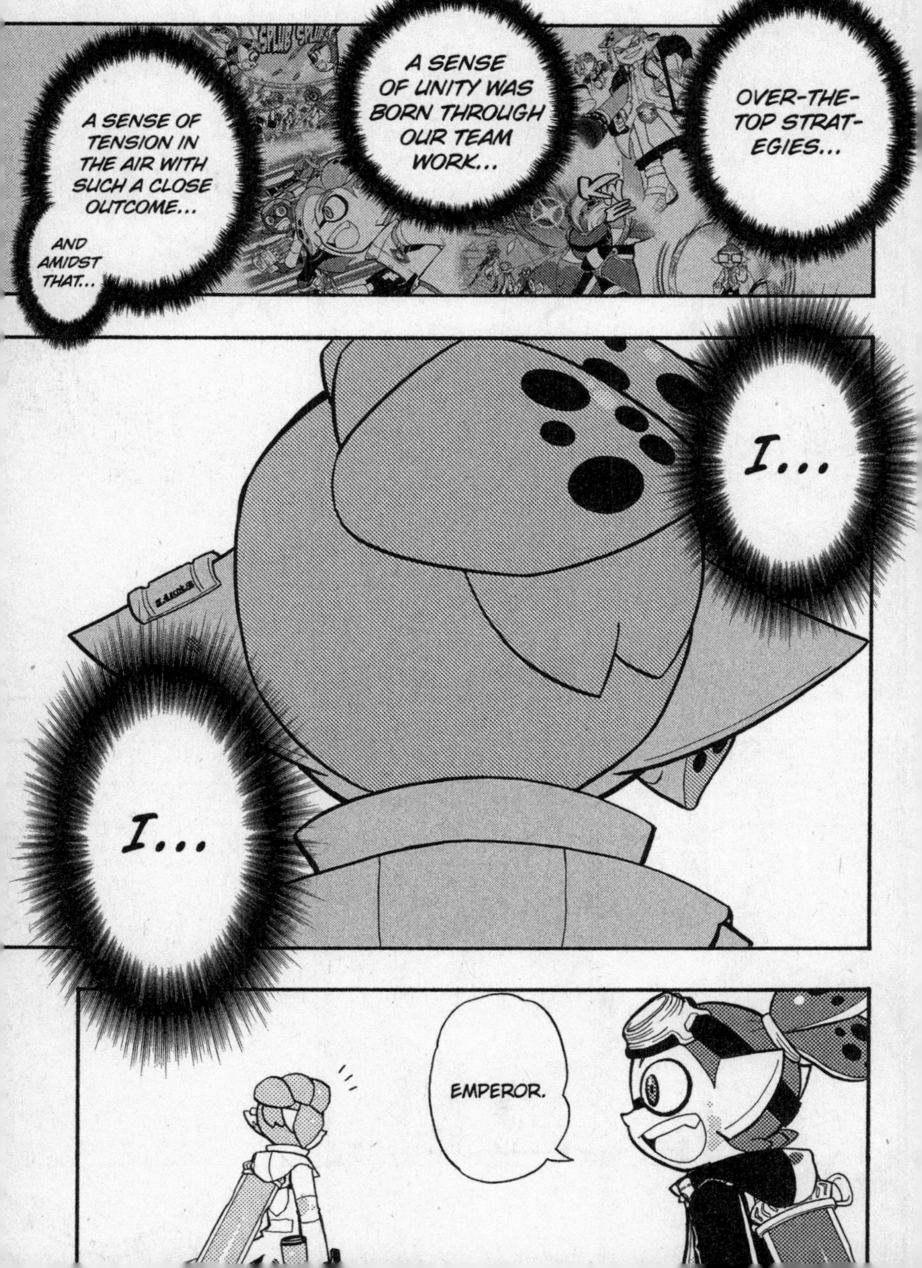
OVER-THE-TOP STRAT-EGIES...
A SENSE OF UNITY WAS BORN THROUGH OUR TEAM WORK...
A SENSE OF TENSION IN THE AIR WITH SUCH A CLOSE OUTCOME...
AND AMIDST THAT...
I...
I...
EMPEROR.

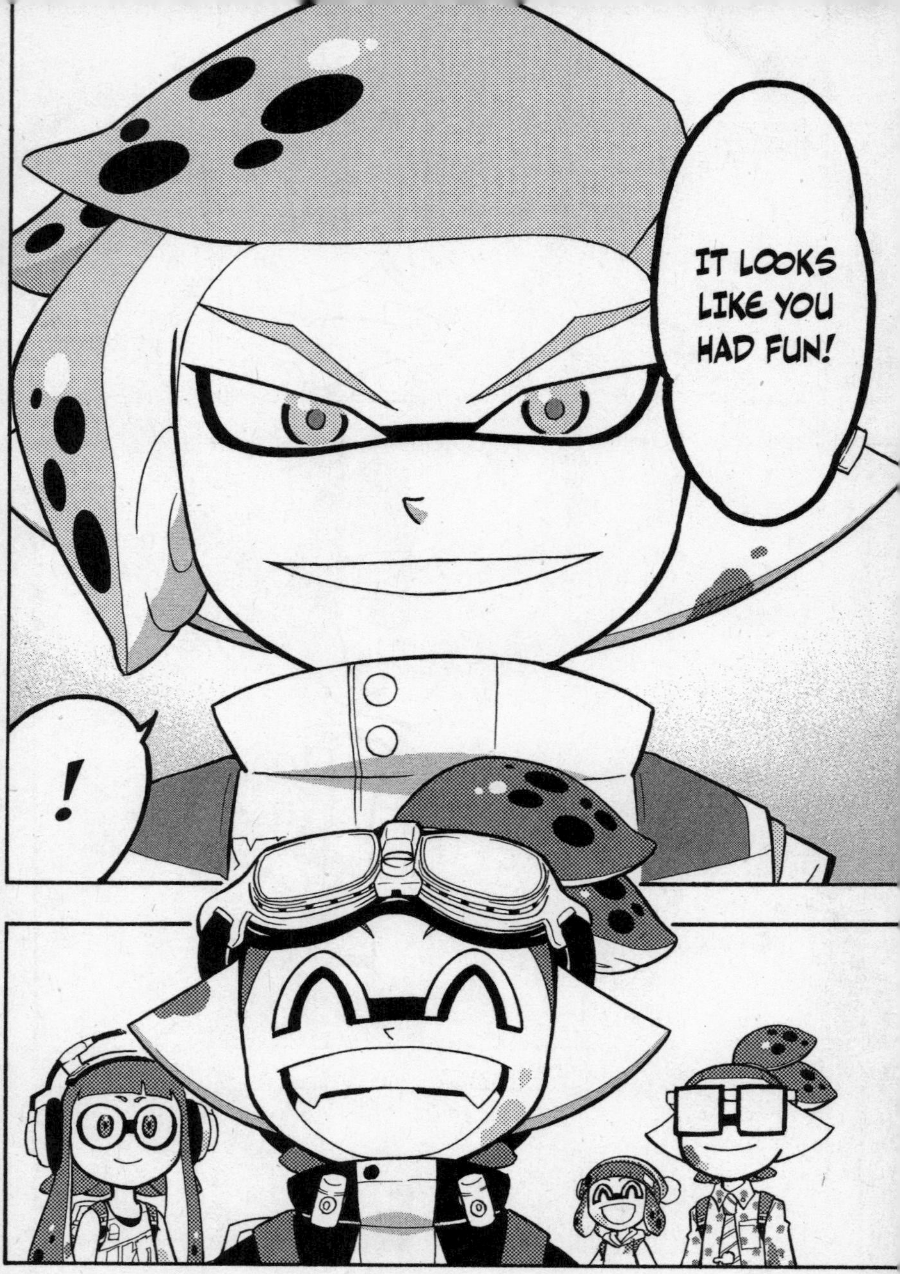
IT LOOKS LIKE YOU HAD FUN!
!

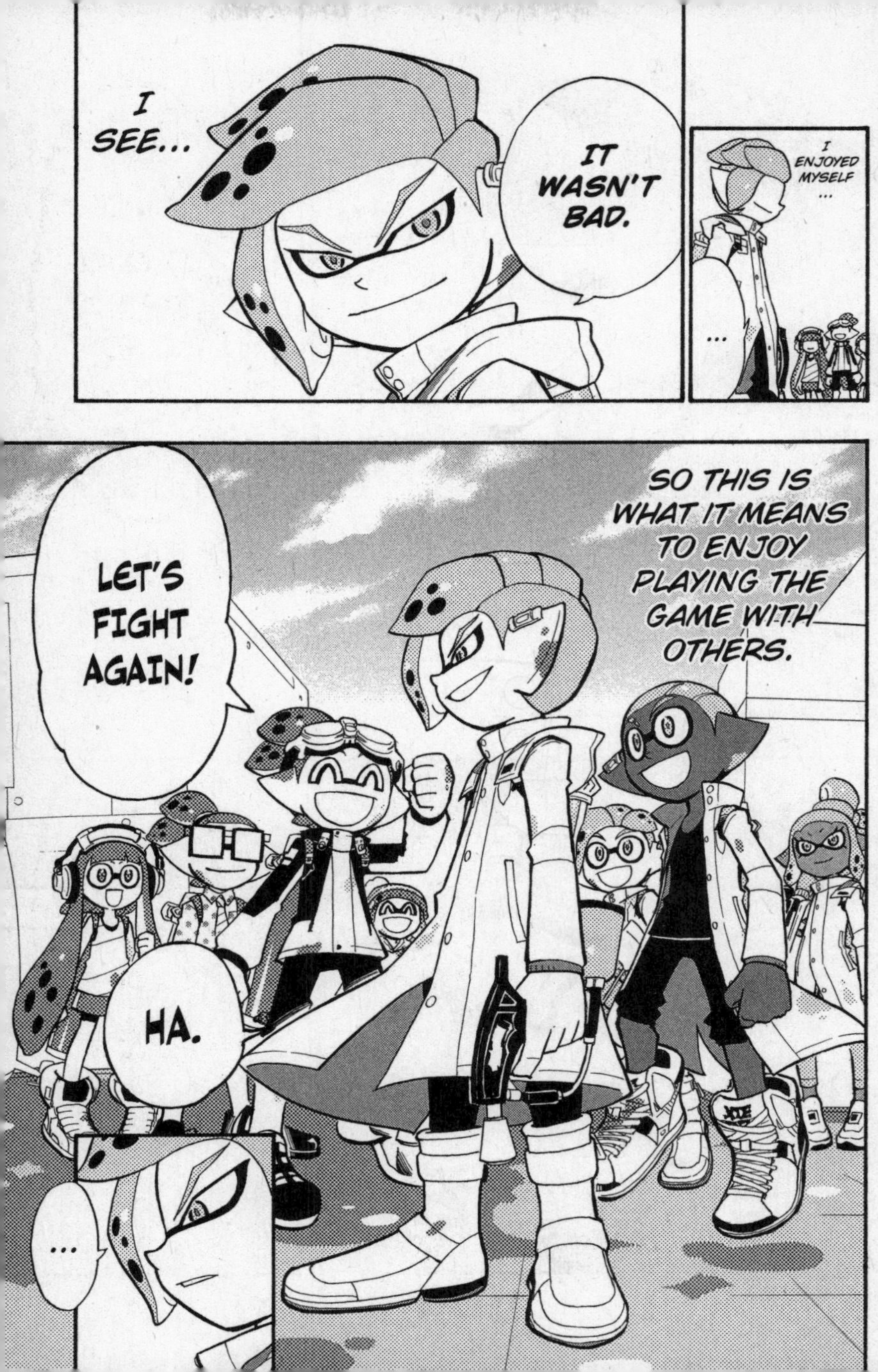
I ENJOYED MYSELF ...
...
I SEE...
IT WASN'T BAD.
SO THIS IS WHAT IT MEANS TO ENJOY PLAYING THE GAME WITH OTHERS.
LET'S FIGHT AGAIN!
HA.
...

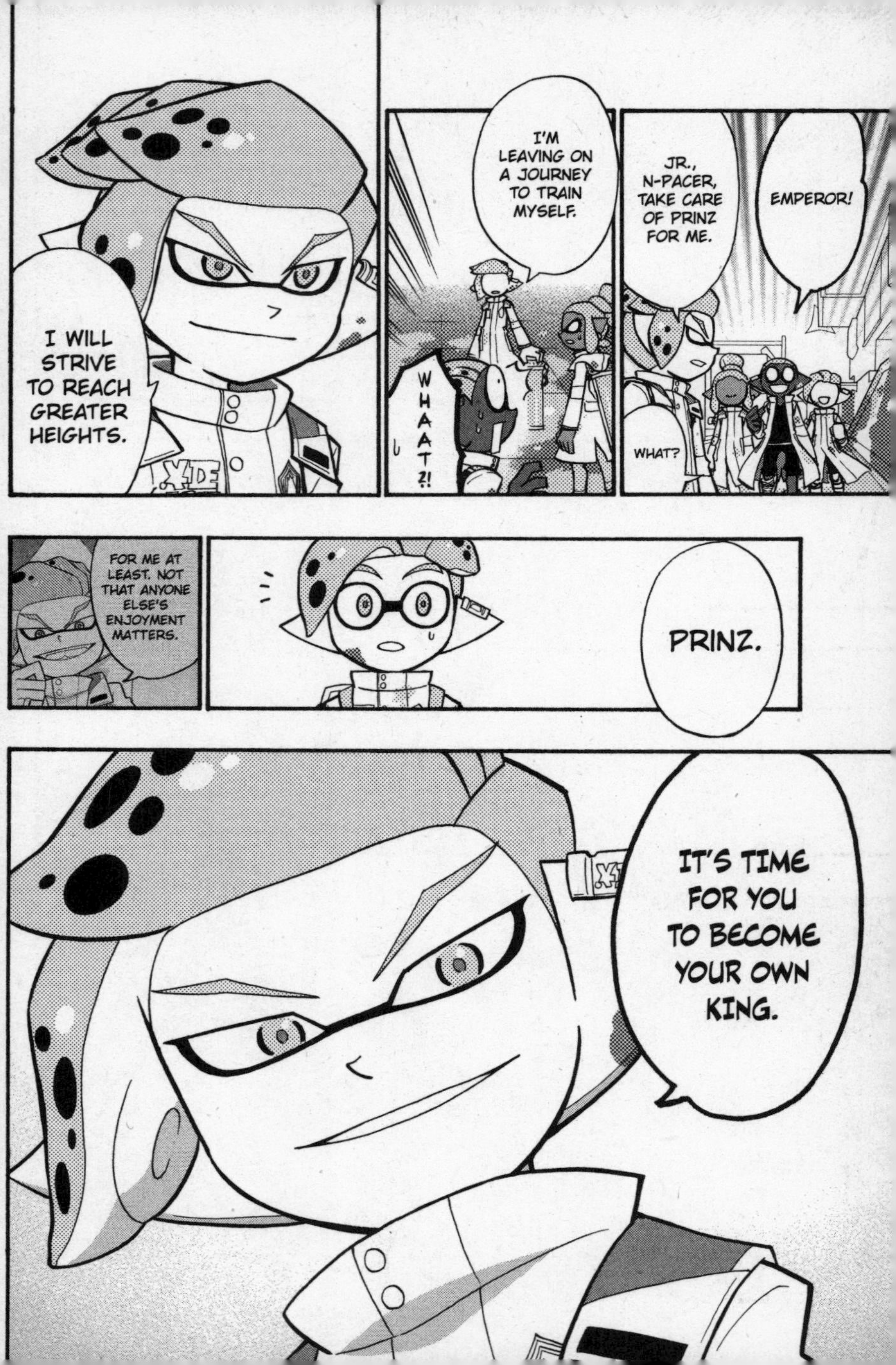
EMPEROR!
JR., N-PACER, TAKE CARE OF PRINZ FOR ME.
WHAT?
I'M LEAVING ON A JOURNEY TO TRAIN MYSELF.
WHAAT?!
I WILL STRIVE TO REACH GREATER HEIGHTS.
PRINZ.
FOR ME AT LEAST. NOT THAT ANYONE ELSE'S ENJOYMENT MATTERS.
IT'S TIME FOR YOU TO BECOME YOUR OWN KING.

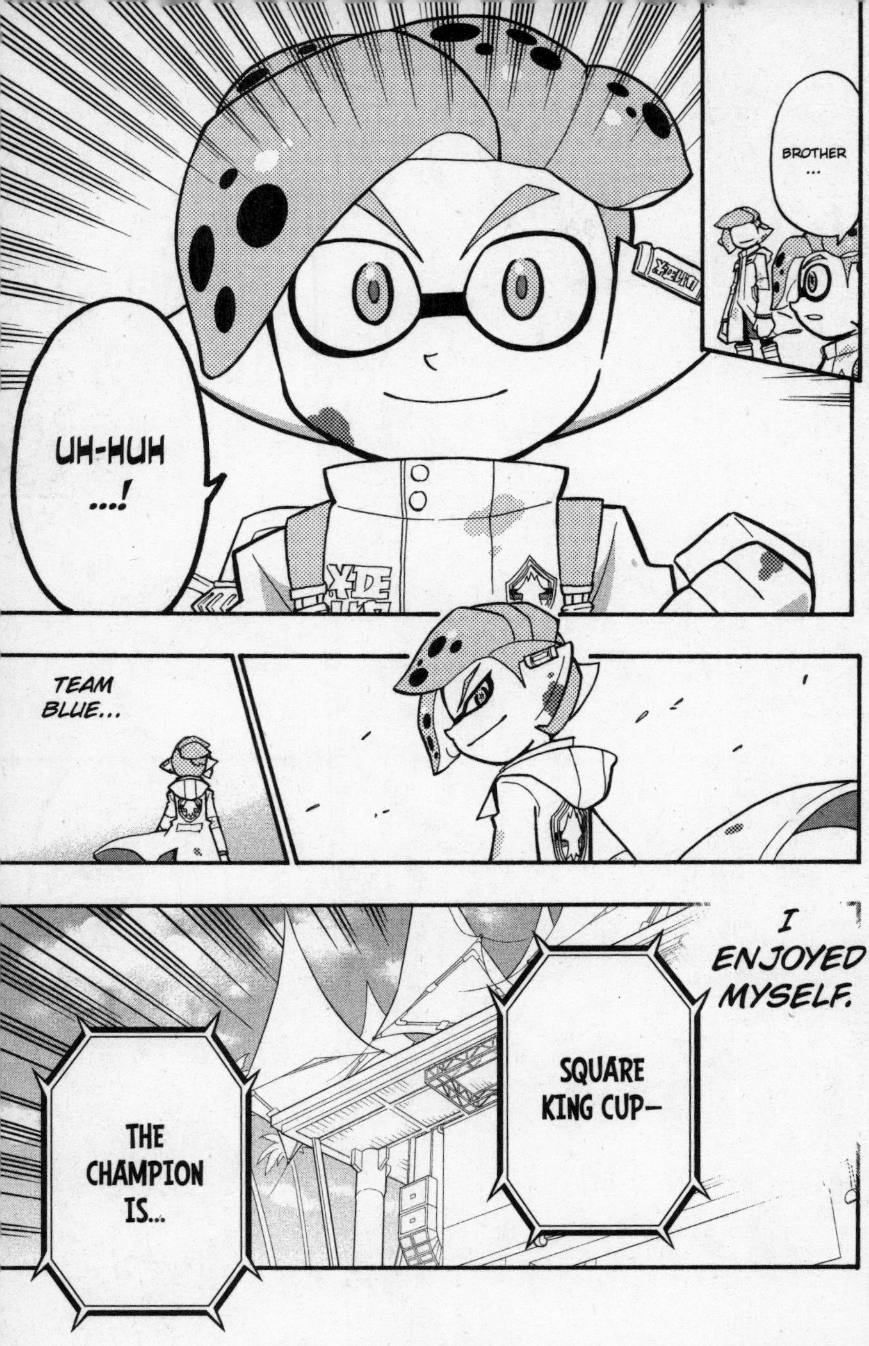
BROTHER ...
UH-HUH ...!
TEAM BLUE...
I ENJOYED MYSELF.
SQUARE KING CUP—
THE CHAMPION IS...

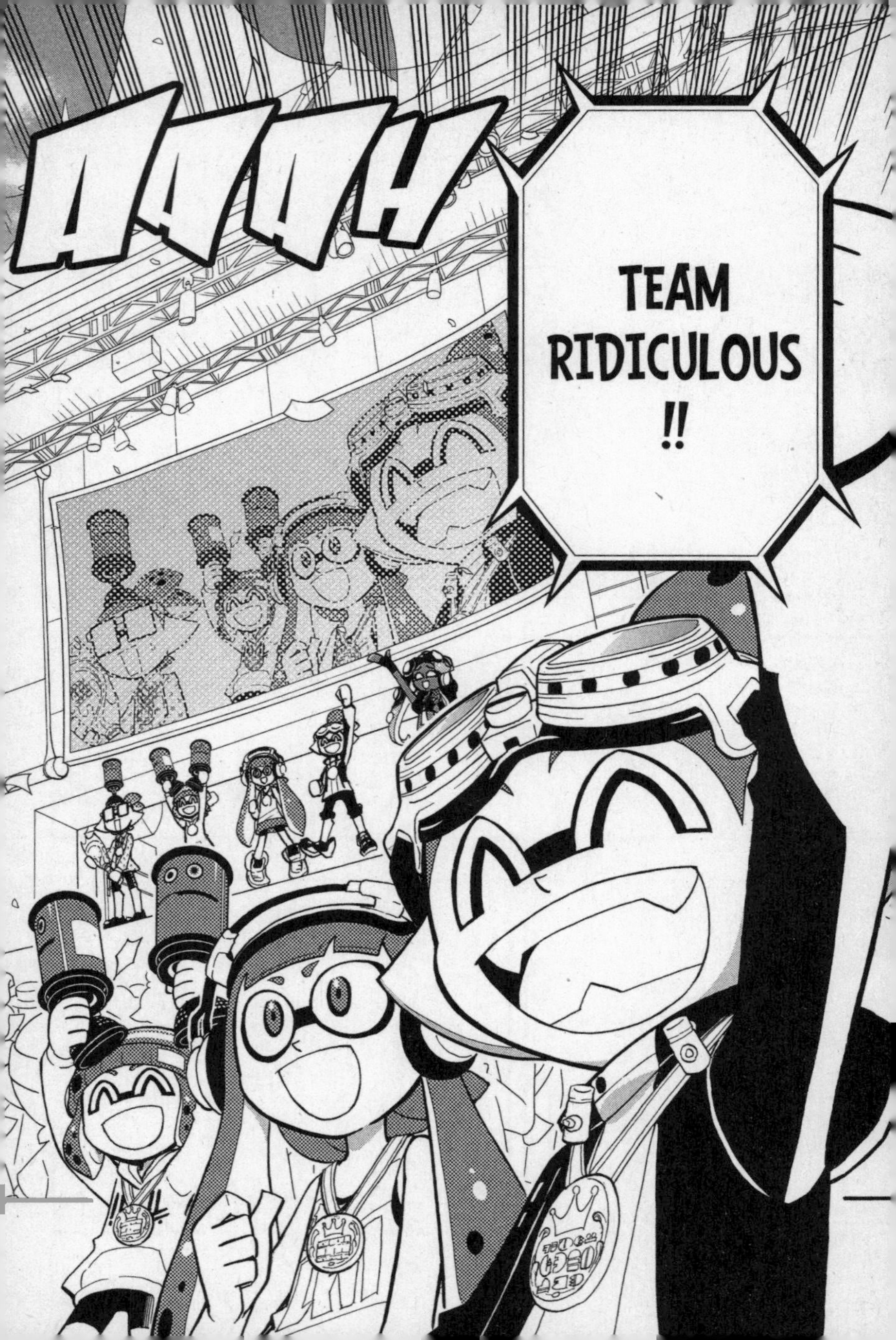
AAAH
TEAM RIDICULOUS!!

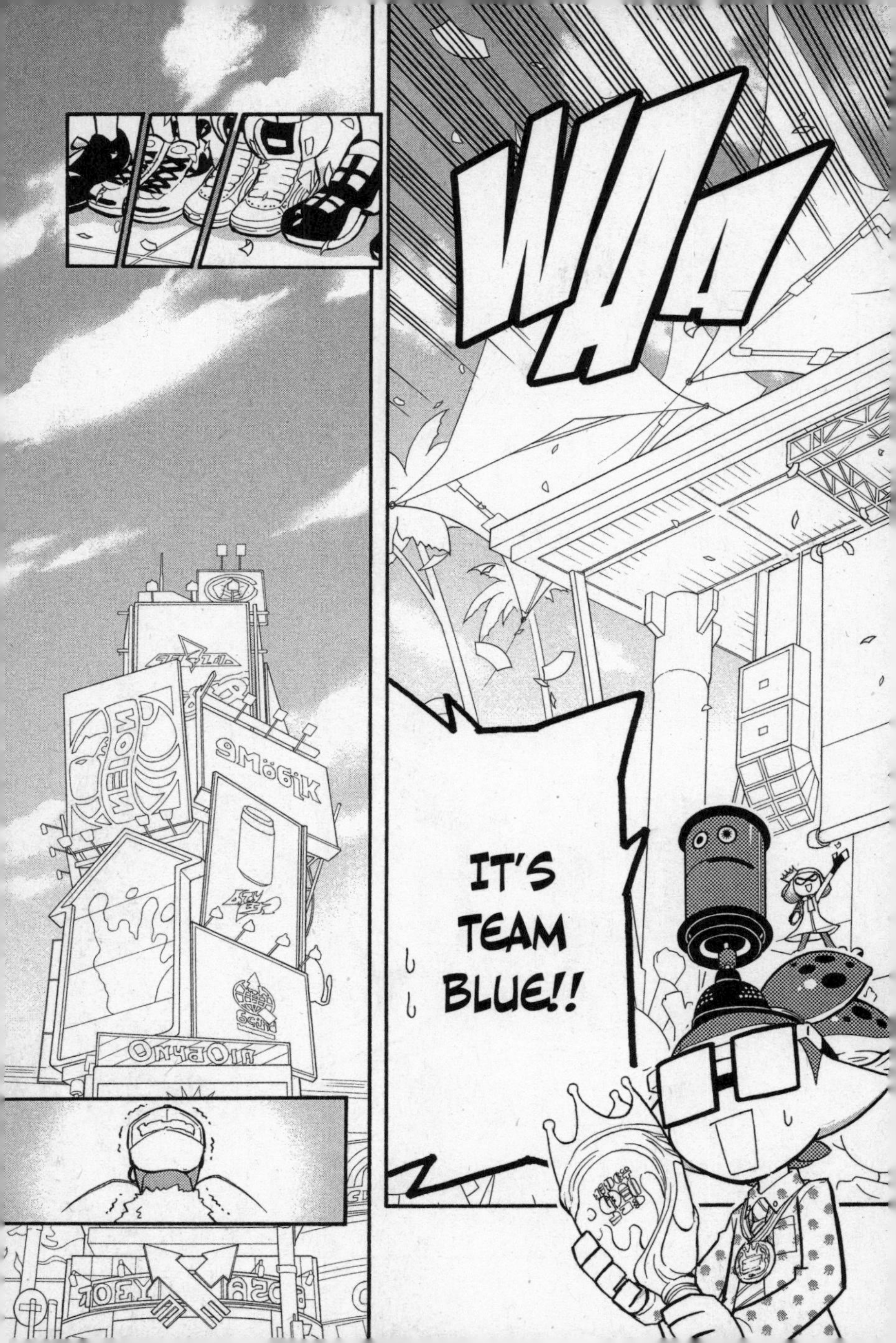
WAA
IT'S TEAM BLUE!!

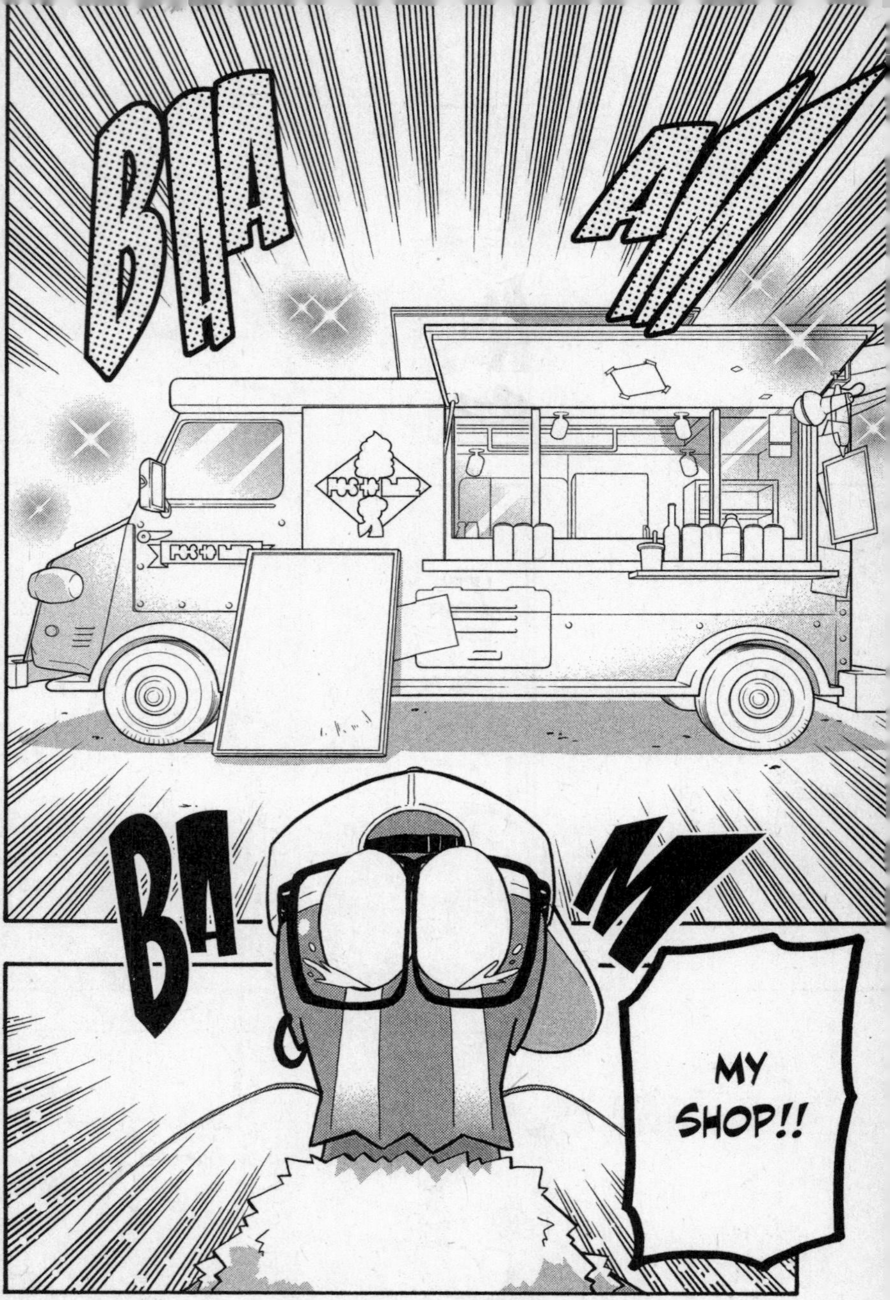
BAAAM
BAM
MY SHOP!!

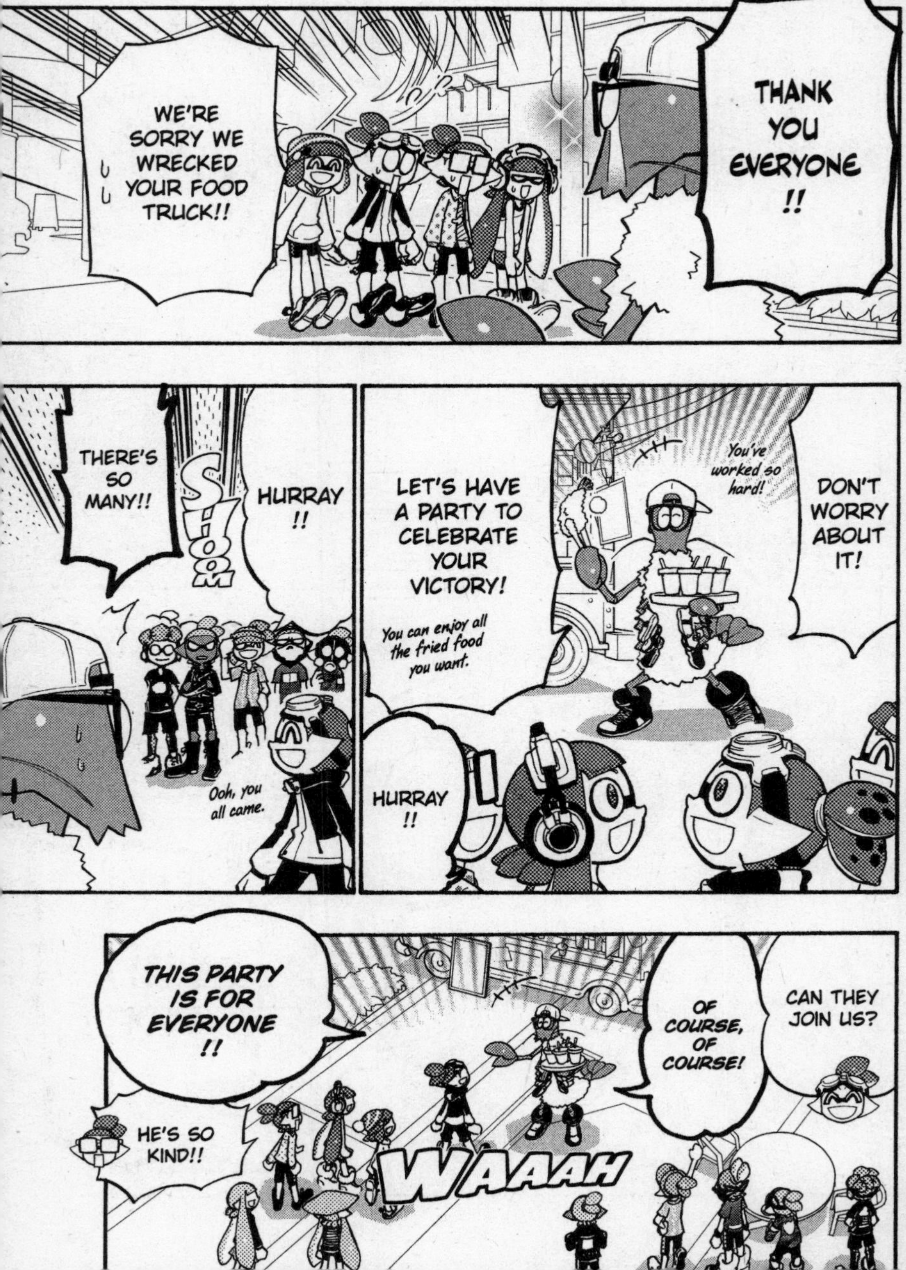
THANK YOU EVERYONE !!
WE'RE SORRY WE WRECKED YOUR FOOD TRUCK!!
DON'T WORRY ABOUT IT!
You've worked so hard!
LET'S HAVE A PARTY TO CELEBRATE YOUR VICTORY!
You can enjoy all the fried food you want.
HURRAY !!
HURRAY !!
SHOOM
THERE'S SO MANY!!
Ooh, you all came.
CAN THEY JOIN US?
OF COURSE, OF COURSE!
THIS PARTY IS FOR EVERYONE !!
WAAAH
HE'S SO KIND!!

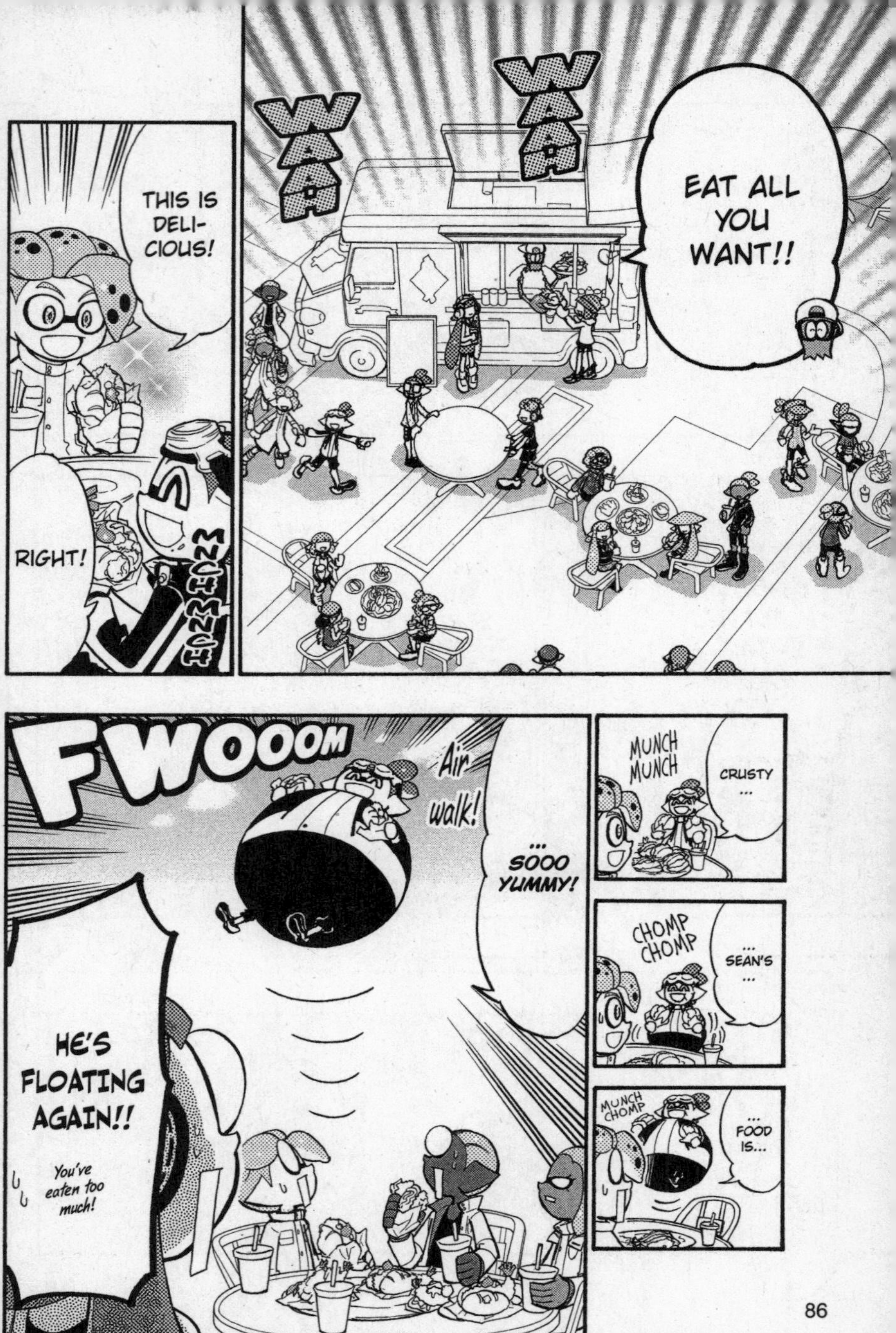

WAA
WAA
EAT ALL YOU WANT!!
THIS IS DELICIOUS!
RIGHT!
MNCH MNCH
MUNCH MUNCH
CRUSTY ...
CHOMP CHOMP
... SEAN'S ...
MUNCH CHOMP
... FOOD IS...
... SOOO YUMMY!
FWOOOM
Air walk!
HE'S FLOATING AGAIN!!
You've eaten too much!

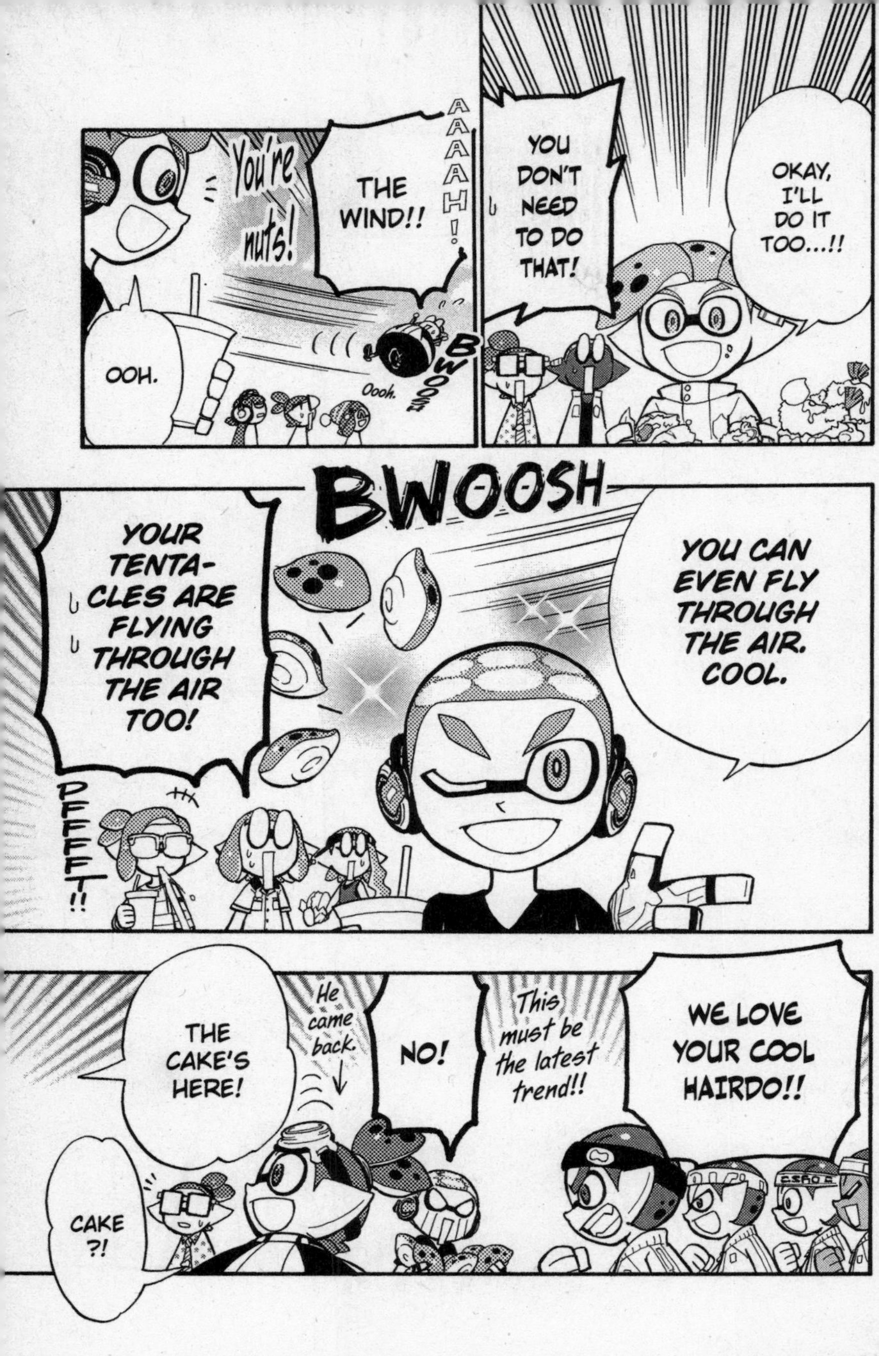
OKAY, I'LL DO IT TOO...!!
YOU DON'T NEED TO DO THAT!
AAAAAH!
THE WIND!!
You're nuts!
Oooh.
OOH.
BWOOSH
YOU CAN EVEN FLY THROUGH THE AIR. COOL.
YOUR TENTACLES ARE FLYING THROUGH THE AIR TOO!
PFFFFT!!
WE LOVE YOUR COOL HAIRDO!!
This must be the latest trend!!
NO!
He came back.
THE CAKE'S HERE!
CAKE?!

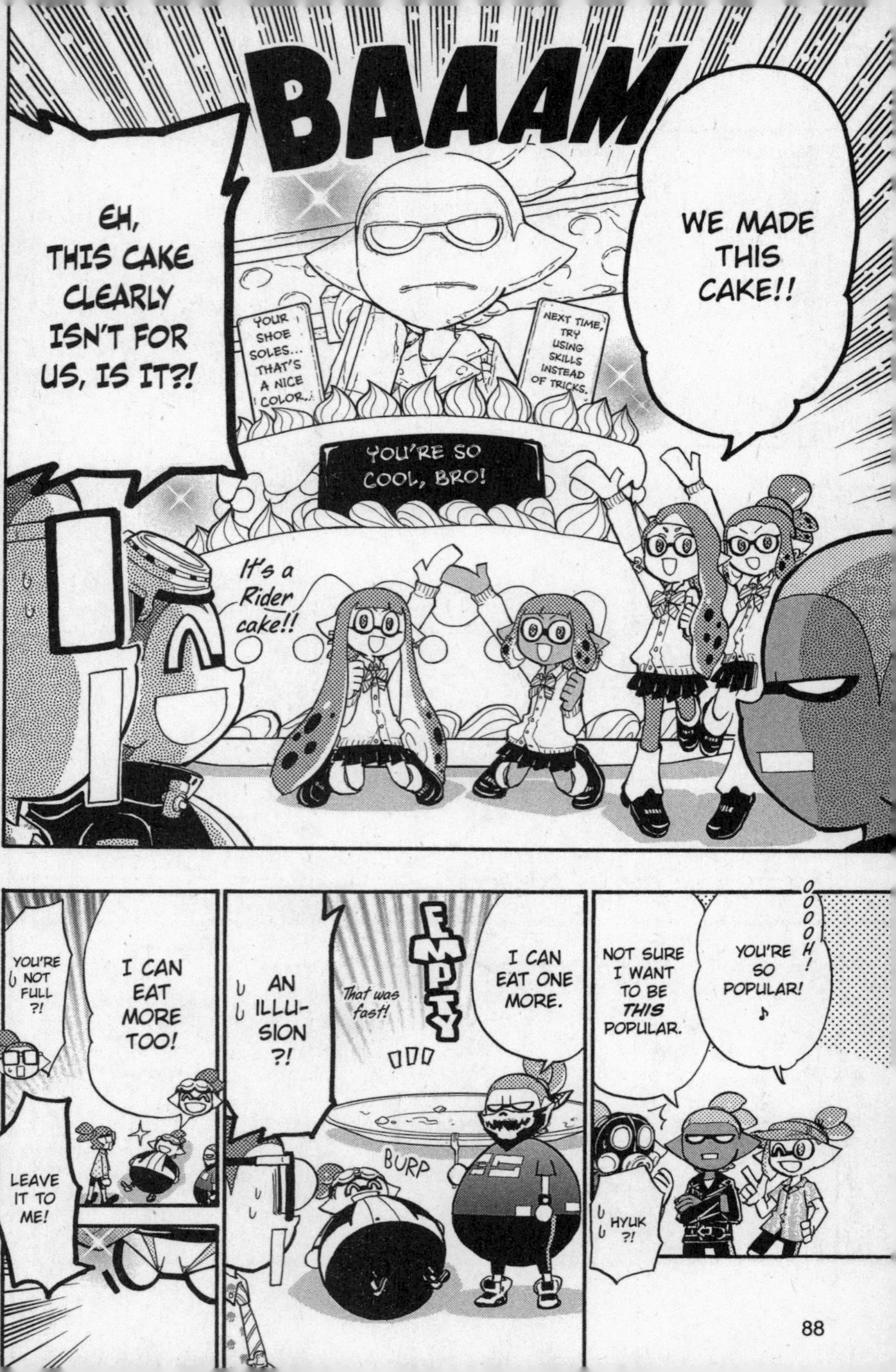
BAAAM
WE MADE THIS CAKE!!
EH, THIS CAKE CLEARLY ISN'T FOR US, IS IT?!
NEXT TIME, TRY USING SKILLS INSTEAD OF TRICKS.
YOUR SHOE SOLES... THAT'S A NICE COLOR.
YOU'RE SO COOL, BRO!
It's a Rider cake!!
OOOOH!
YOU'RE SO POPULAR! ♪
NOT SURE I WANT TO BE THIS POPULAR.
HYUK ?!
EMPTY
I CAN EAT ONE MORE.
That was fast!
AN ILLUSION?!
BURP
I CAN EAT MORE TOO!
YOU'RE NOT FULL ?!
LEAVE IT TO ME!

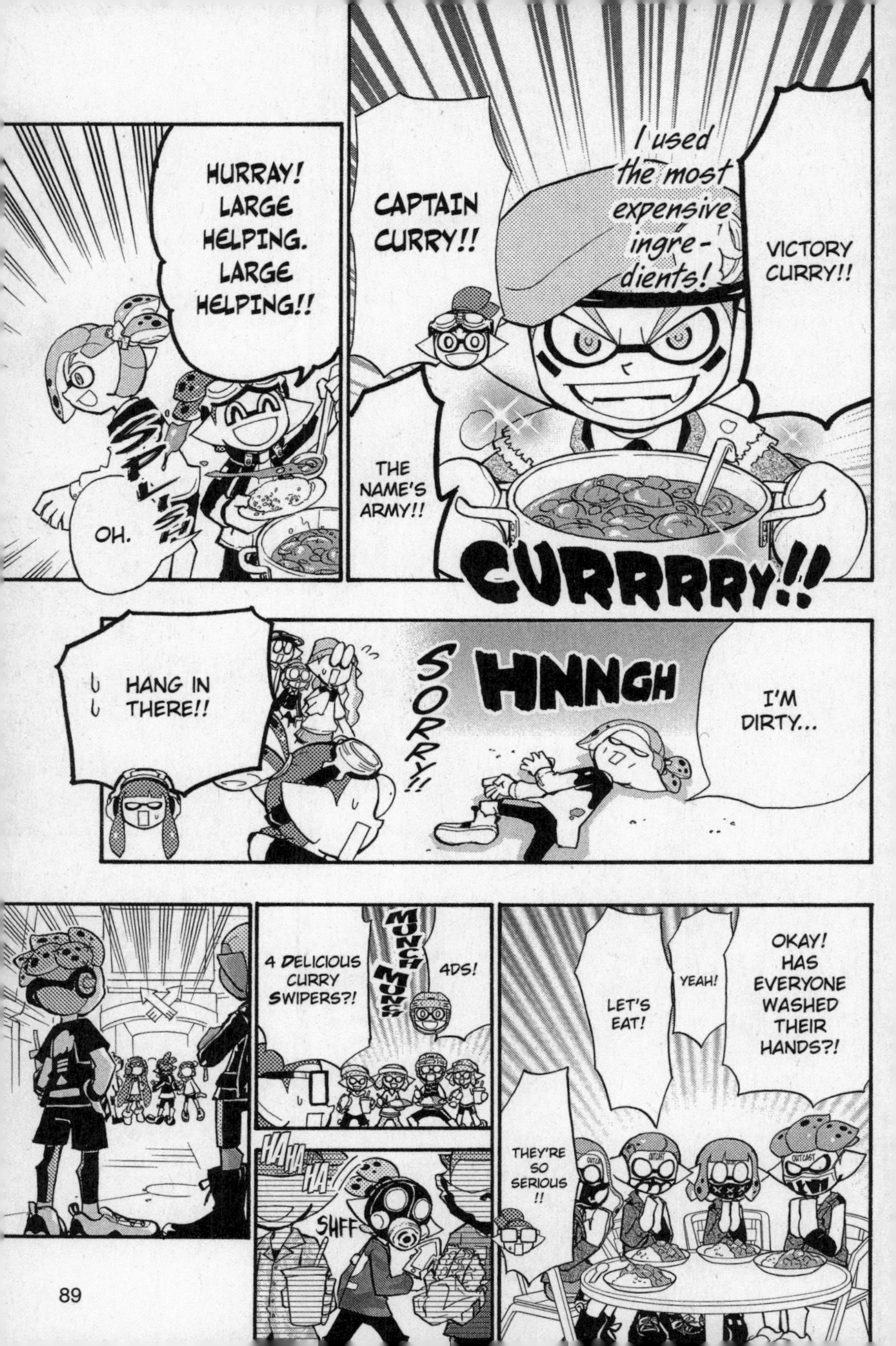
VICTORY CURRY!!
I used the most expensive ingre-dients!
CAPTAIN CURRY!!
THE NAME'S ARMY!!
CURRRRY!!
HURRAY! LARGE HELPING. LARGE HELPING!!
OH.
I'M DIRTY...
HNNGH
SORRY!!
HANG IN THERE!!
OKAY! HAS EVERYONE WASHED THEIR HANDS?!
YEAH!
LET'S EAT!
THEY'RE SO SERIOUS !!
4DS!
MUNCH MUNCH
4 DELICIOUS CURRY SWIPERS?!
HAHAHA
SHFF

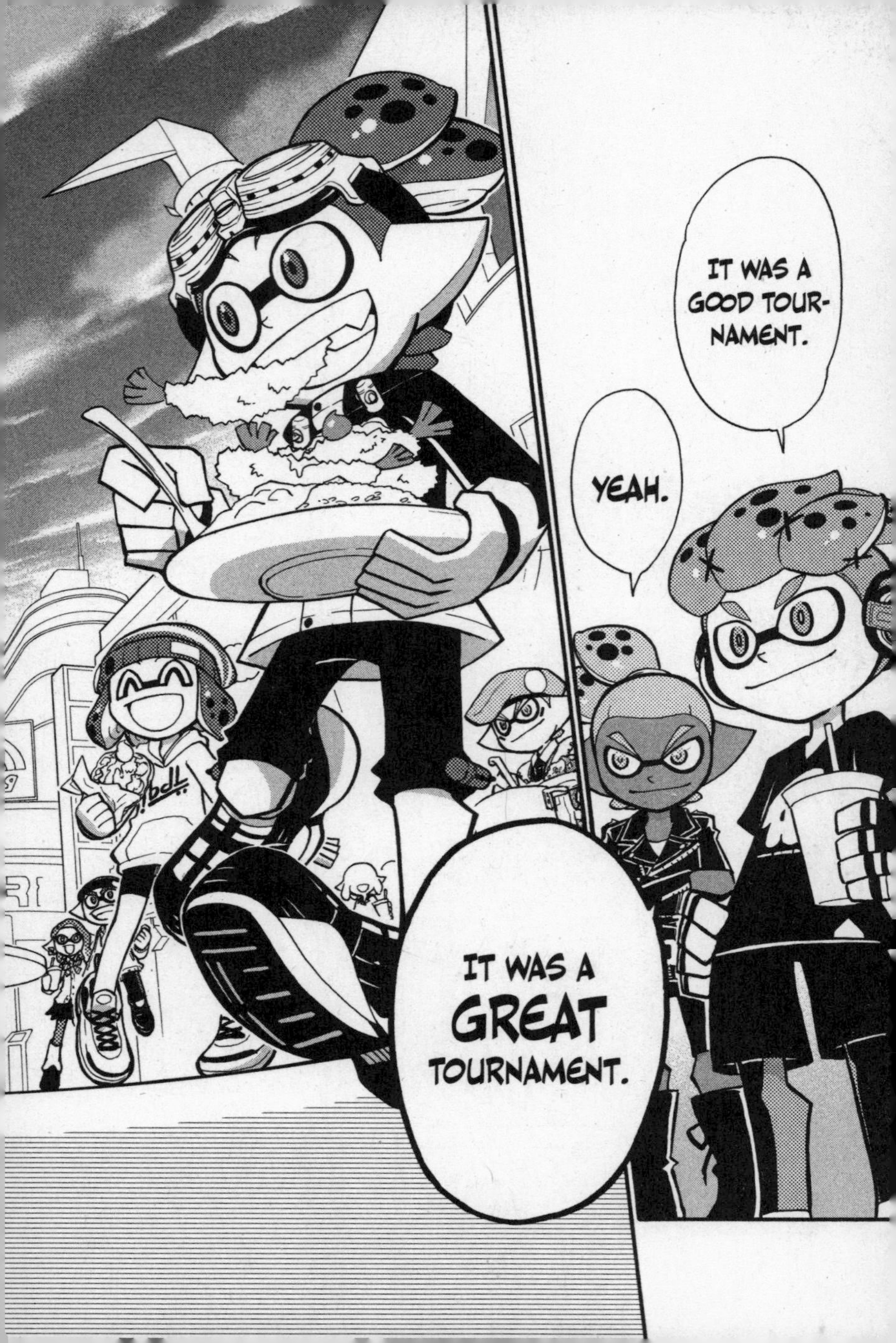
IT WAS A GOOD TOUR- NAMENT.
YEAH.
IT WAS A GREAT TOURNAMENT.

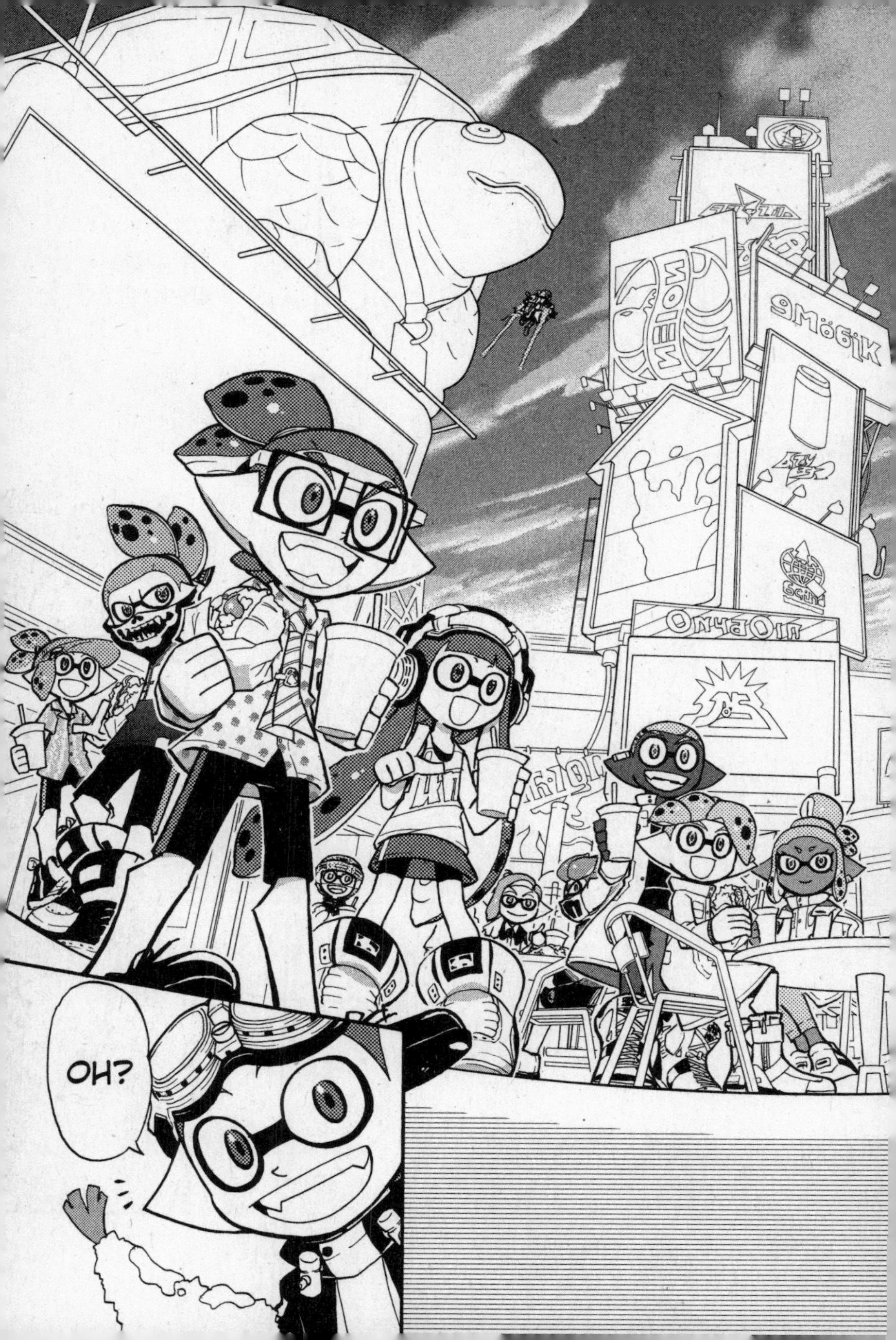
OH?

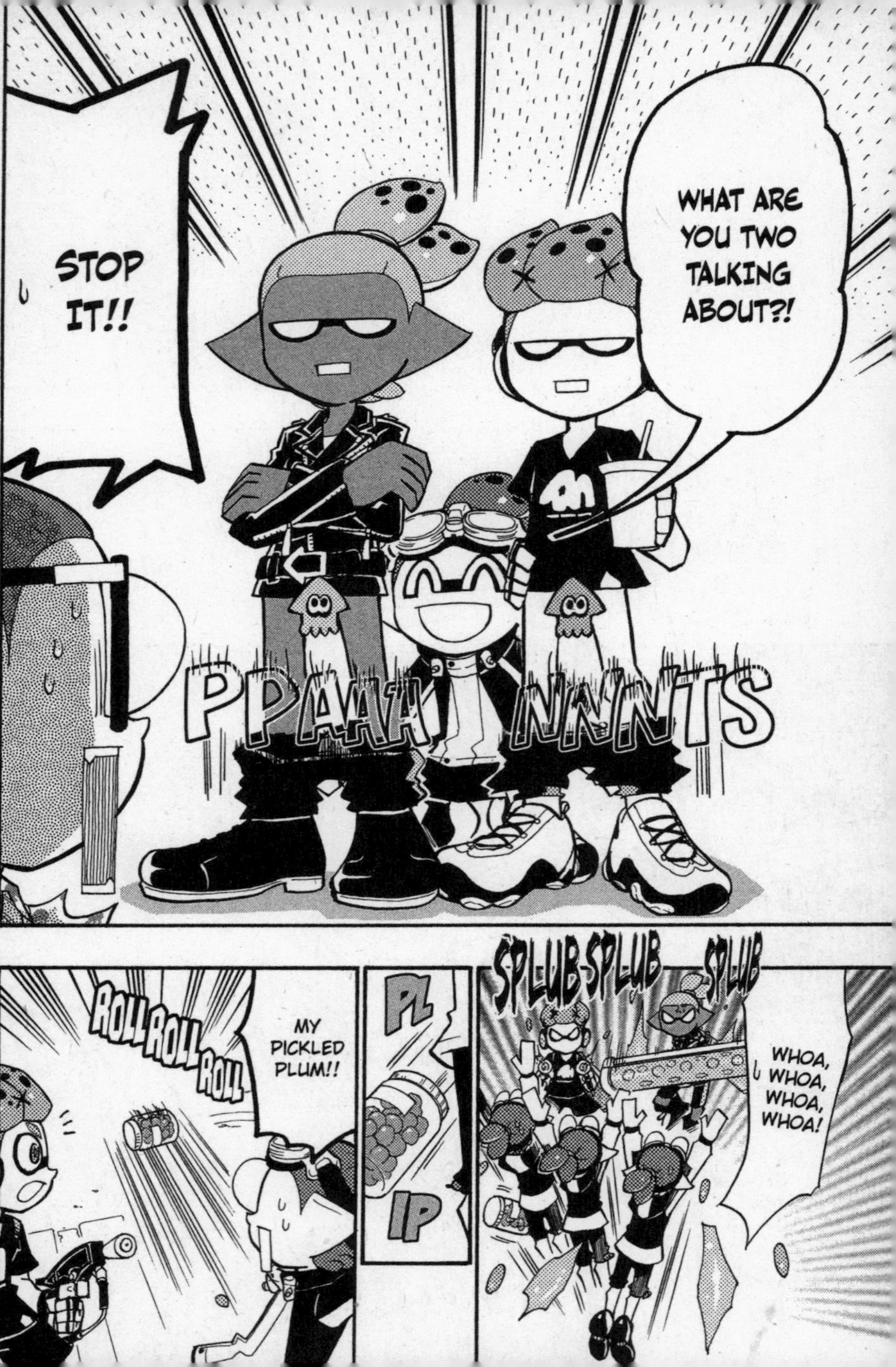
WHAT ARE YOU TWO TALKING ABOUT?!
STOP IT!!
PPAAAA NNNNTS
SPLUB SPLUB SPLUB
WHOA, WHOA, WHOA, WHOA!
PL IP
ROLL ROLL ROLL
MY PICKLED PLUM!!

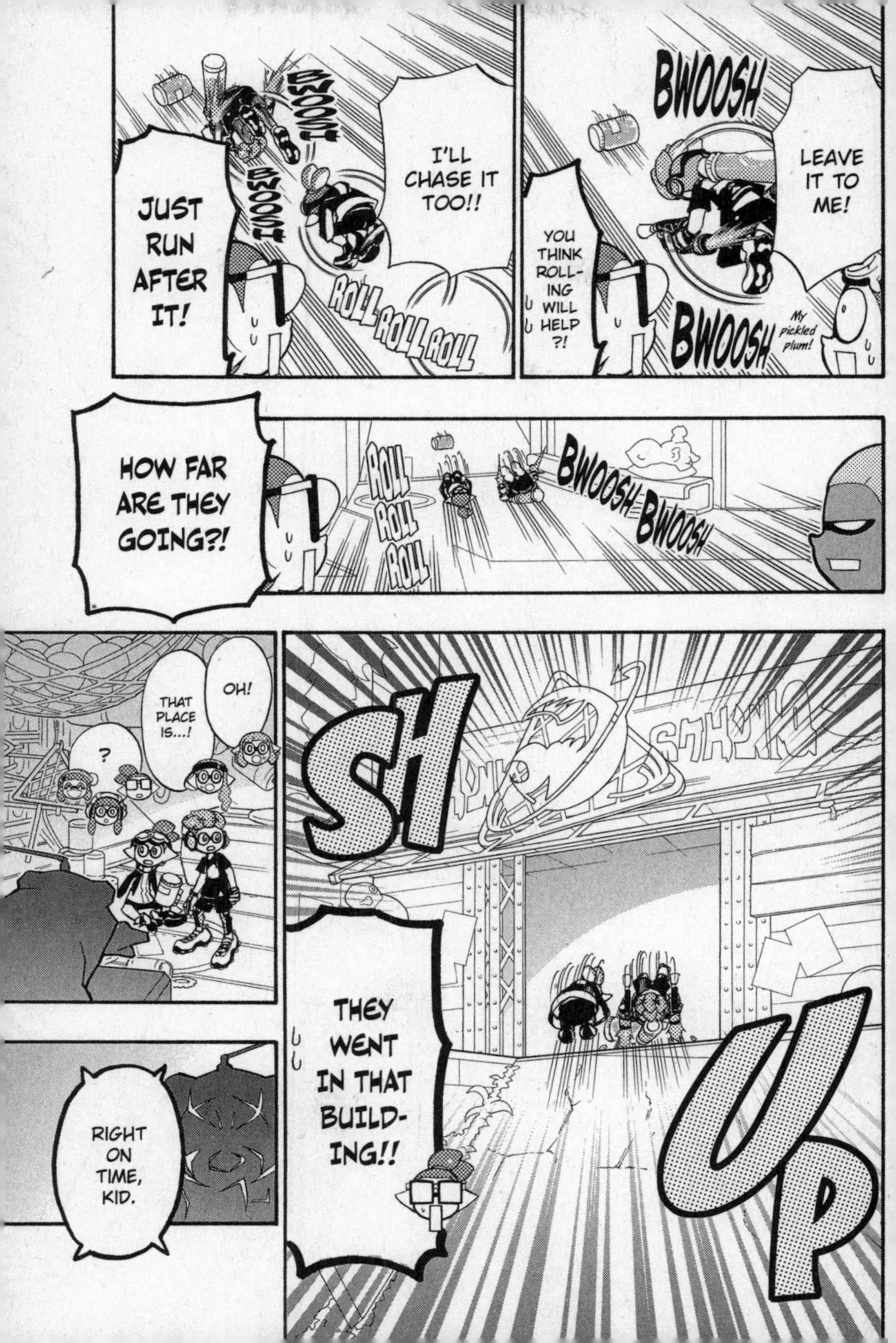
BWOOSH
LEAVE IT TO ME!
YOU THINK ROLLING WILL HELP?!
BWOOSH
My pickled plum!
BWOOSH
I'LL CHASE IT TOO!!
BWOOSH
JUST RUN AFTER IT!
ROLL ROLL ROLL
BWOOSH BWOOSH
ROLL ROLL ROLL
HOW FAR ARE THEY GOING?!
SH
UP
THEY WENT IN THAT BUILDING!!
OH!
THAT PLACE IS...!
?
RIGHT ON TIME, KID.

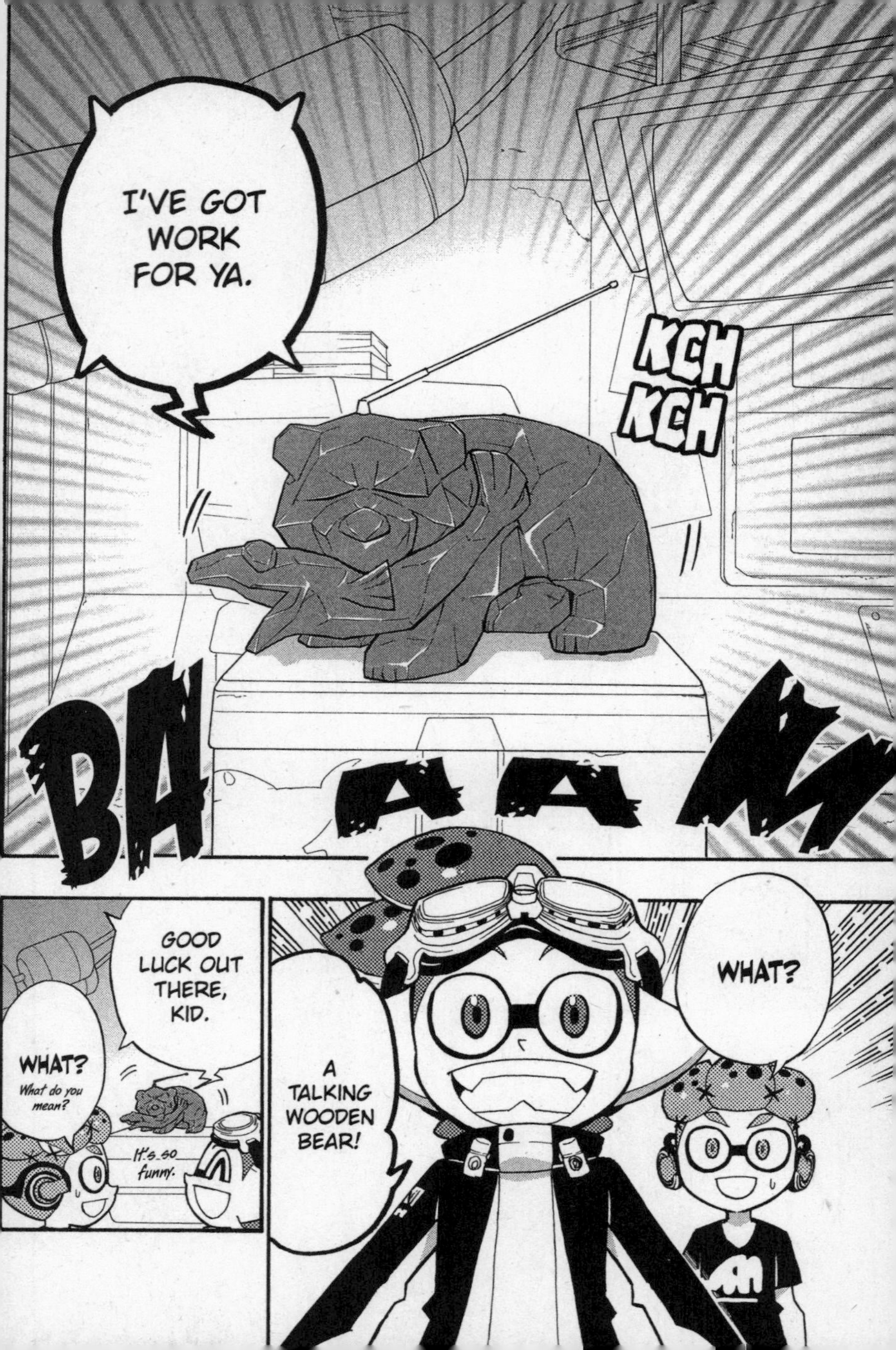
I'VE GOT WORK FOR YA.
KCH KCH
BAAAM
WHAT?
A TALKING WOODEN BEAR!
GOOD LUCK OUT THERE, KID.
WHAT?
What do you mean?
It's so funny.

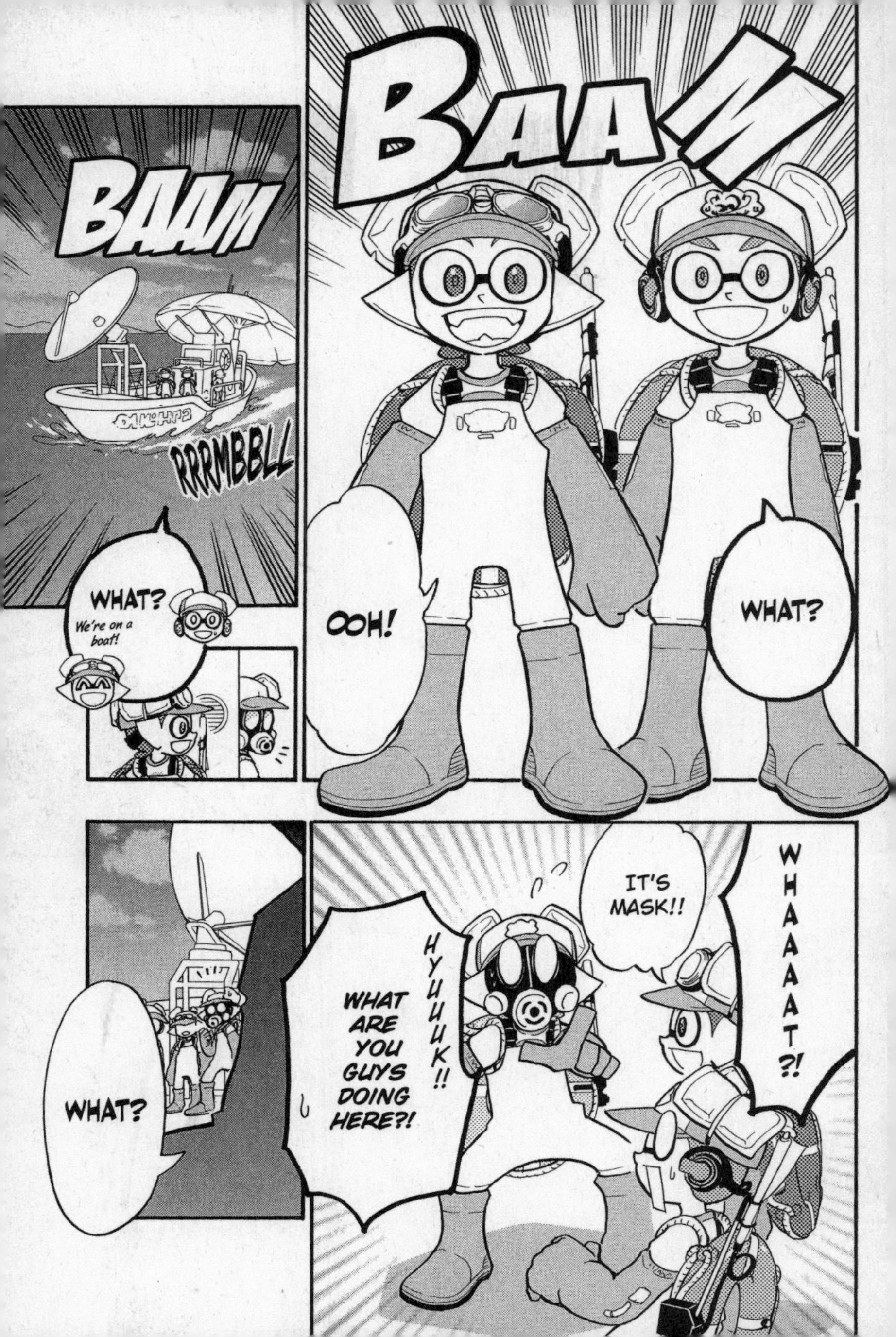
BAAAM
WHAT?
OOH!
BAAM
RRRMBBLL
WHAT?
We're on a boat!
WHAAAAT?!
IT'S MASK!!
HYUUUK!!
WHAT ARE YOU GUYS DOING HERE?!
WHAT?

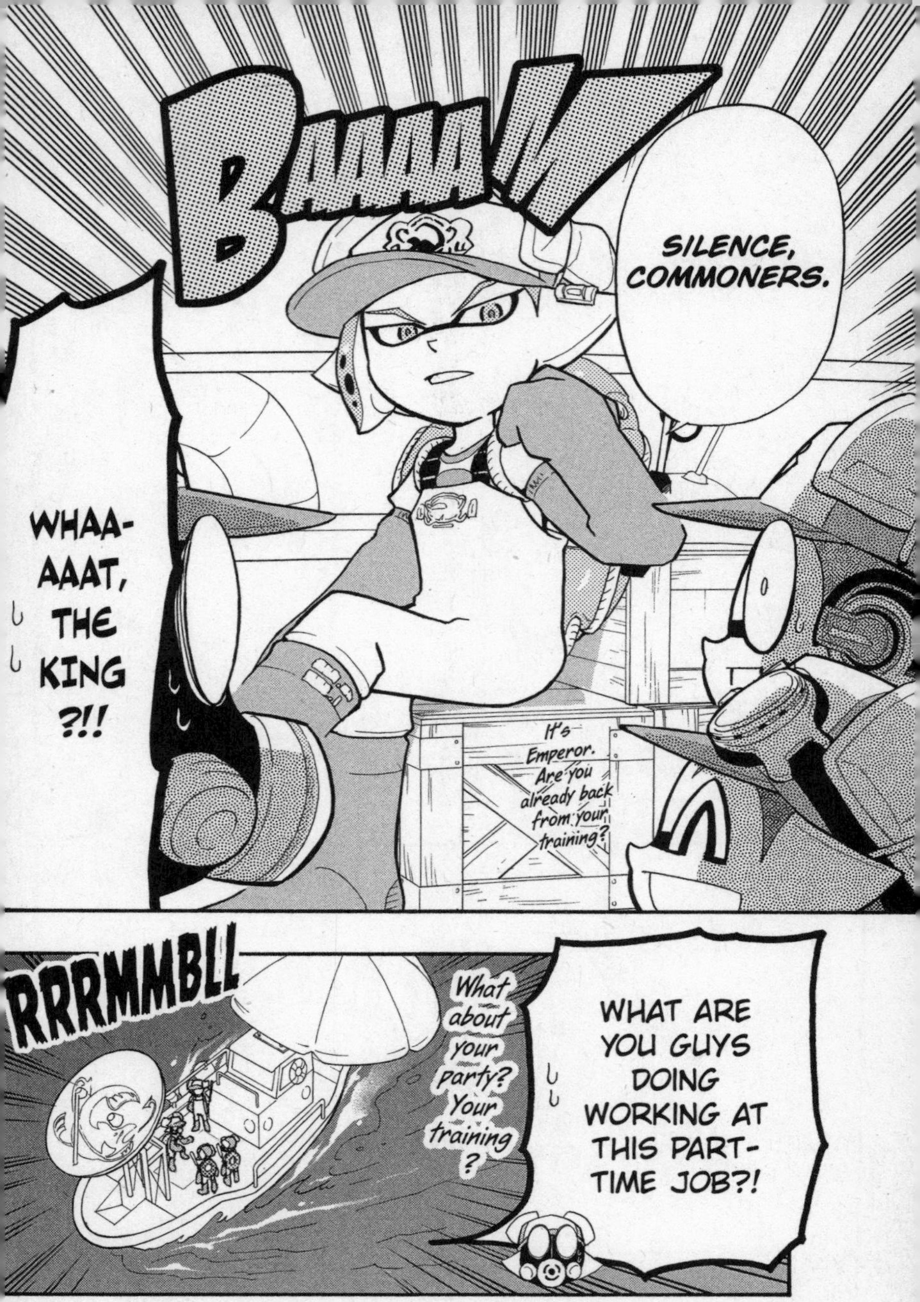
BAAAAM
SILENCE, COMMONERS.
WHAA-AAAT, THE KING ?!!
It's Emperor. Are you already back from your training?
WHAT ARE YOU GUYS DOING WORKING AT THIS PART-TIME JOB?!
What about your party? Your training ?
RRRMMBLL

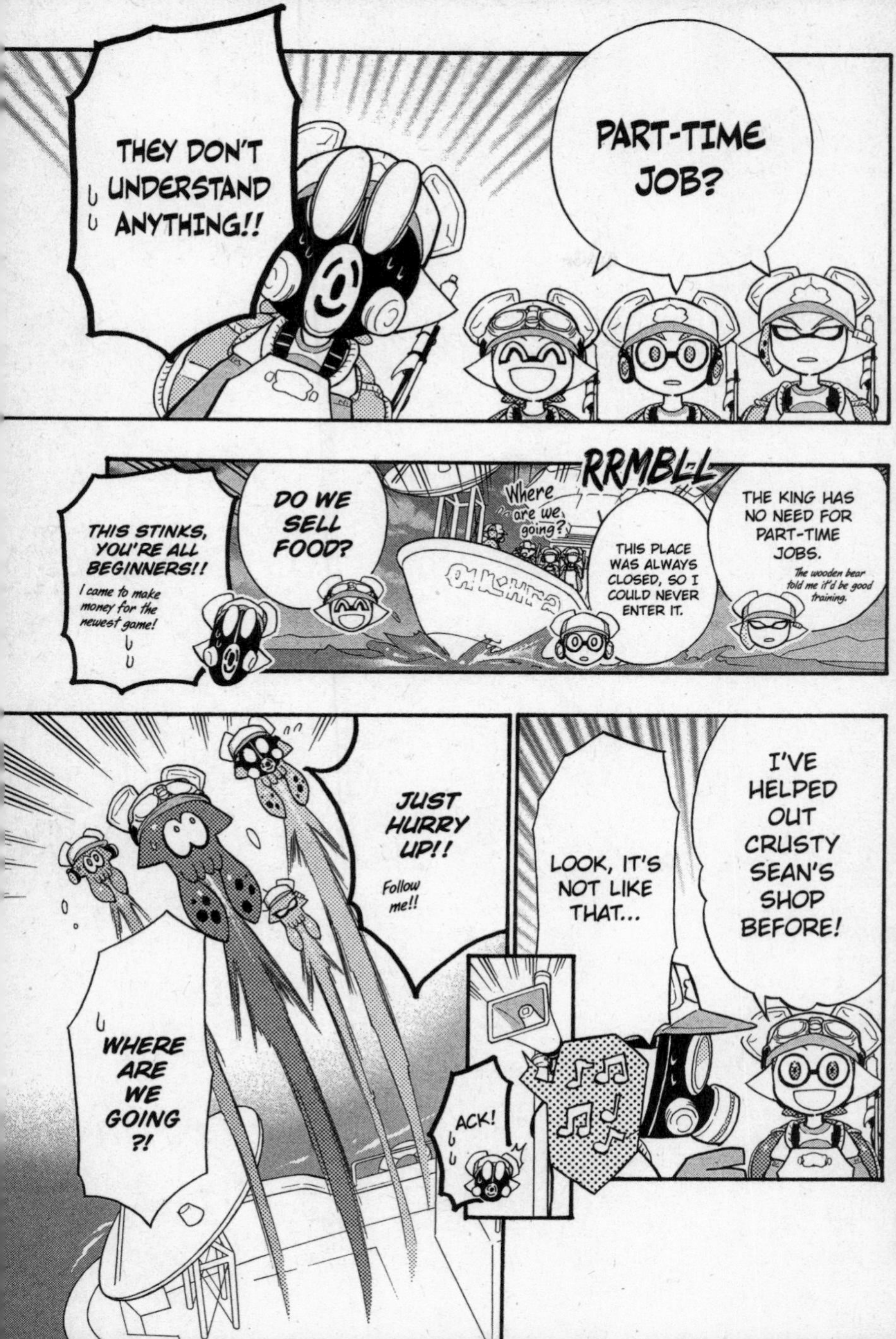
PART-TIME JOB?
THEY DON'T UNDERSTAND ANYTHING!!
RRMBL-L
THE KING HAS NO NEED FOR PART-TIME JOBS.
The wooden bear told me it'd be good training.
THIS PLACE WAS ALWAYS CLOSED, SO I COULD NEVER ENTER IT.
Where are we going?
DO WE SELL FOOD?
THIS STINKS, YOU'RE ALL BEGINNERS!!
I came to make money for the newest game!
I'VE HELPED OUT CRUSTY SEAN'S SHOP BEFORE!
LOOK, IT'S NOT LIKE THAT...
ACK!
JUST HURRY UP!!
Follow me!!
WHERE ARE WE GOING?!

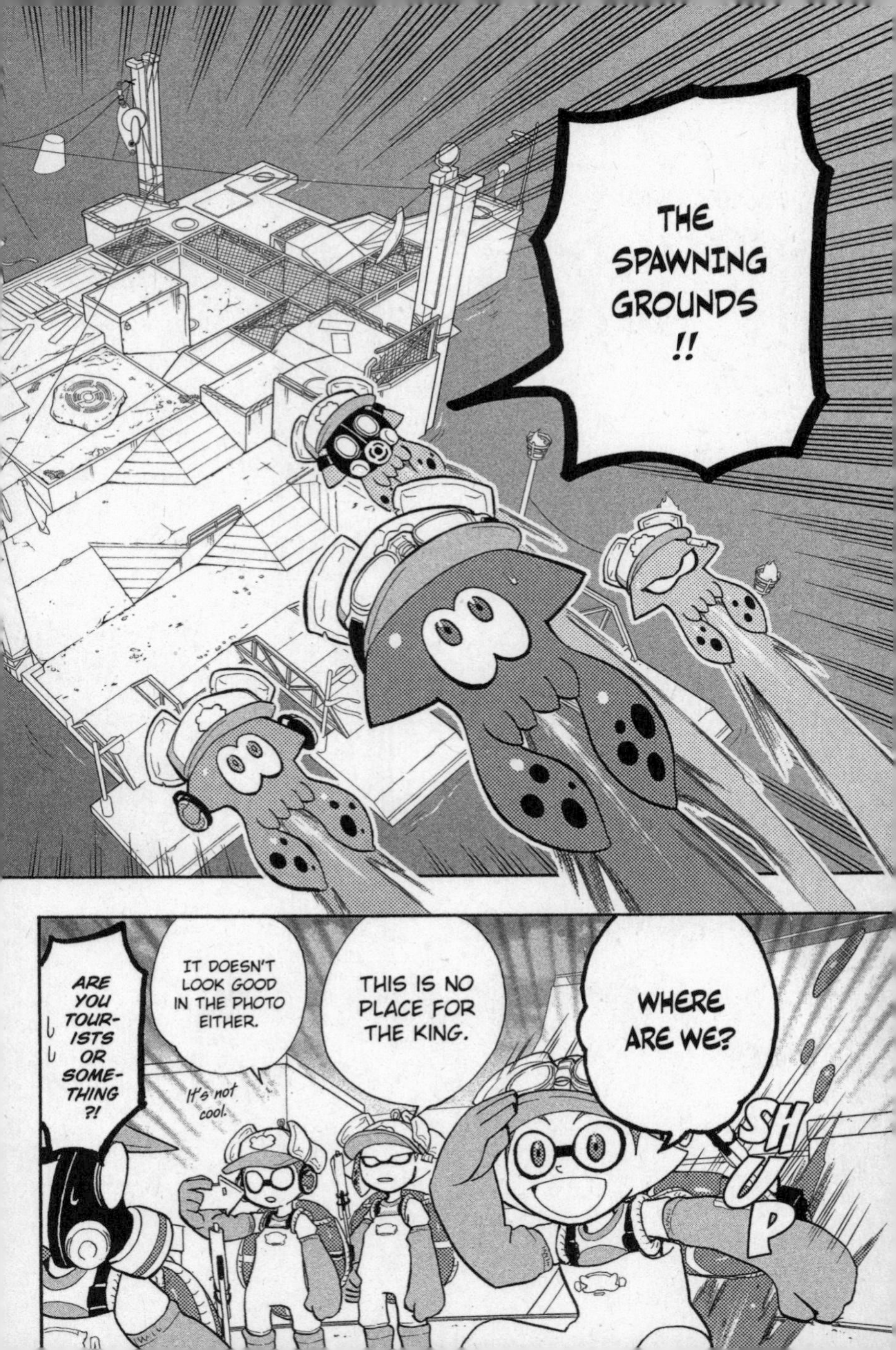
THE SPAWNING GROUNDS !!
WHERE ARE WE?
SHUP
THIS IS NO PLACE FOR THE KING.
IT DOESN'T LOOK GOOD IN THE PHOTO EITHER.
It's not cool.
ARE YOU TOURISTS OR SOMETHING ?!

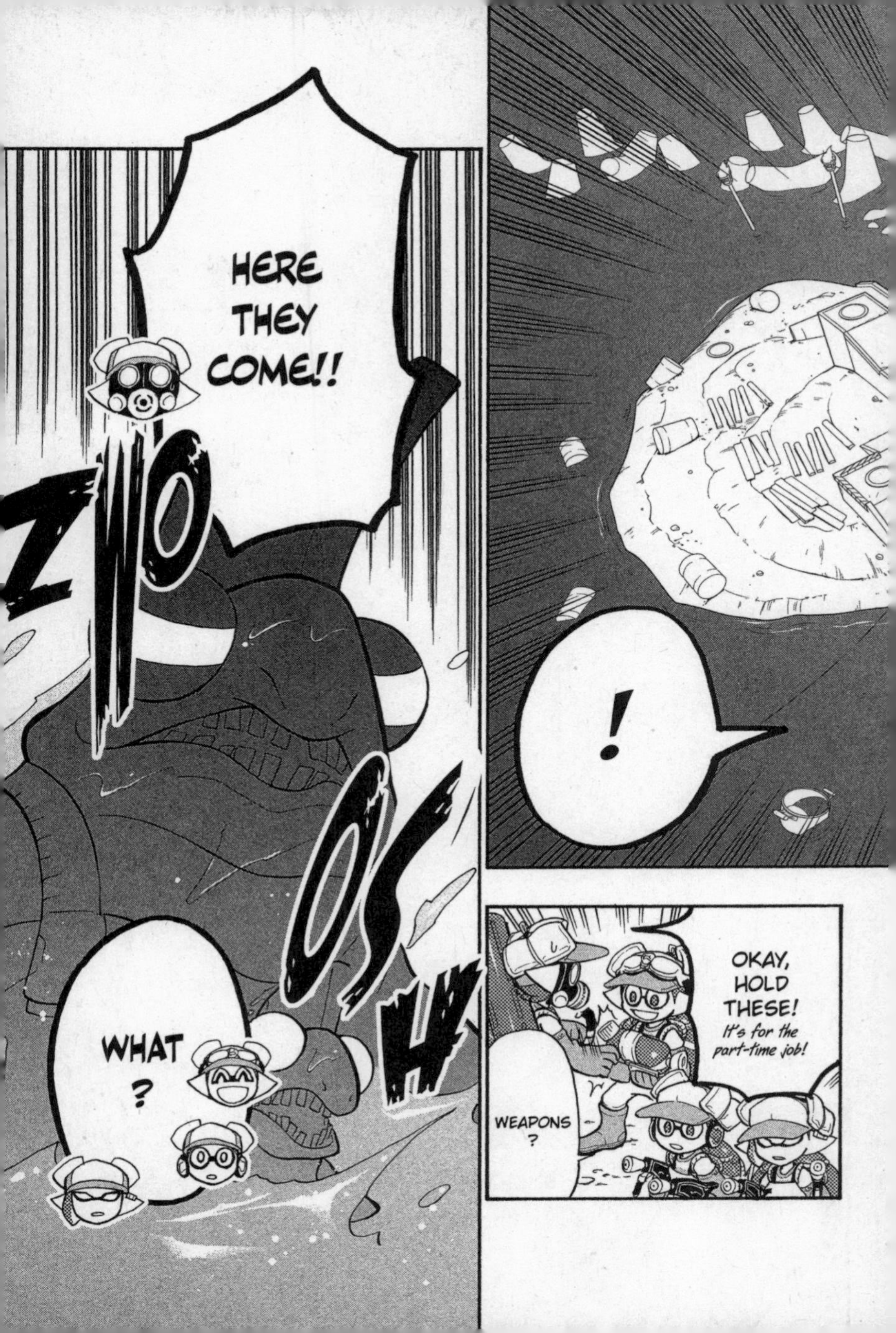
!
OKAY, HOLD THESE! It's for the part-time job!
WEAPONS?
HERE THEY COME!!
ZWOOSH
WHAT?

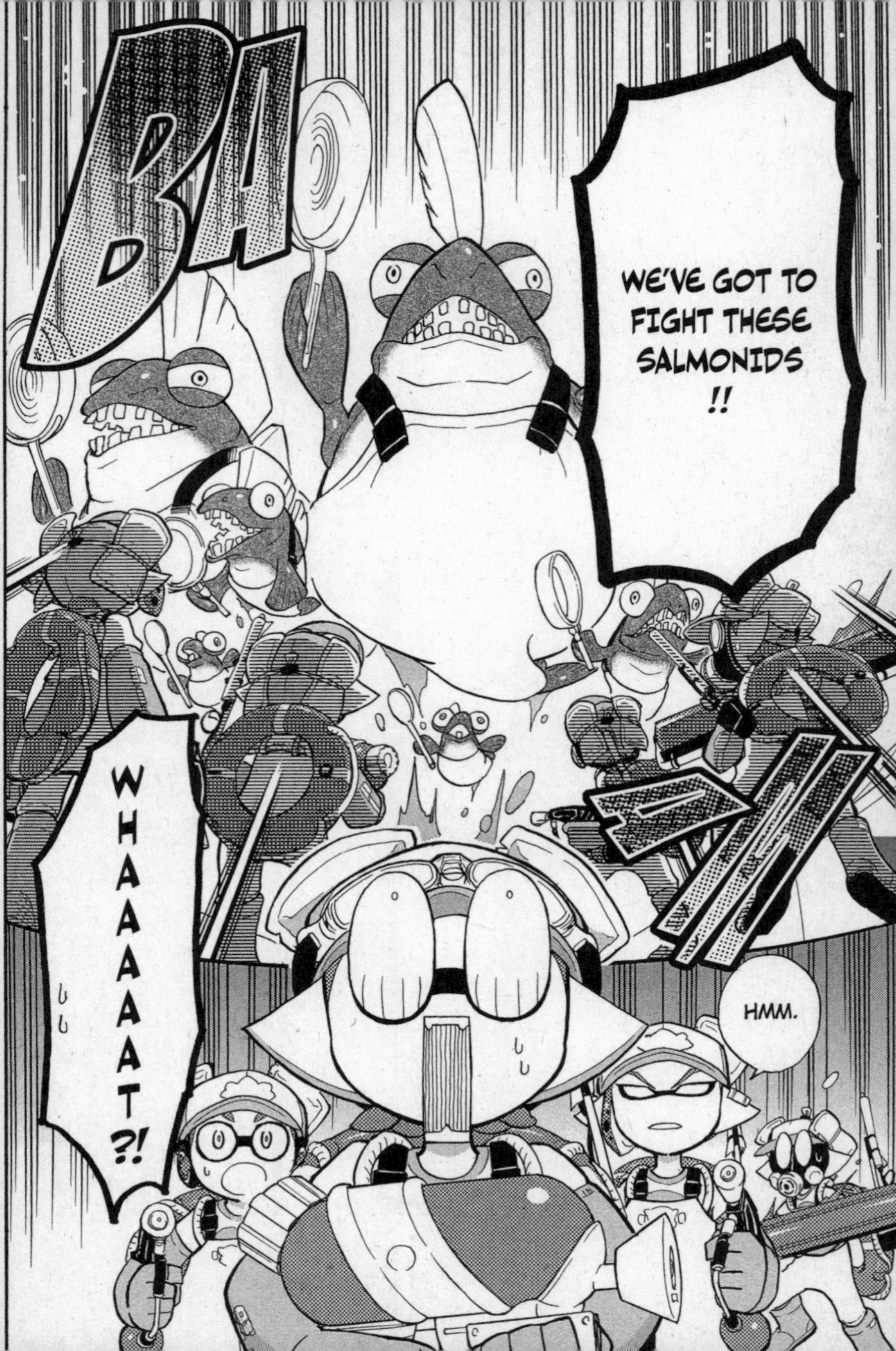
WE'VE GOT TO FIGHT THESE SALMONIDS !!
BA
HMM.
WHAAAAAT?!

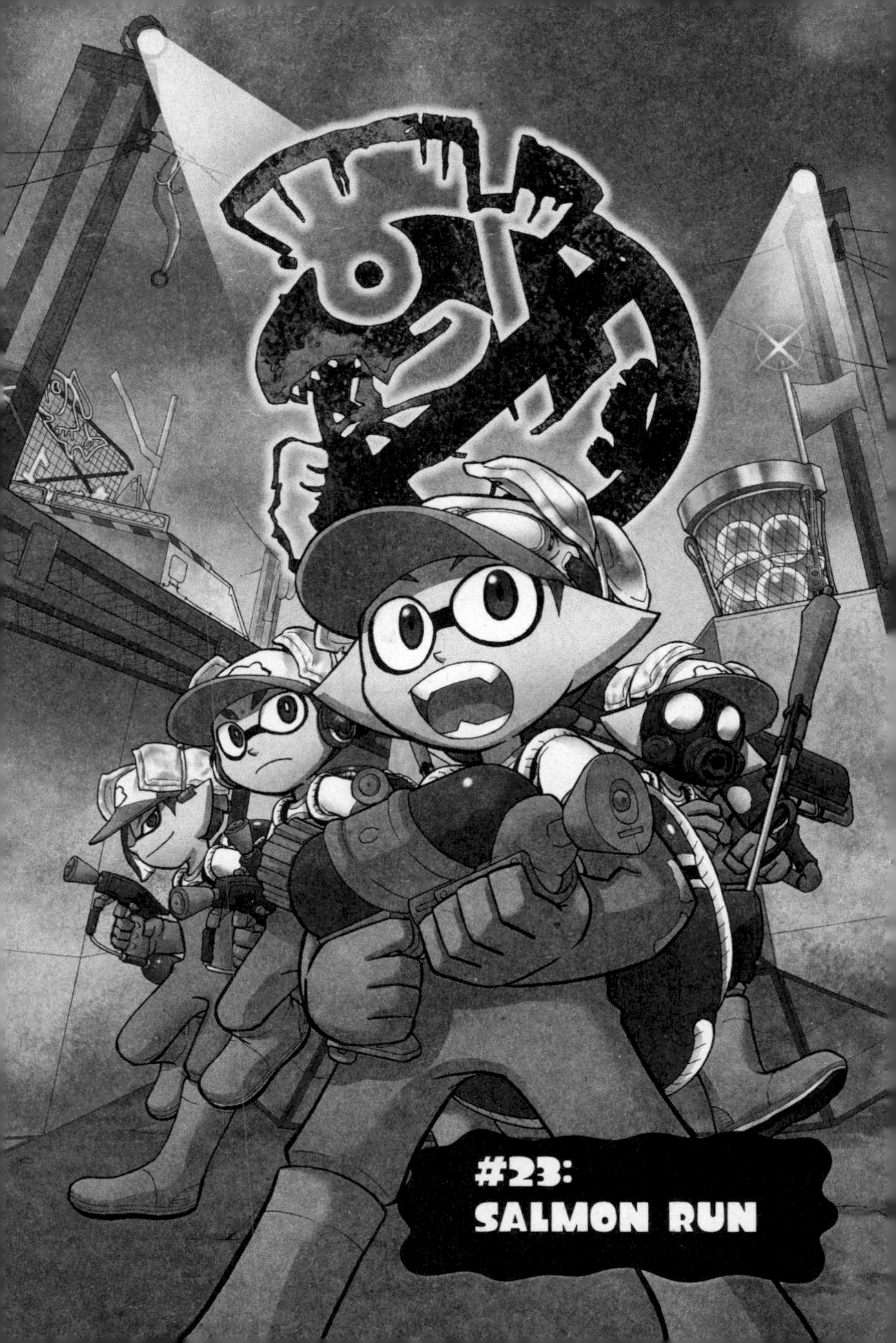
#23:
SALMON RUN

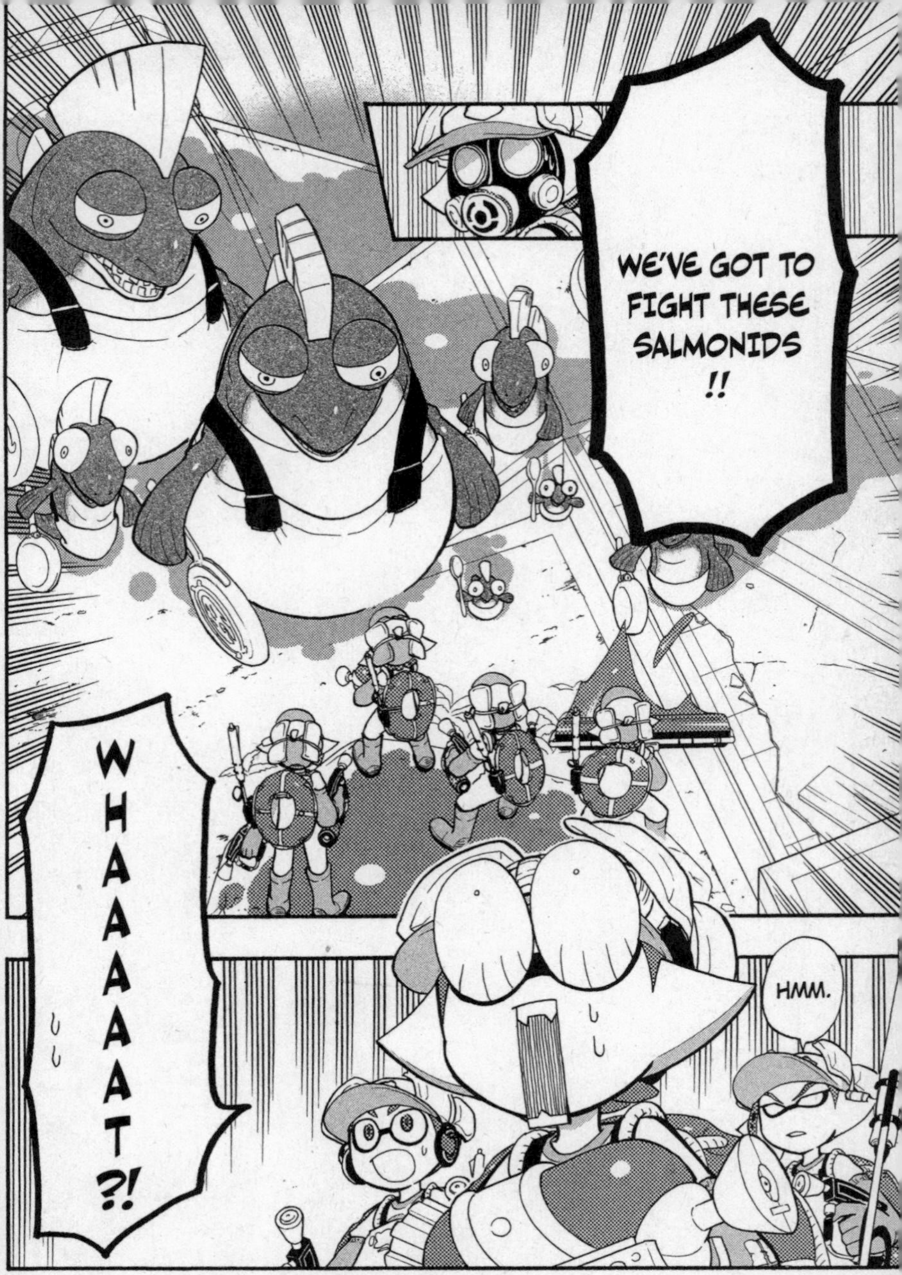

WE'VE GOT TO FIGHT THESE SALMONIDS!!
HMM.
WHAAAAAT?!

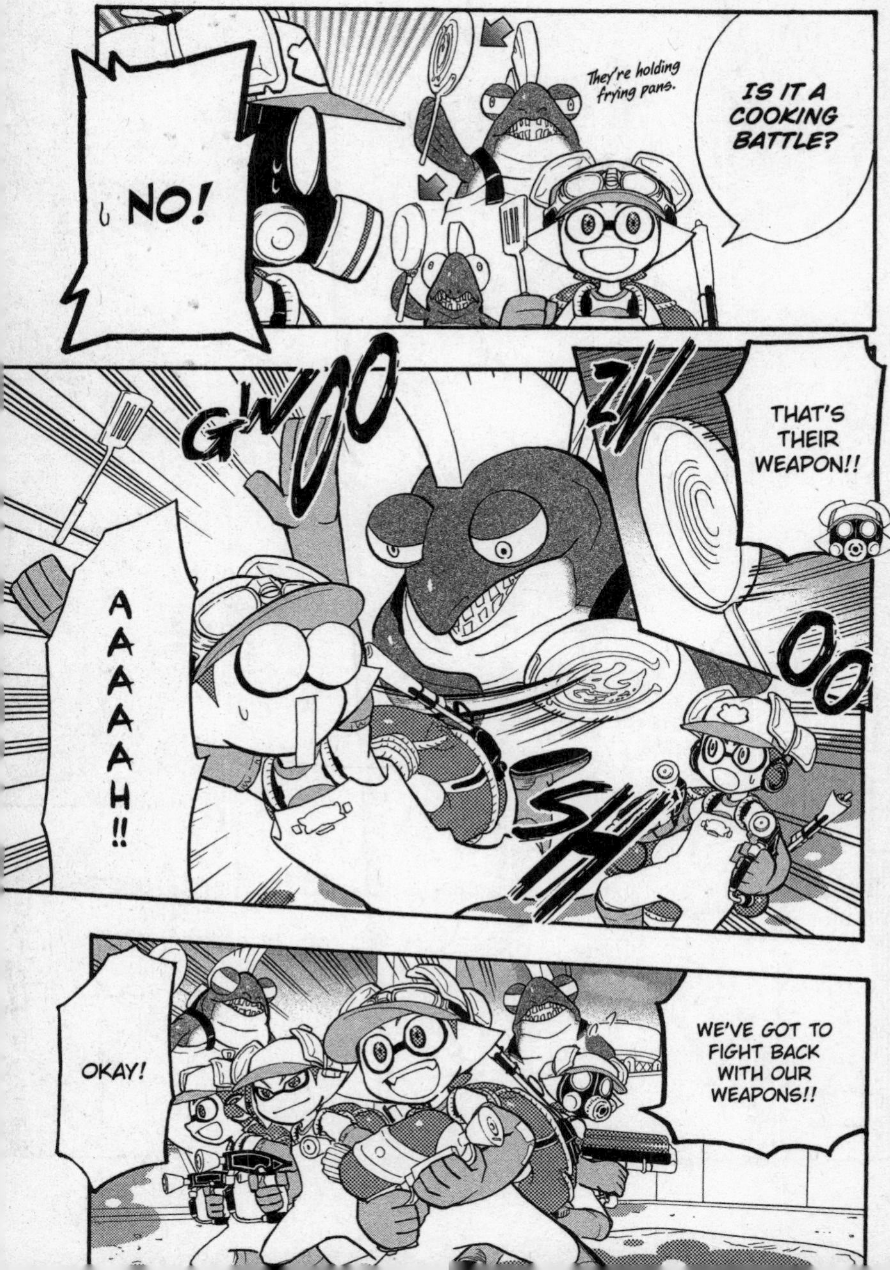
IS IT A COOKING BATTLE?
They're holding frying pans.
NO!
THAT'S THEIR WEAPON!!
ZW
OO
SH
GWOO
AAAAAH!!
WE'VE GOT TO FIGHT BACK WITH OUR WEAPONS!!
OKAY!

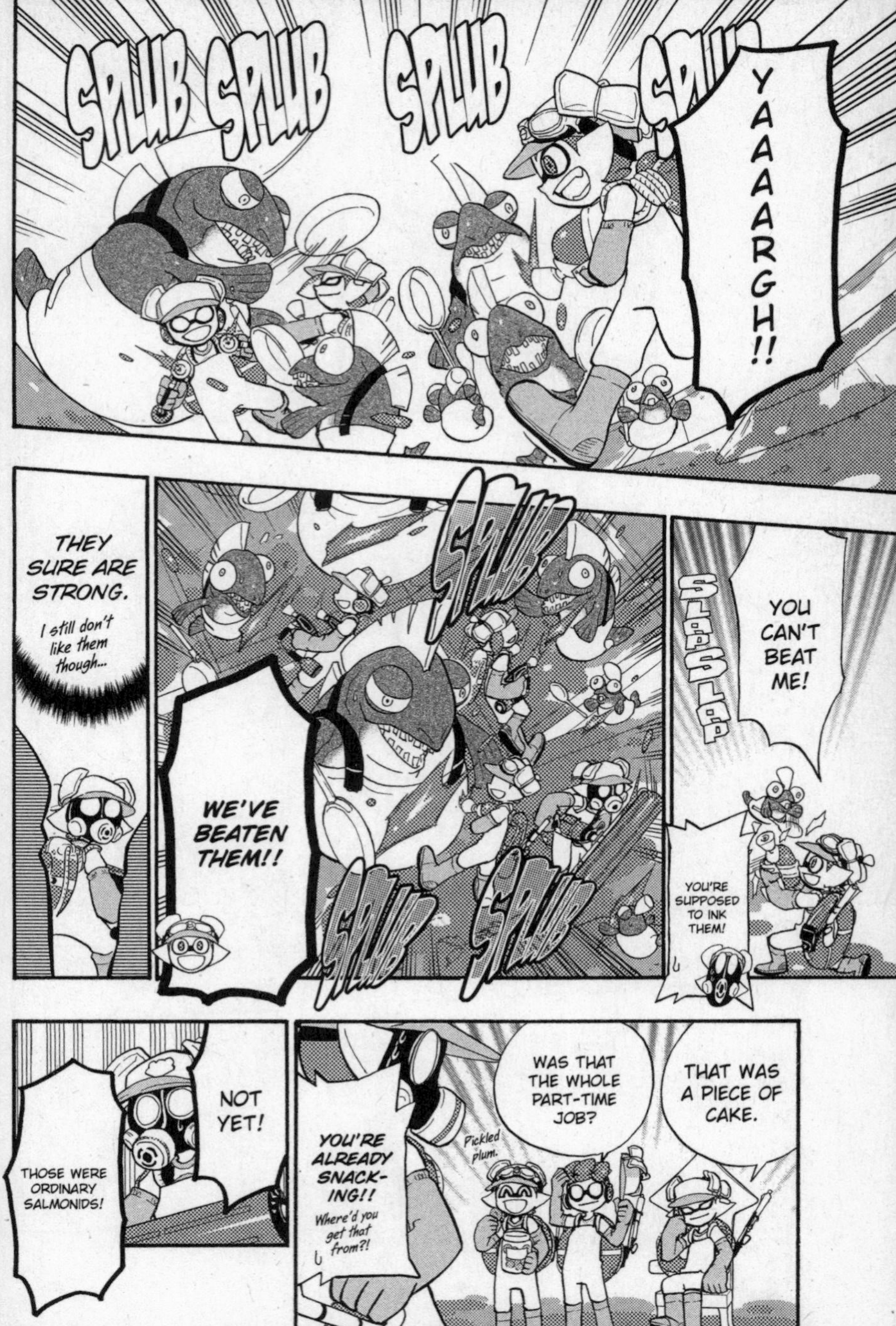
YAAAARGH!!
SPLUB
SPLUB
SPLUB
SPLUB
YOU CAN'T BEAT ME!
SLAP SLAP
YOU'RE SUPPOSED TO INK THEM!
SPLUB
WE'VE BEATEN THEM!!
SPLUB
SPLUB
THEY SURE ARE STRONG.
I still don't like them though...
THAT WAS A PIECE OF CAKE.
WAS THAT THE WHOLE PART-TIME JOB?
Pickled plum.
YOU'RE ALREADY SNACKING!!
Where'd you get that from?!
NOT YET!
THOSE WERE ORDINARY SALMONIDS!

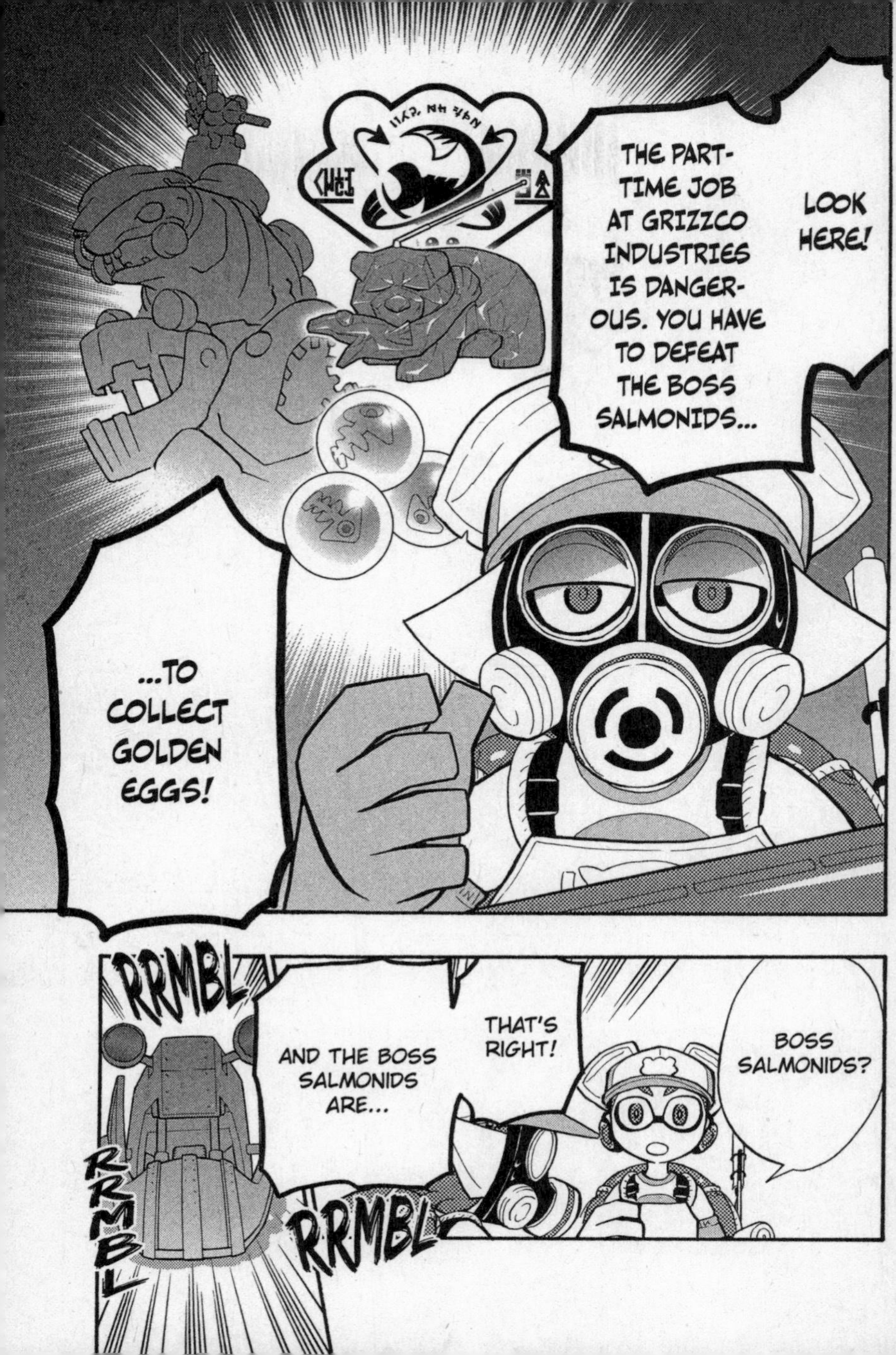
LOOK HERE!
THE PART-TIME JOB AT GRIZZCO INDUSTRIES IS DANGER-OUS. YOU HAVE TO DEFEAT THE BOSS SALMONIDS...
...TO COLLECT GOLDEN EGGS!
BOSS SALMONIDS?
THAT'S RIGHT!
AND THE BOSS SALMONIDS ARE...
RRMBL
RRMBL
RRMBL

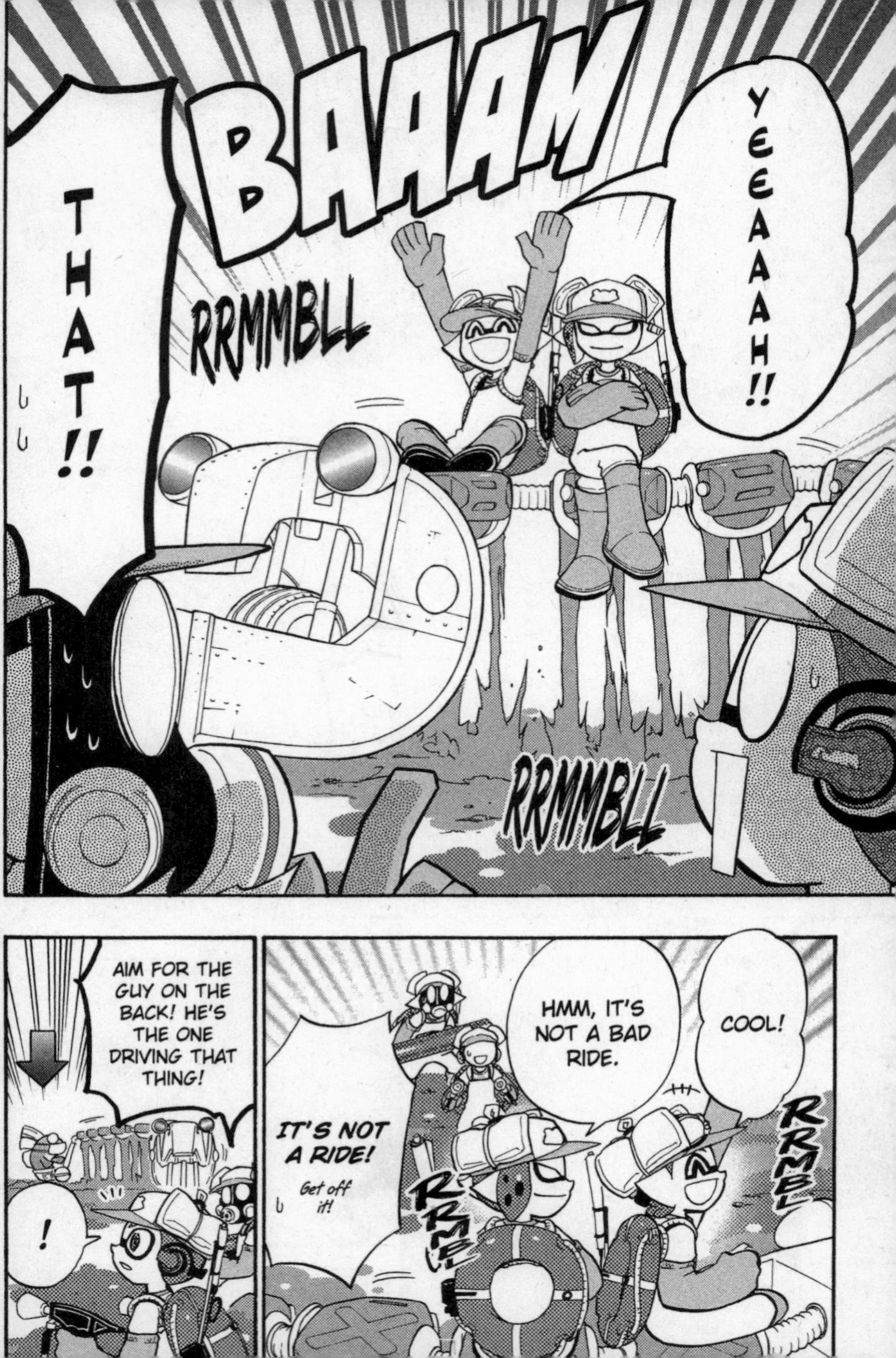
YEEAAAAH!!
BAAAM
THAT!!
RRMMBLL
RRMMBLL
COOL!
HMM, IT'S NOT A BAD RIDE.
RRMMBL
IT'S NOT A RIDE!
Get off it!
RRMMBL
AIM FOR THE GUY ON THE BACK! HE'S THE ONE DRIVING THAT THING!
!

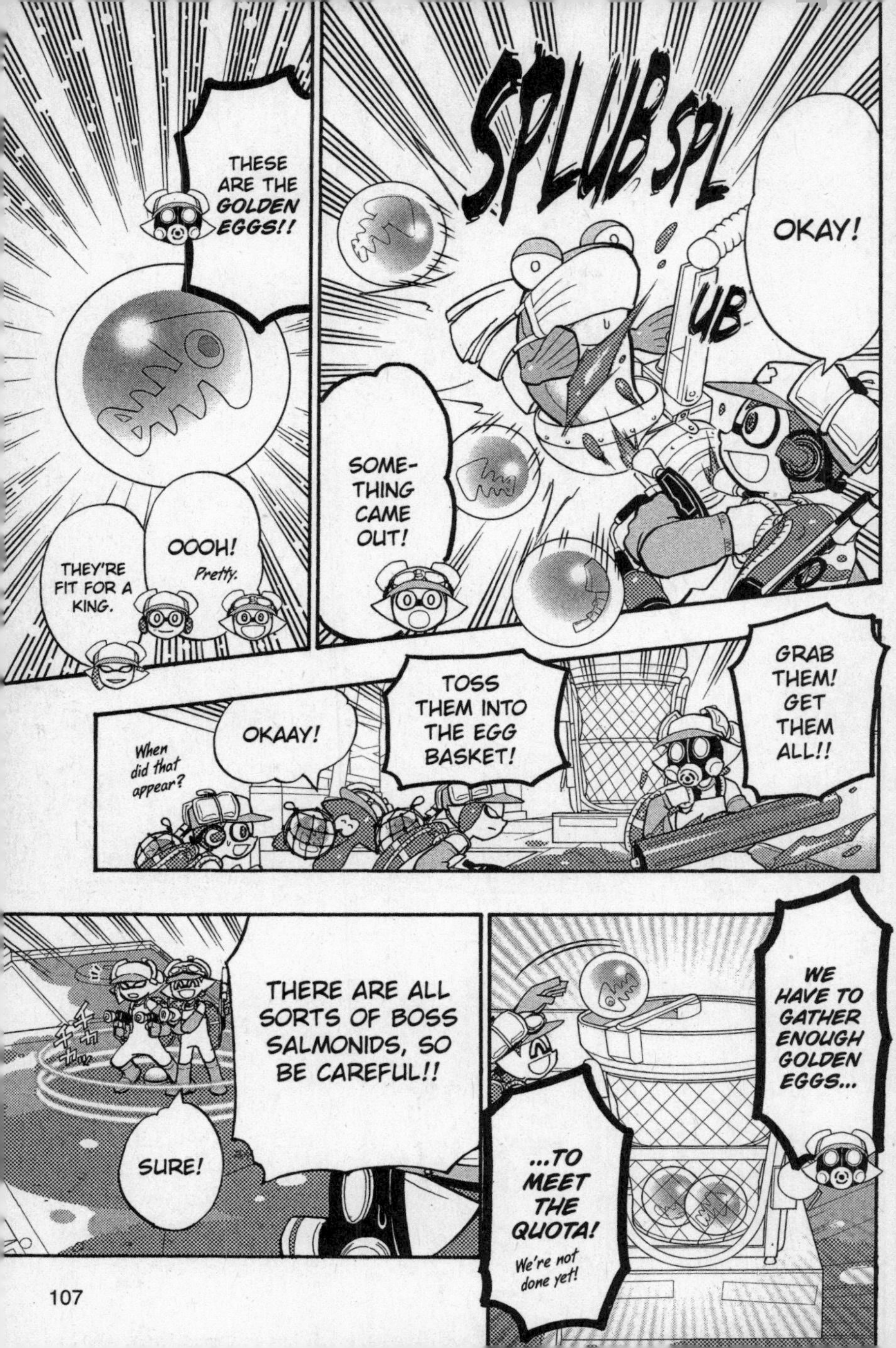
SPLUB SPL
UB
OKAY!
SOME-THING CAME OUT!
THESE ARE THE GOLDEN EGGS!!
OOOH!
Pretty.
THEY'RE FIT FOR A KING.
GRAB THEM! GET THEM ALL!!
TOSS THEM INTO THE EGG BASKET!
OKAAY!
When did that appear?
WE HAVE TO GATHER ENOUGH GOLDEN EGGS...
...TO MEET THE QUOTA!
We're not done yet!
THERE ARE ALL SORTS OF BOSS SALMONIDS, SO BE CAREFUL!!
SURE!

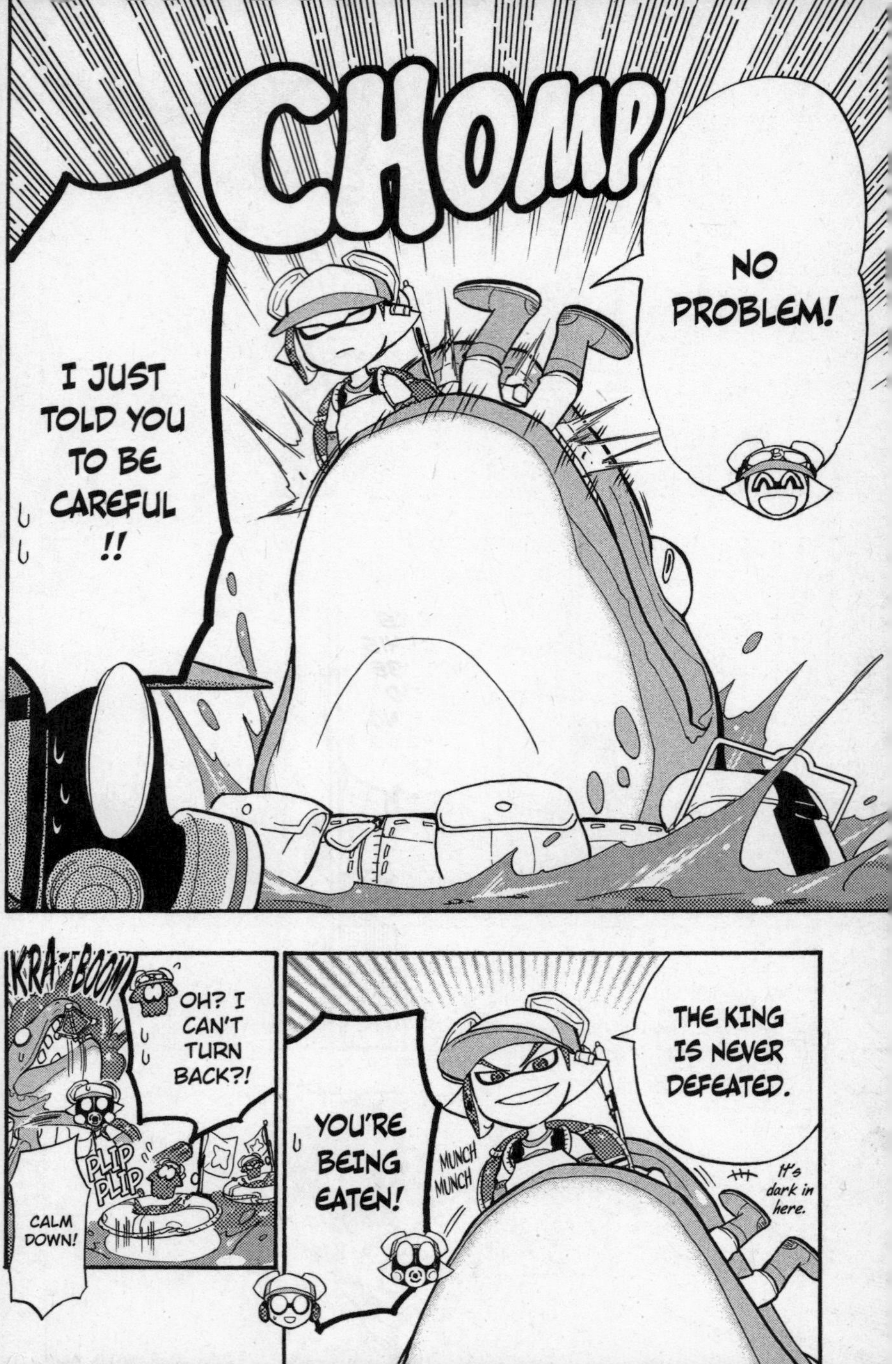
CHOMP
NO PROBLEM!
I JUST TOLD YOU TO BE CAREFUL!!
THE KING IS NEVER DEFEATED.
It's dark in here.
MUNCH MUNCH
YOU'RE BEING EATEN!
KRA-BOOM
OH? I CAN'T TURN BACK?!
PLIP PLIP
CALM DOWN!

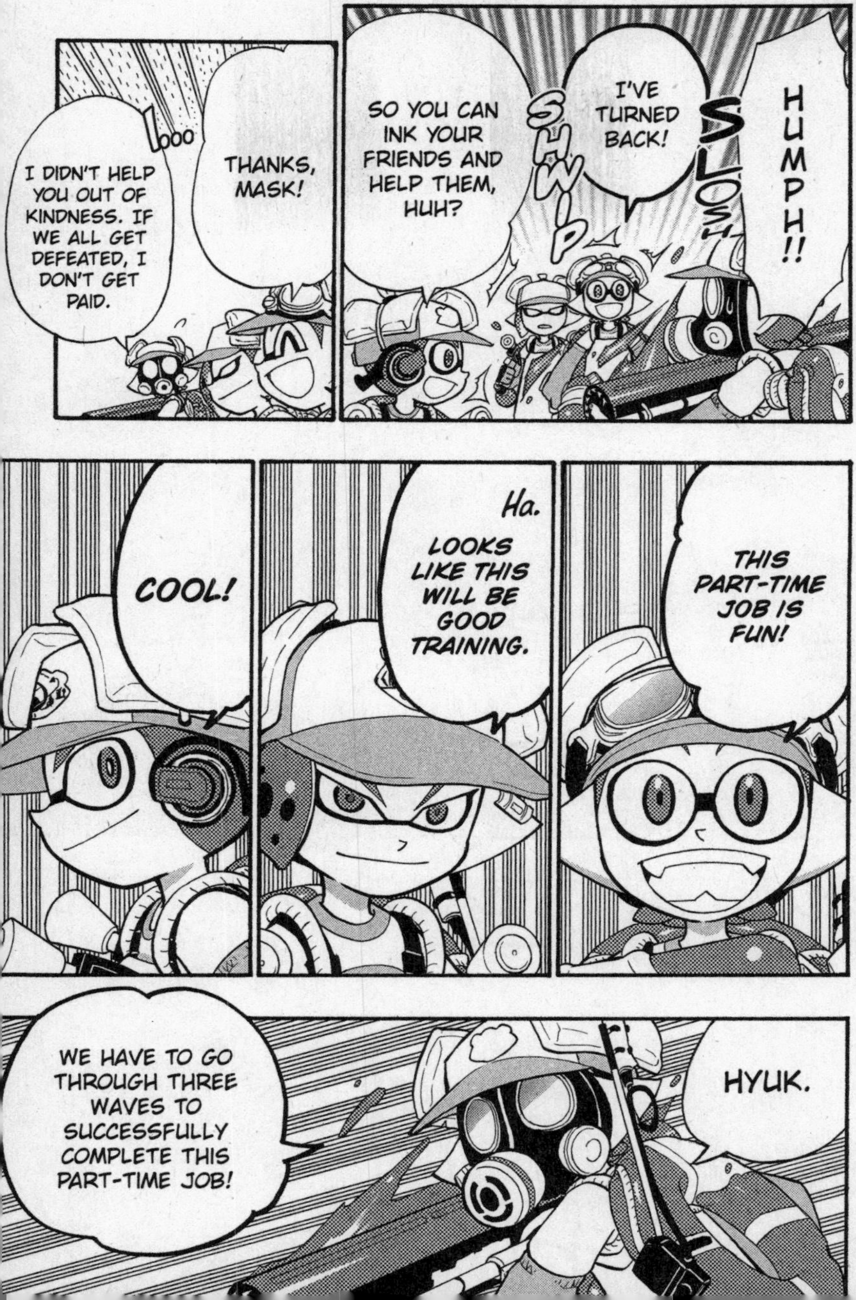
HUMPH!!
SLOSH
I'VE TURNED BACK!
SHWIP
SO YOU CAN INK YOUR FRIENDS AND HELP THEM, HUH?
THANKS, MASK!
I DIDN'T HELP YOU OUT OF KINDNESS. IF WE ALL GET DEFEATED, I DON'T GET PAID.
THIS PART-TIME JOB IS FUN!
Ha.
LOOKS LIKE THIS WILL BE GOOD TRAINING.
COOL!
HYUK.
WE HAVE TO GO THROUGH THREE WAVES TO SUCCESSFULLY COMPLETE THIS PART-TIME JOB!

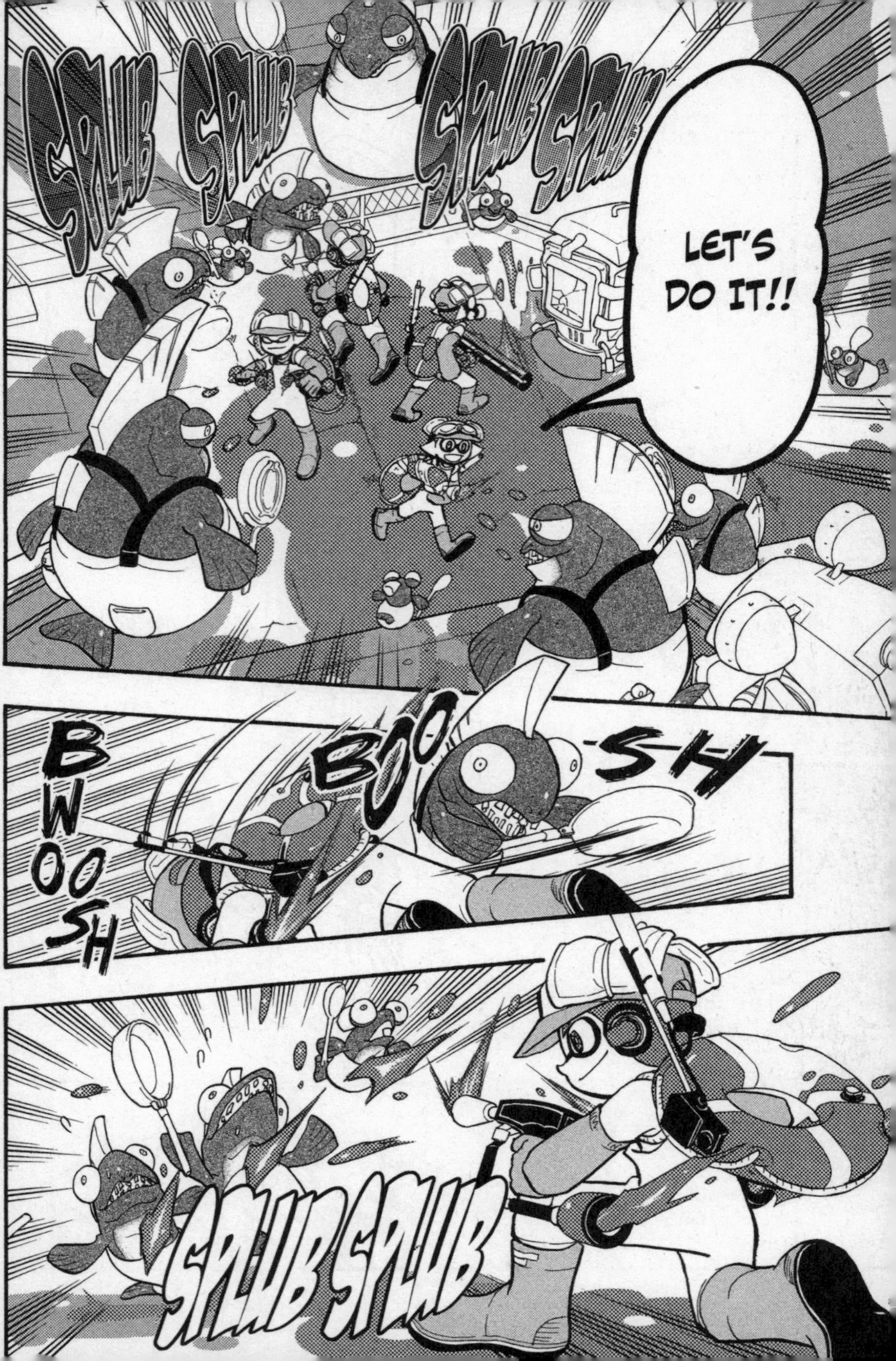
LET'S DO IT!!
SPLUB SPLUB
SPLUB SPLUB
BOOSH
BWOOSH
SPLUB SPLUB

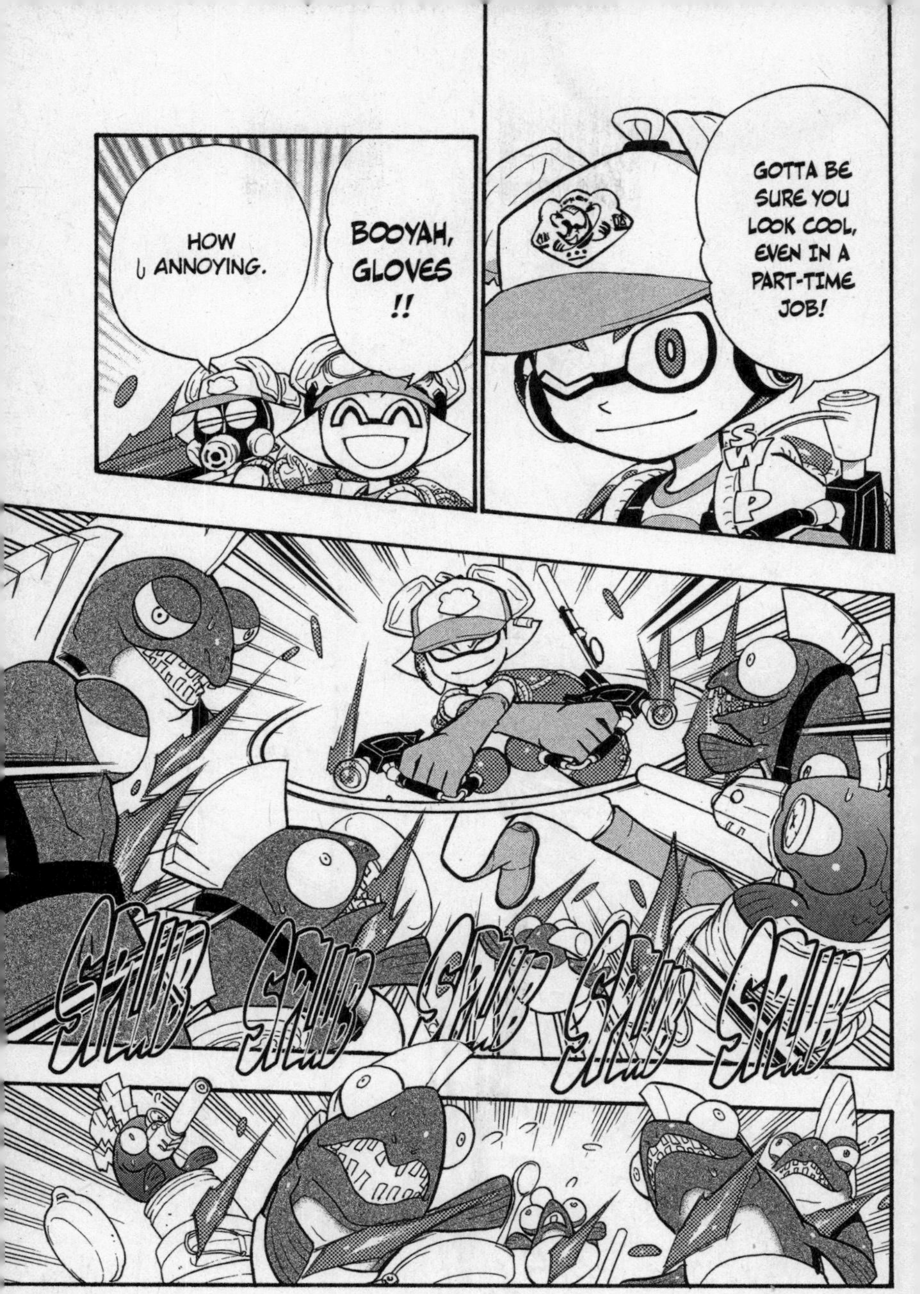
GOTTA BE SURE YOU LOOK COOL, EVEN IN A PART-TIME JOB!
BOOYAH, GLOVES !!
HOW ANNOYING.
SCRUB SCRUB SCRUB SCRUB SCRUB

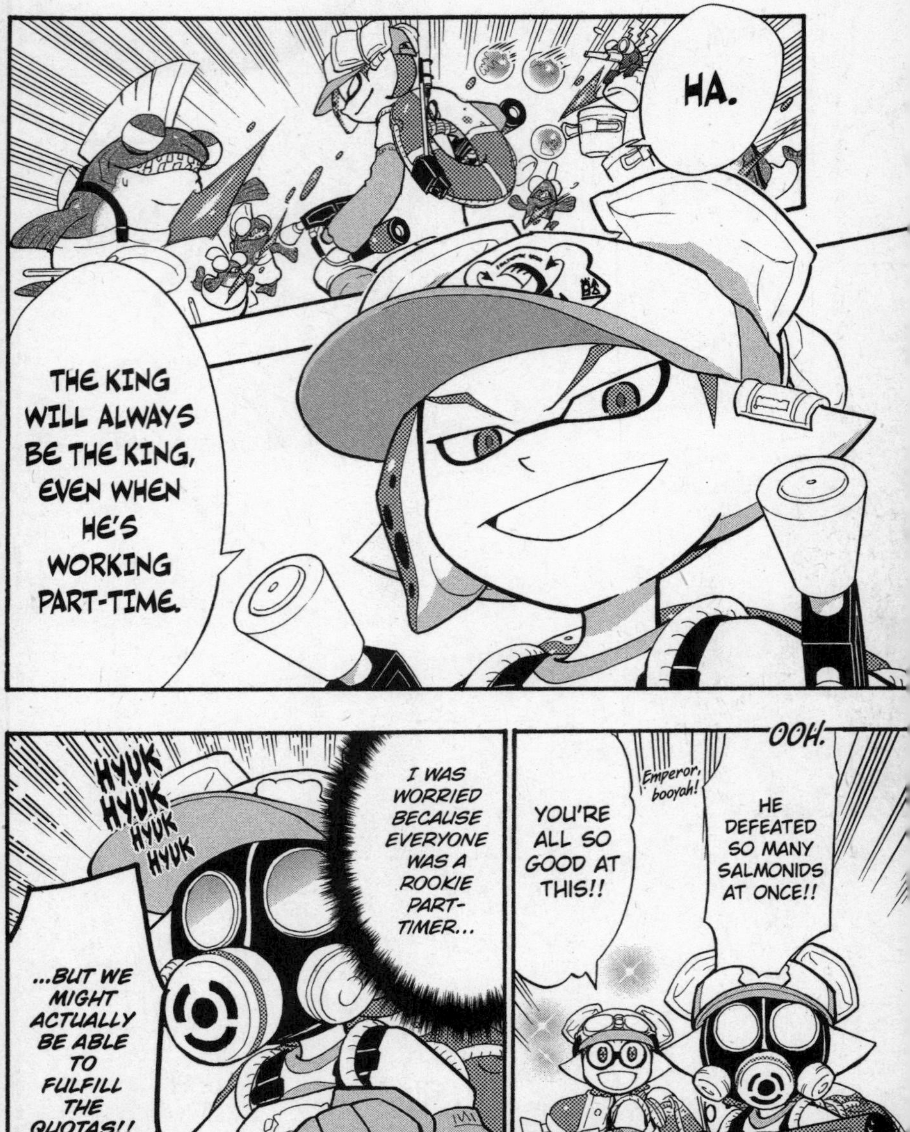
HA.
THE KING WILL ALWAYS BE THE KING, EVEN WHEN HE'S WORKING PART-TIME.
OOH.
HE DEFEATED SO MANY SALMONIDS AT ONCE!!
Emperor, booyah!
YOU'RE ALL SO GOOD AT THIS!!
I WAS WORRIED BECAUSE EVERYONE WAS A ROOKIE PART-TIMER...
HYUK HYUK HYUK HYUK
...BUT WE MIGHT ACTUALLY BE ABLE TO FULFILL THE QUOTAS!!

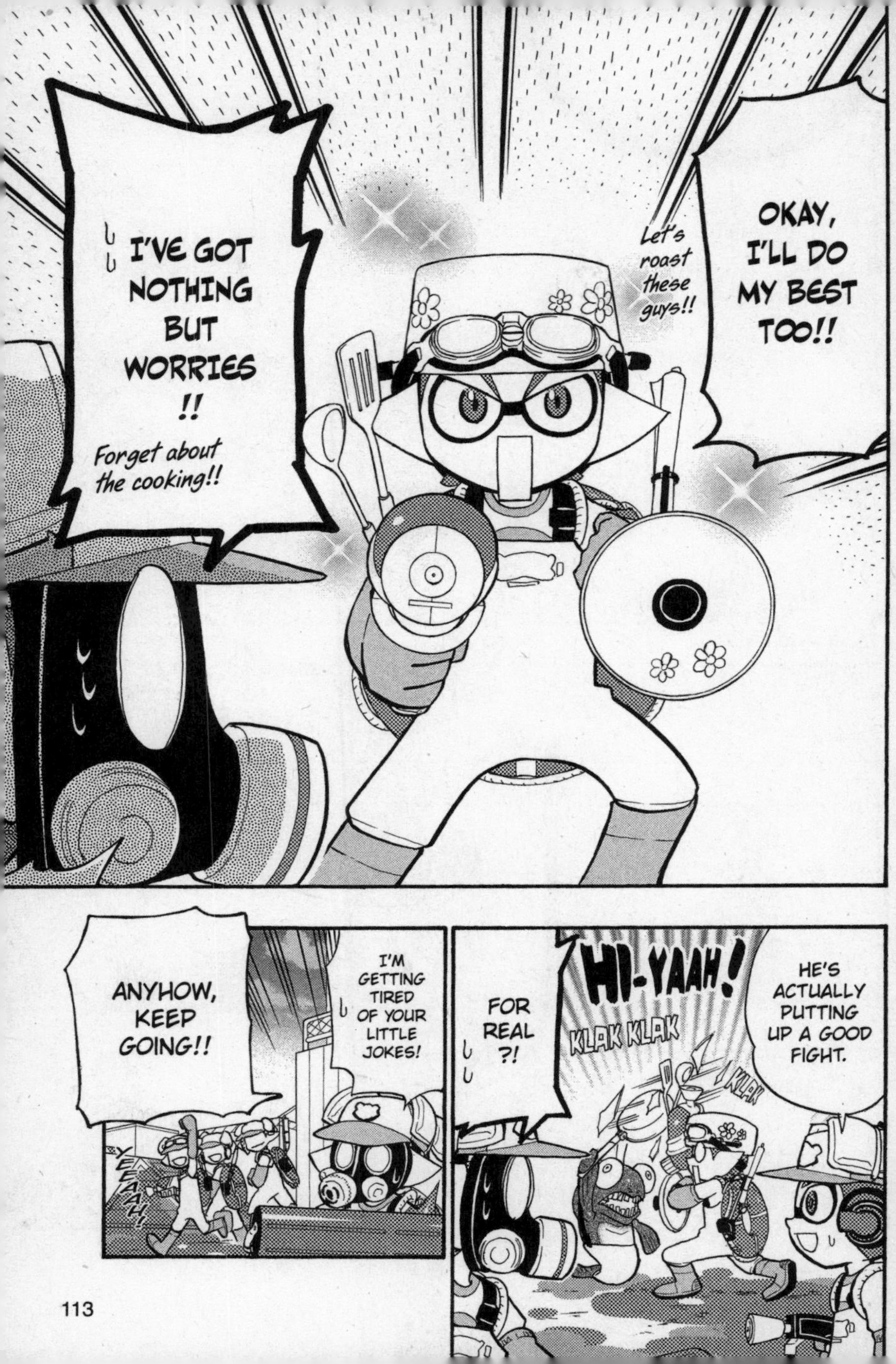
OKAY, I'LL DO MY BEST TOO!!
Let's roast these guys!!
I'VE GOT NOTHING BUT WORRIES!!
Forget about the cooking!!
HE'S ACTUALLY PUTTING UP A GOOD FIGHT.
HI-YAAH!
KLAK KLAK
KLAK
FOR REAL?!
I'M GETTING TIRED OF YOUR LITTLE JOKES!
ANYHOW, KEEP GOING!!
YEEAAH!

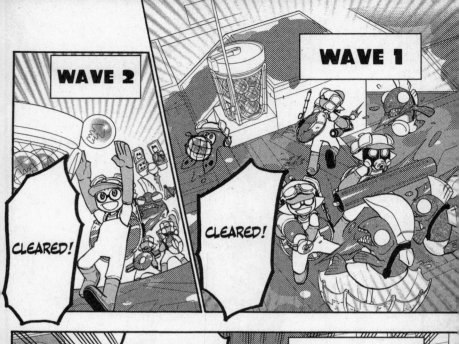

WAVE 2

WAVE 1

CLEARED!

CLEARED!

FINAL WAVE

WE GET THROUGH THIS WAVE AND WE'RE DONE!

OKAY !!

ACK!!

OH? THE WATER LEVEL IS RISING?

SH WA^A^AA

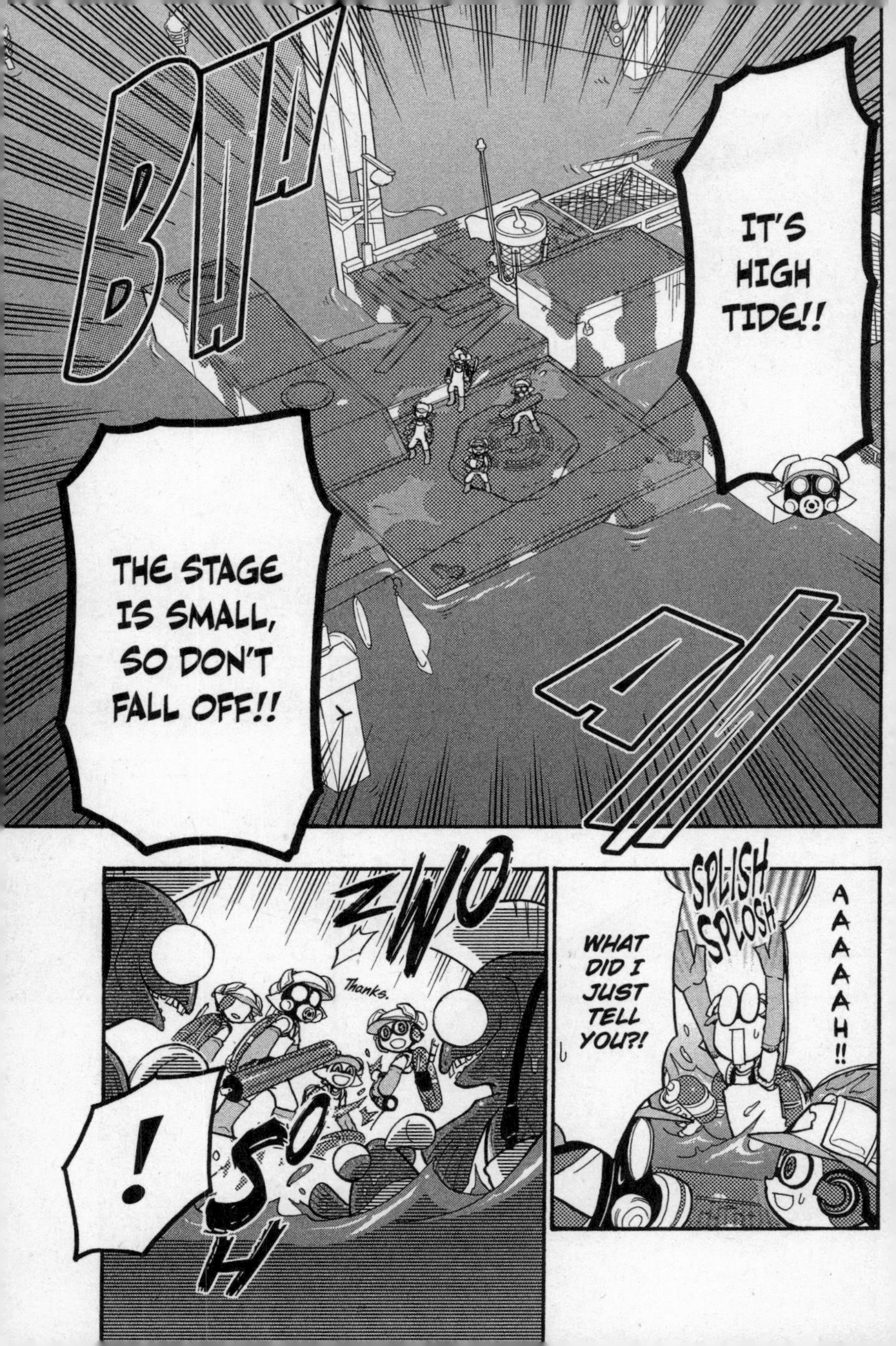
IT'S HIGH TIDE!!
BWAH
THE STAGE IS SMALL, SO DON'T FALL OFF!!
A
SPLISH SPLOSH
AAAAAH!!
WHAT DID I JUST TELL YOU?!
ZWO
Thanks.
!
SOH

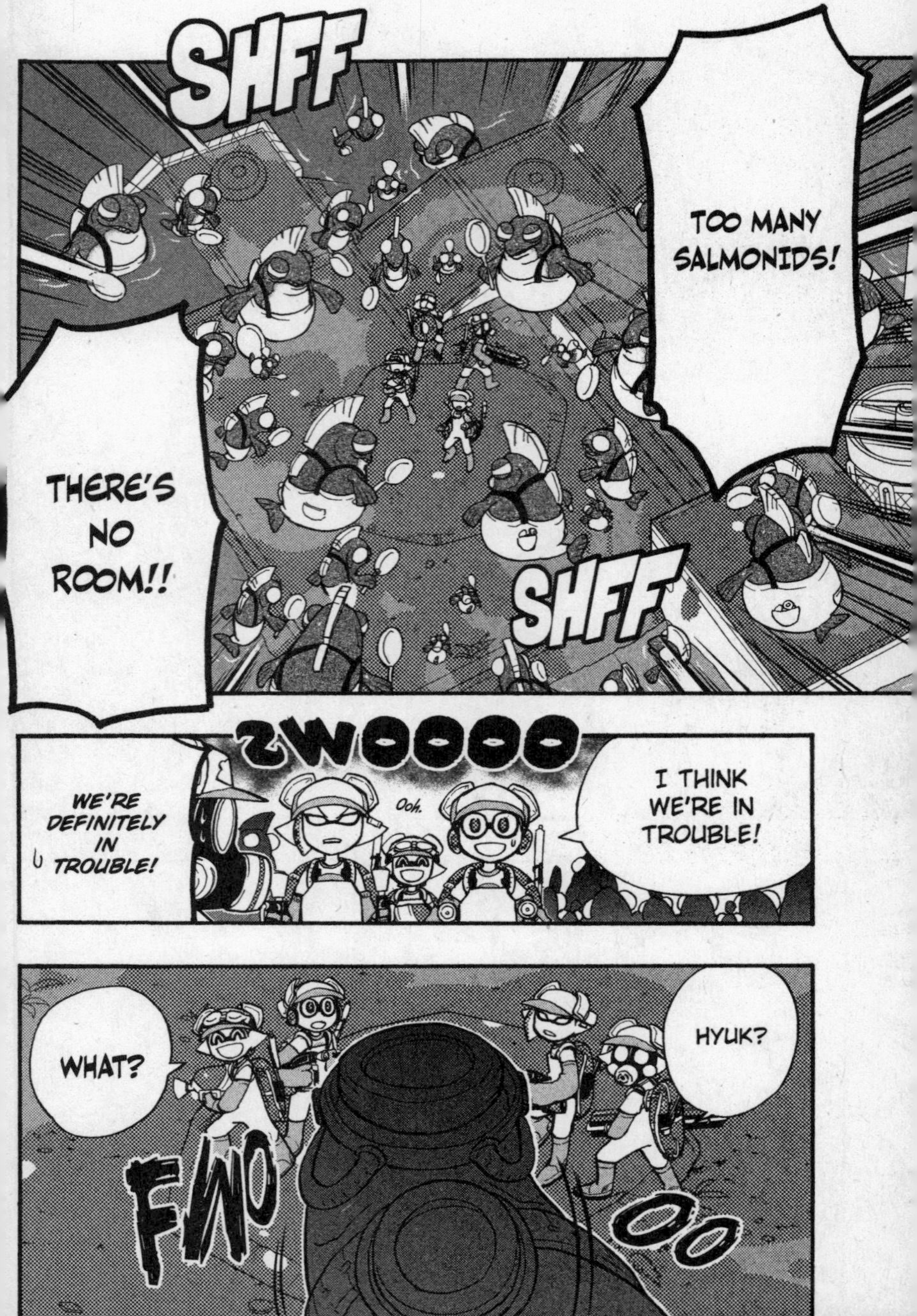
TOO MANY SALMONIDS!
SHFF
THERE'S NO ROOM!!
SHFF
ZWOOOOO
I THINK WE'RE IN TROUBLE!
Ooh.
WE'RE DEFINITELY IN TROUBLE!
HYUK?
WHAT?
FWOOO

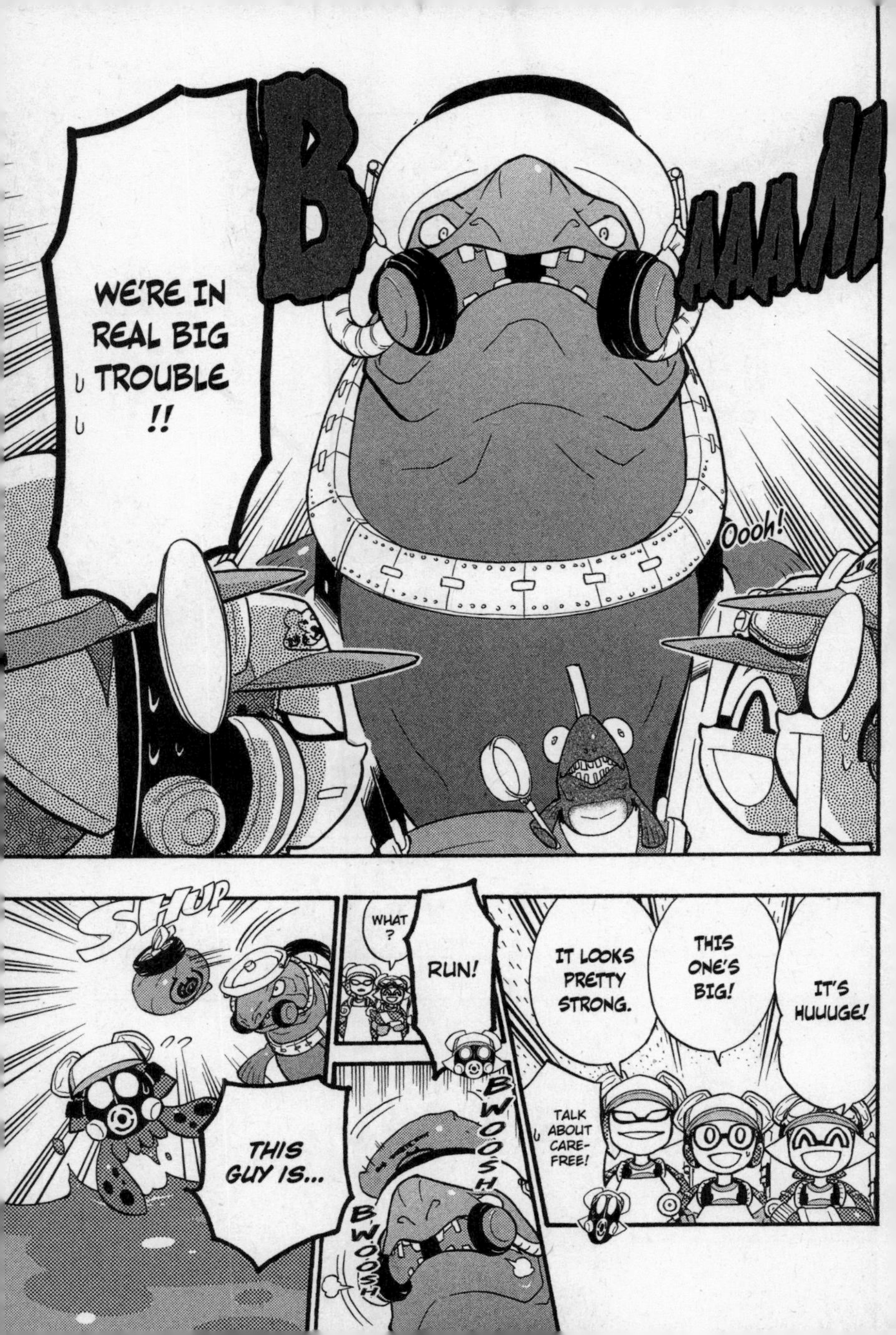
BAAAAM
WE'RE IN REAL BIG TROUBLE !!
Oooh!
IT'S HUUUGE!
THIS ONE'S BIG!
IT LOOKS PRETTY STRONG.
TALK ABOUT CARE-FREE!
WHAT ?
RUN!
BWOOSH
BWOOSH
SHUP
??
THIS GUY IS...

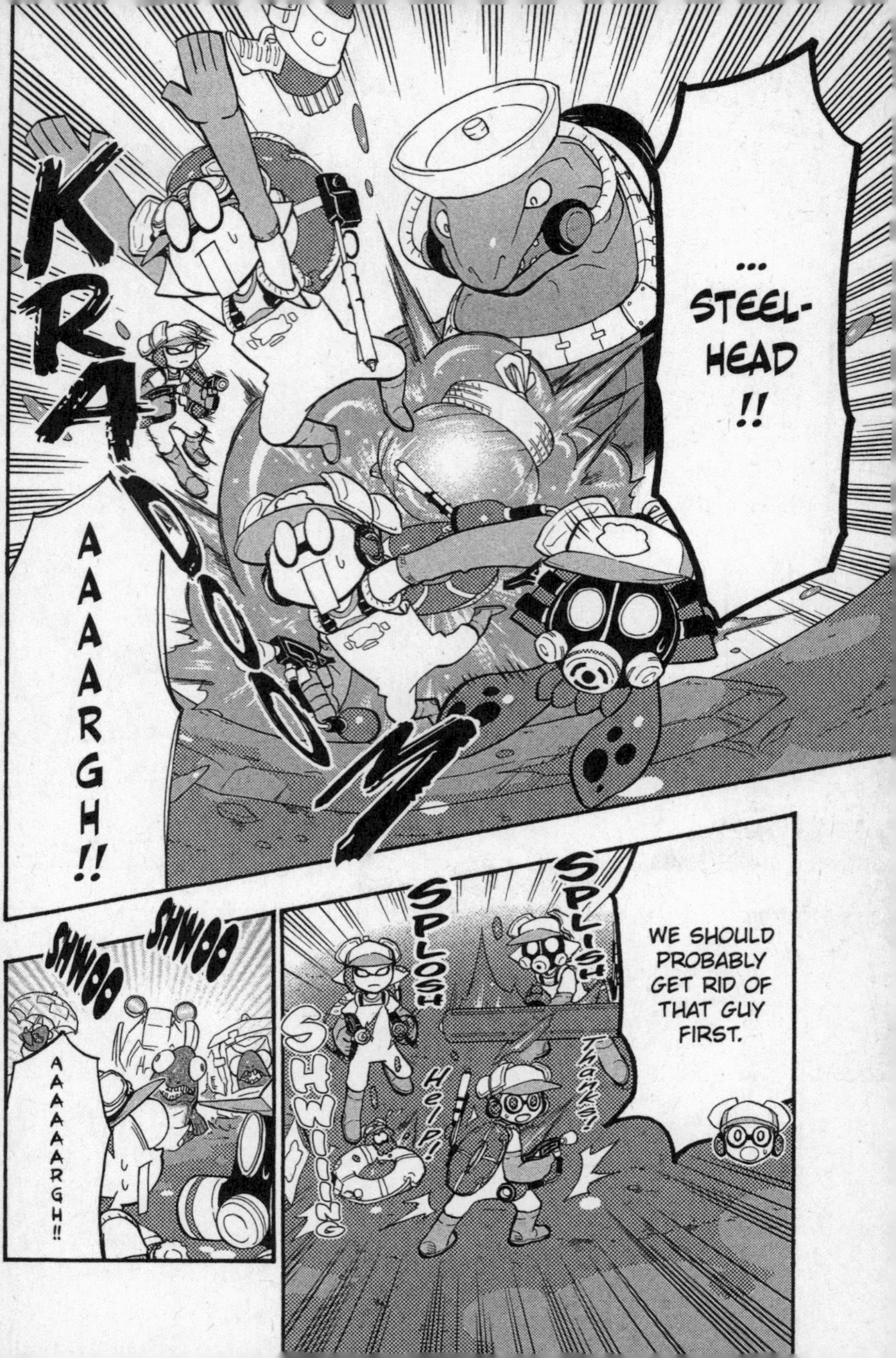
...STEEL-HEAD!!
KRADOOOM
AAAARGH!!
WE SHOULD PROBABLY GET RID OF THAT GUY FIRST.
SPLISH
SPLOSH
Thanks!
Help!
SHWIIING
SHWOO
SHWOO
AAAAAAARGH!!

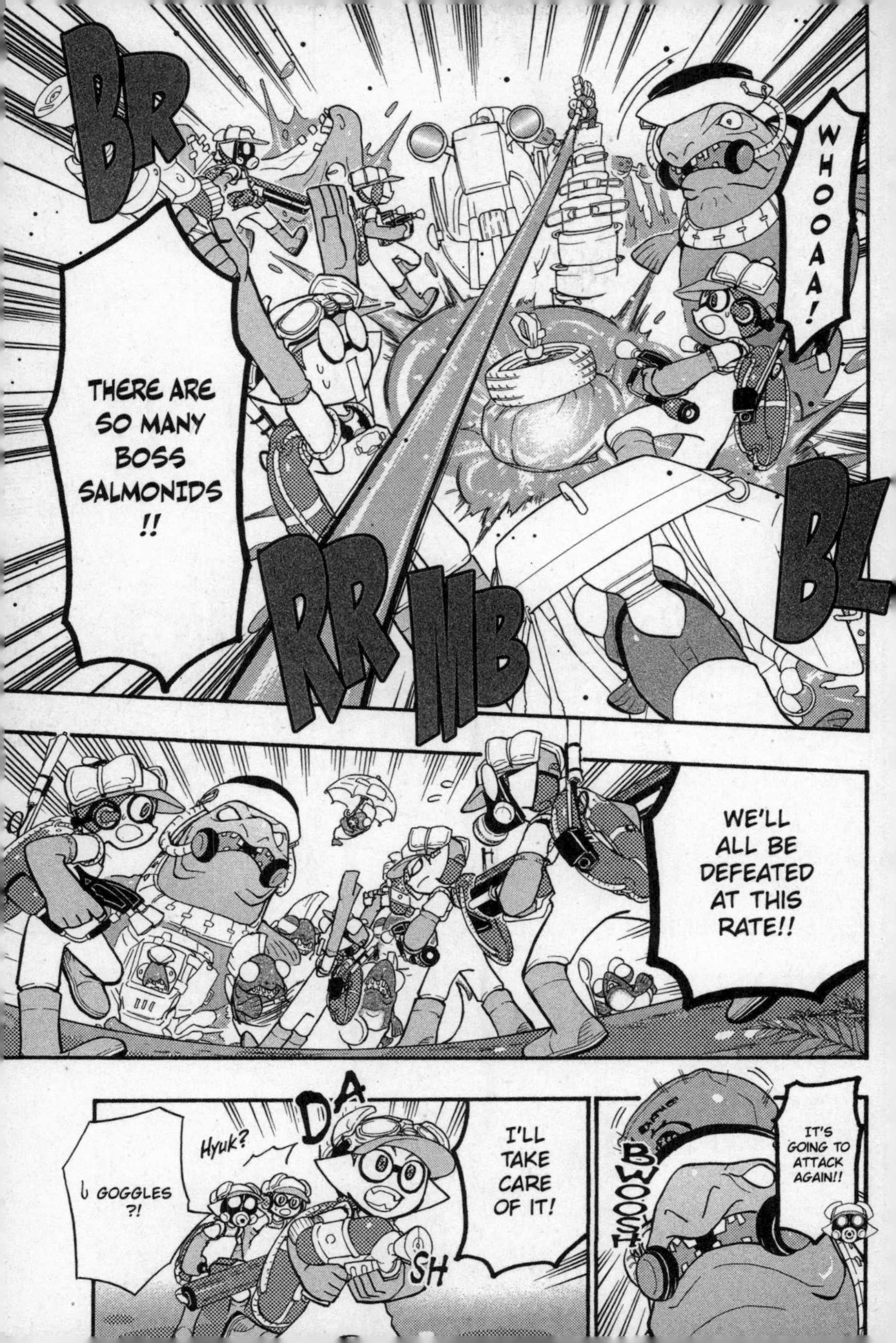
WHOOAAA!
BL
BR
RR
MB
THERE ARE SO MANY BOSS SALMONIDS!!
WE'LL ALL BE DEFEATED AT THIS RATE!!
IT'S GOING TO ATTACK AGAIN!!
BWOOSH
I'LL TAKE CARE OF IT!
DA
SH
Hyuk?
GOGGLES?!

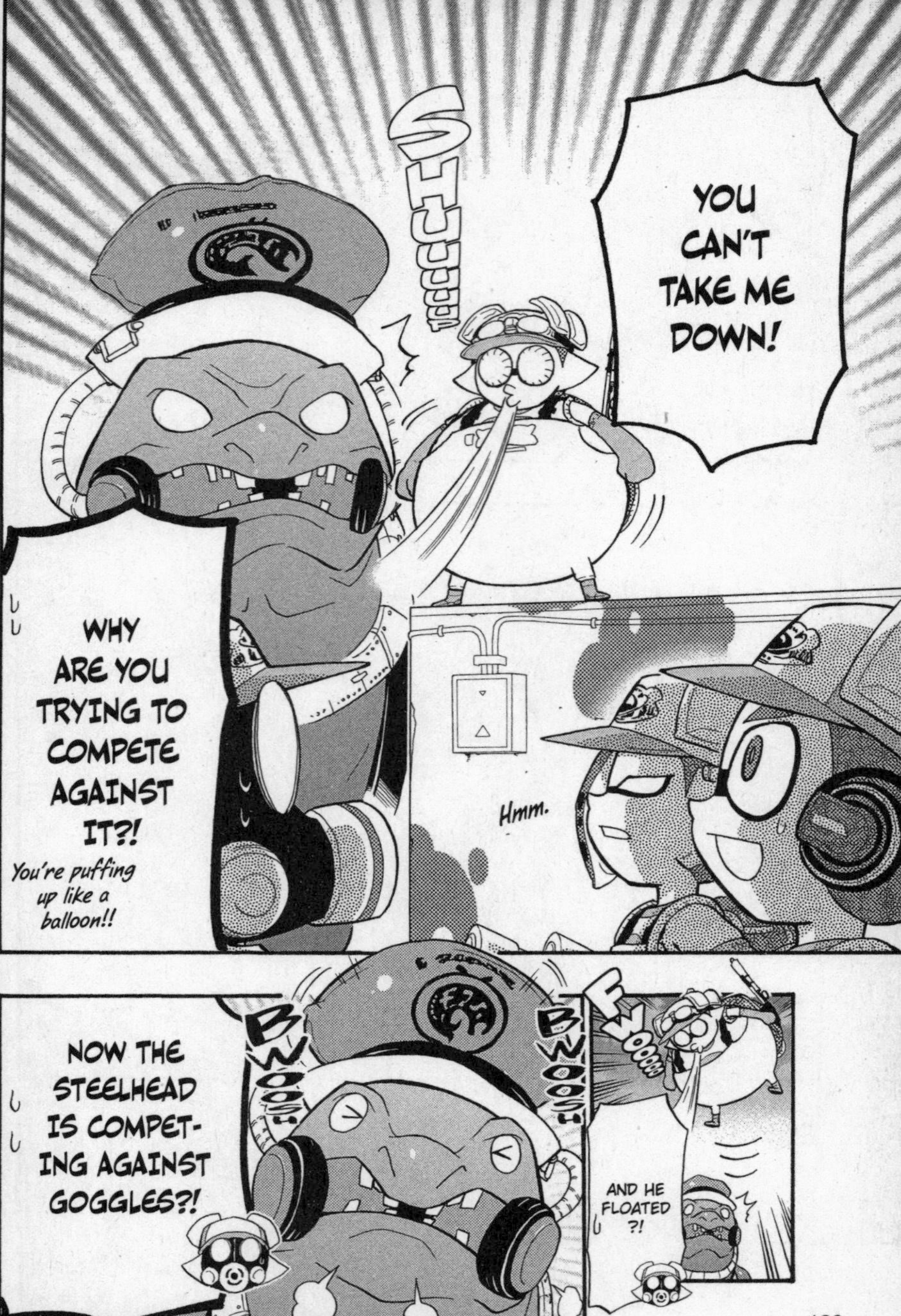
SHUUUUUU
YOU CAN'T TAKE ME DOWN!
WHY ARE YOU TRYING TO COMPETE AGAINST IT?!
You're puffing up like a balloon!!
Hmm.
FWOOOM
AND HE FLOATED?!
BWOOSH
BWOOSH
NOW THE STEELHEAD IS COMPET-ING AGAINST GOGGLES?!

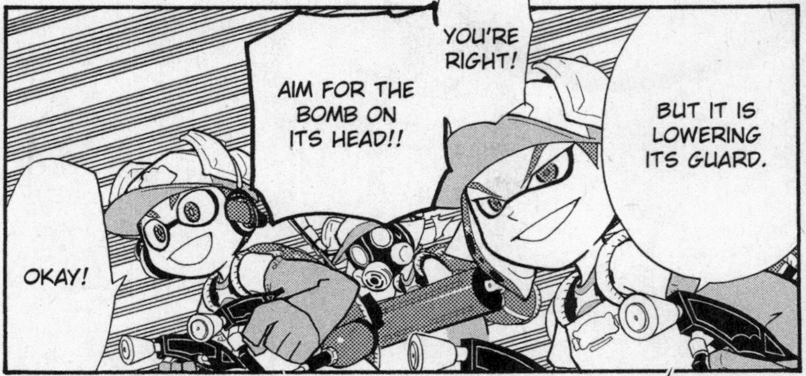
BUT IT IS LOWERING ITS GUARD.
YOU'RE RIGHT!
AIM FOR THE BOMB ON ITS HEAD!!
OKAY!
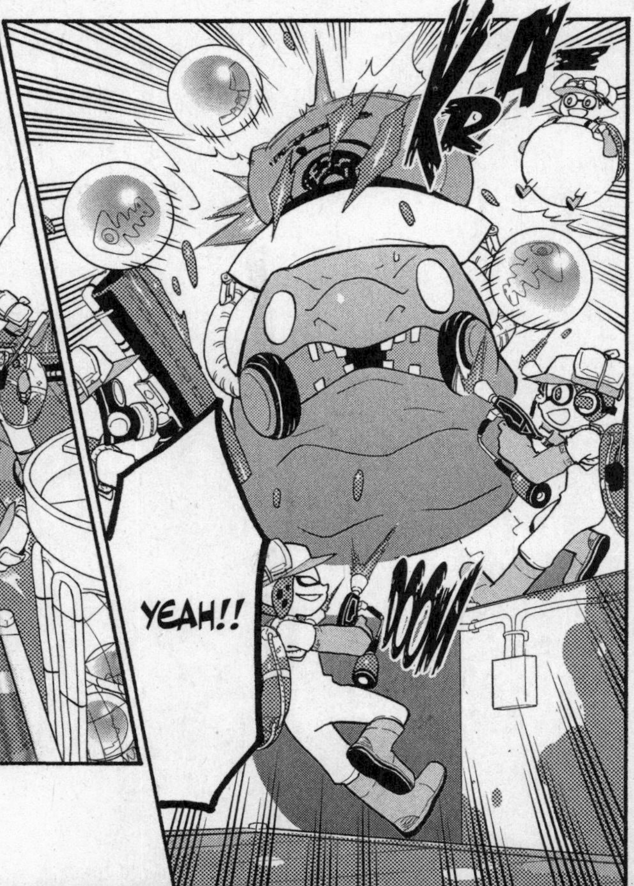
YEAH!!
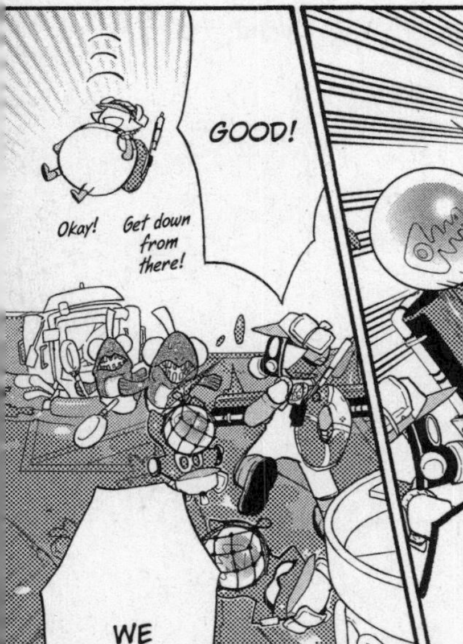
GOOD!
Get down from there!
Okay!
WE STILL HAVE TIME!

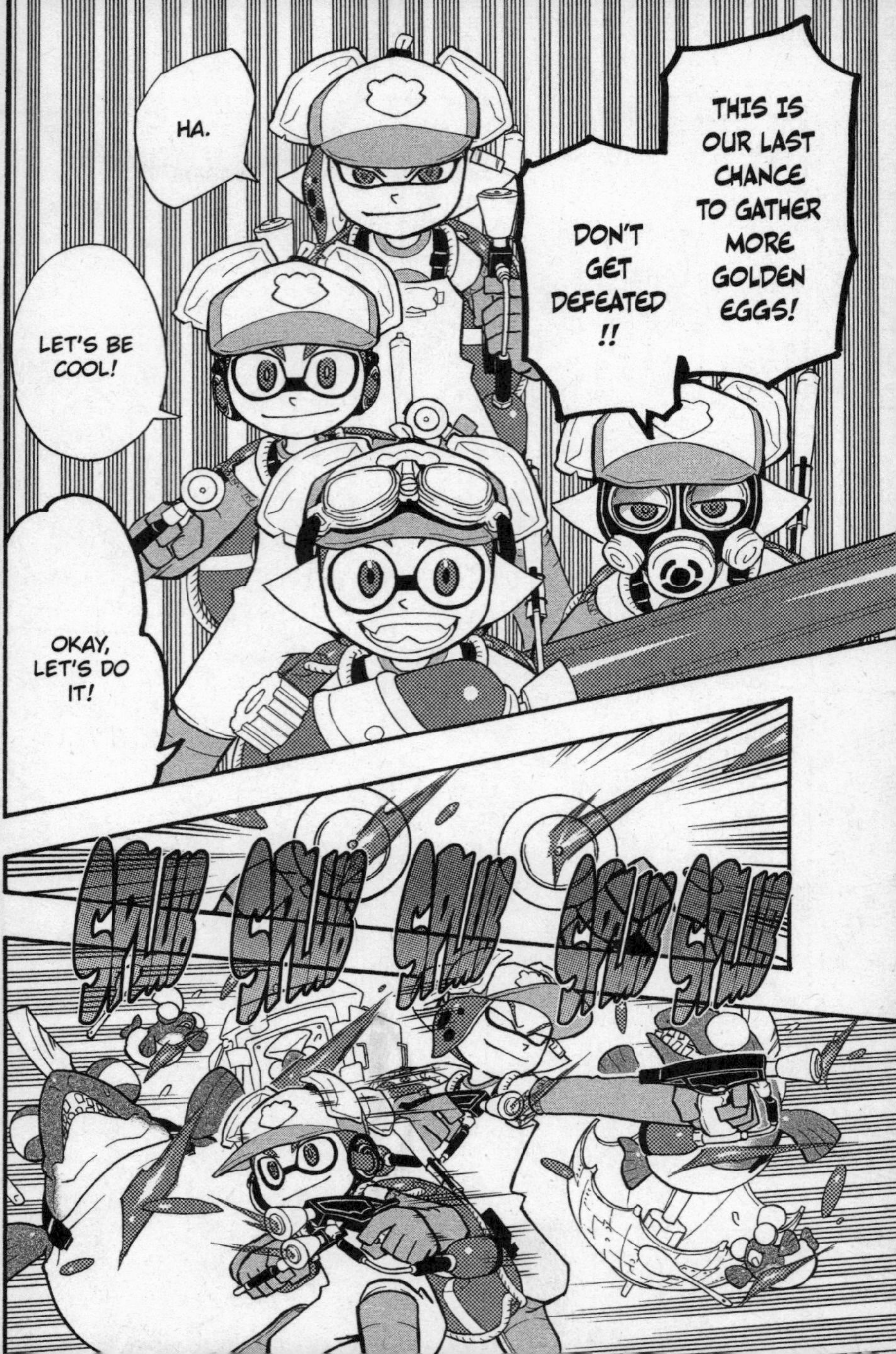
THIS IS OUR LAST CHANCE TO GATHER MORE GOLDEN EGGS!
DON'T GET DEFEATED!!
HA.
LET'S BE COOL!
OKAY, LET'S DO IT!

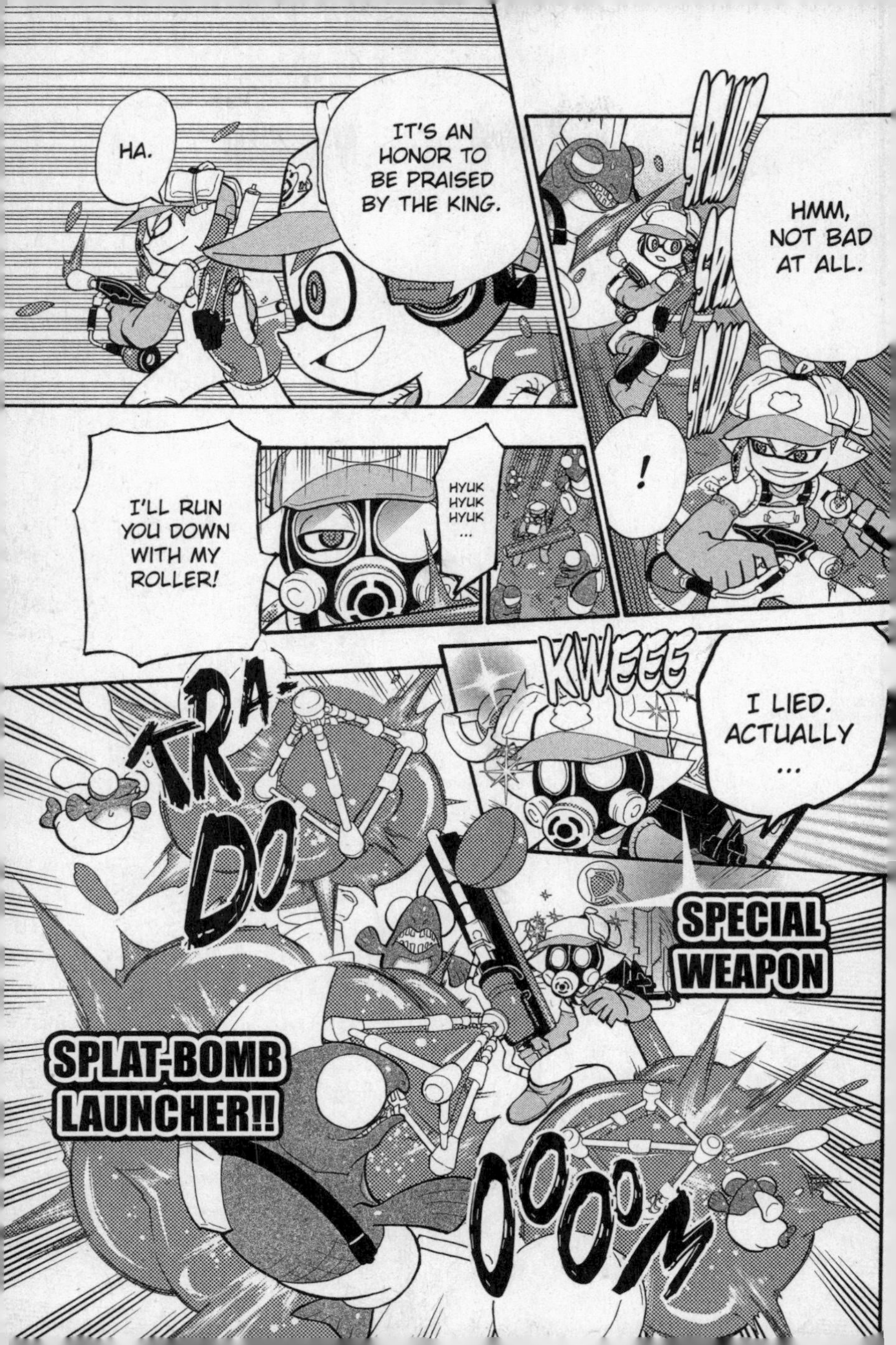
HMM, NOT BAD AT ALL.
IT'S AN HONOR TO BE PRAISED BY THE KING.
HA.
!
HYUK HYUK HYUK ...
I'LL RUN YOU DOWN WITH MY ROLLER!
I LIED. ACTUALLY ...
KWEEE
SPECIAL WEAPON
TRA-
DO
SPLAT-BOMB LAUNCHER!!
OOOOM

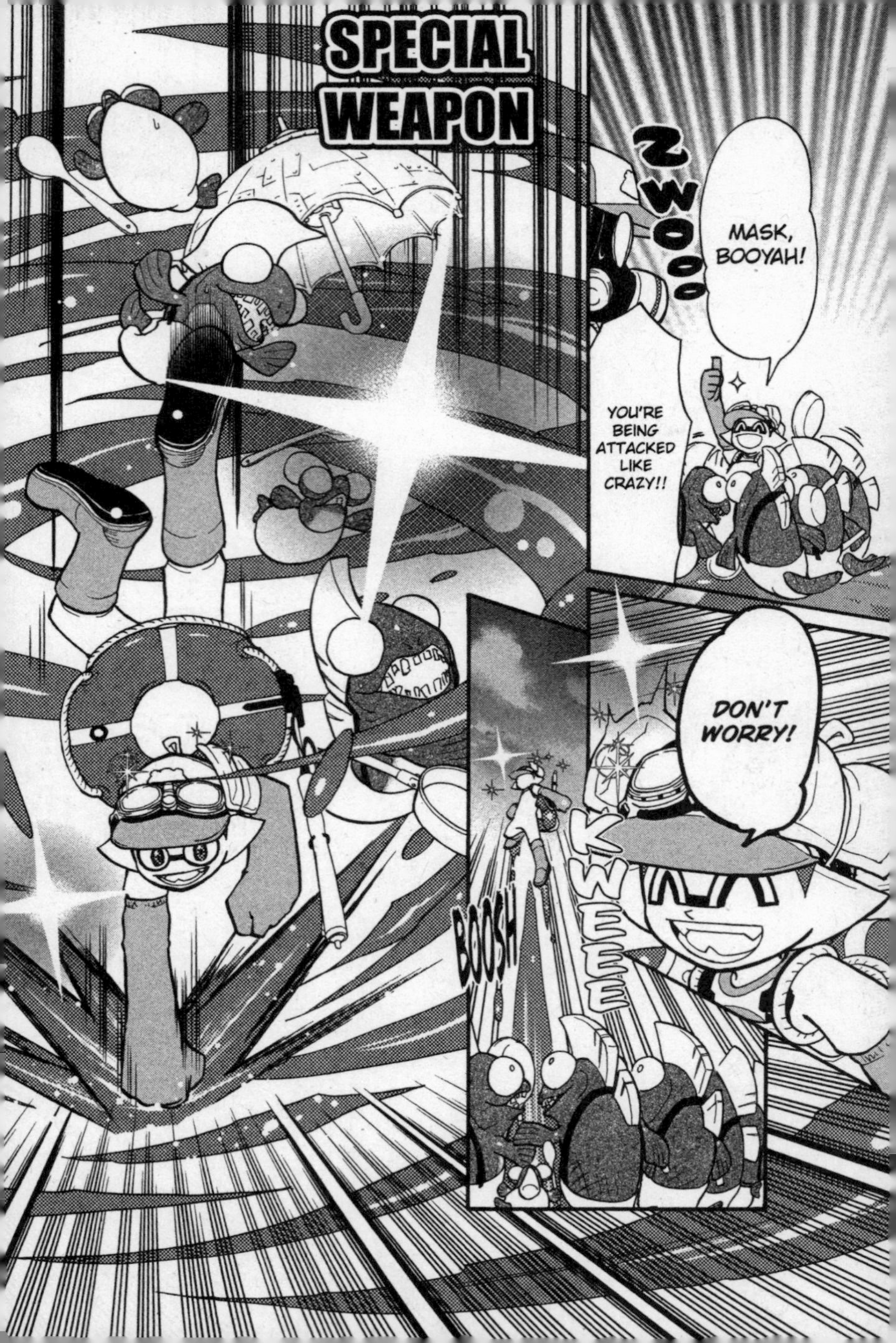
ZWOOO
MASK, BOOYAH!
YOU'RE BEING ATTACKED LIKE CRAZY!!
DON'T WORRY!
KWEEE
BOOSH
SPECIAL WEAPON

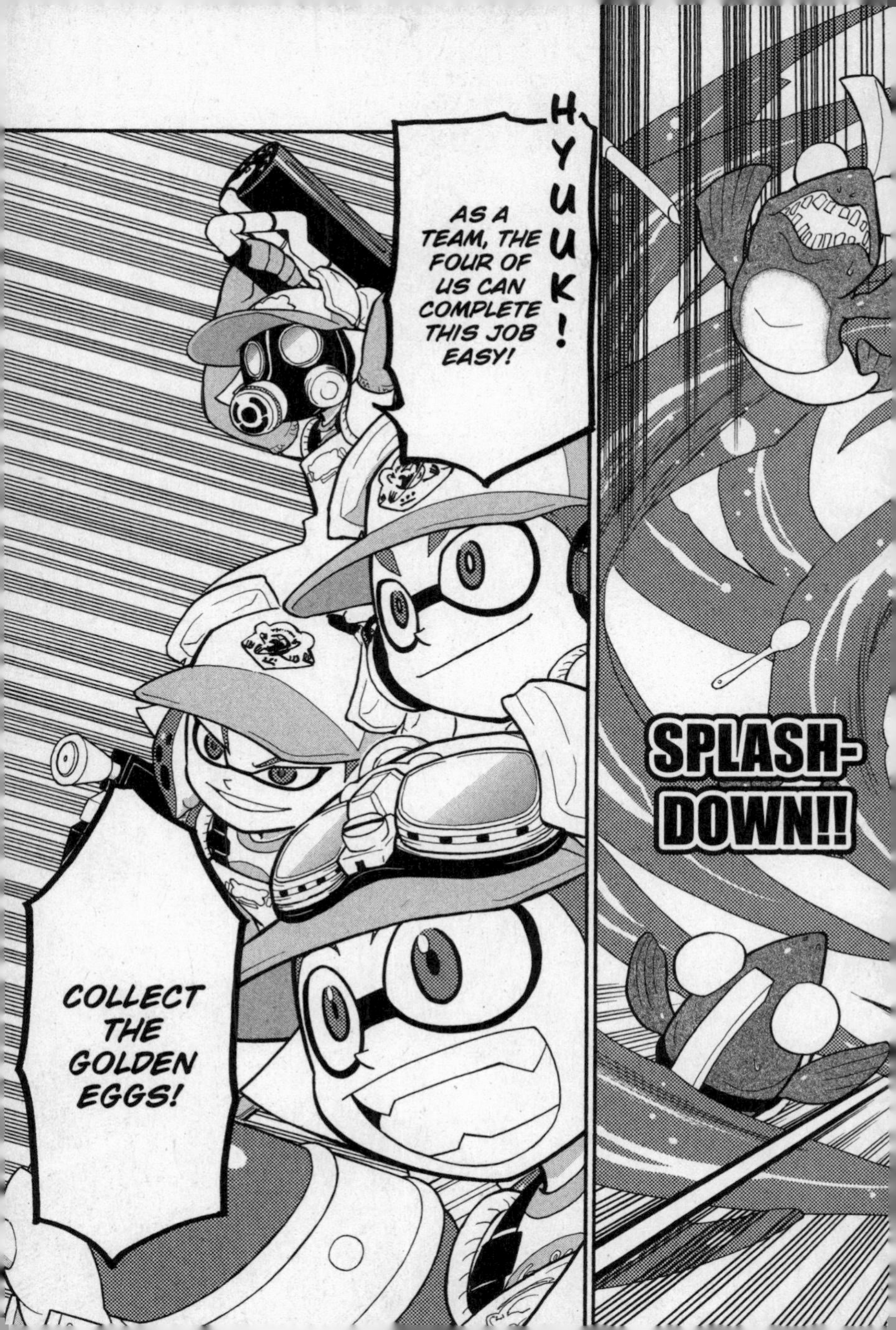
SPLASH-DOWN!!
HYUUK!
AS A TEAM, THE FOUR OF US CAN COMPLETE THIS JOB EASY!
COLLECT THE GOLDEN EGGS!

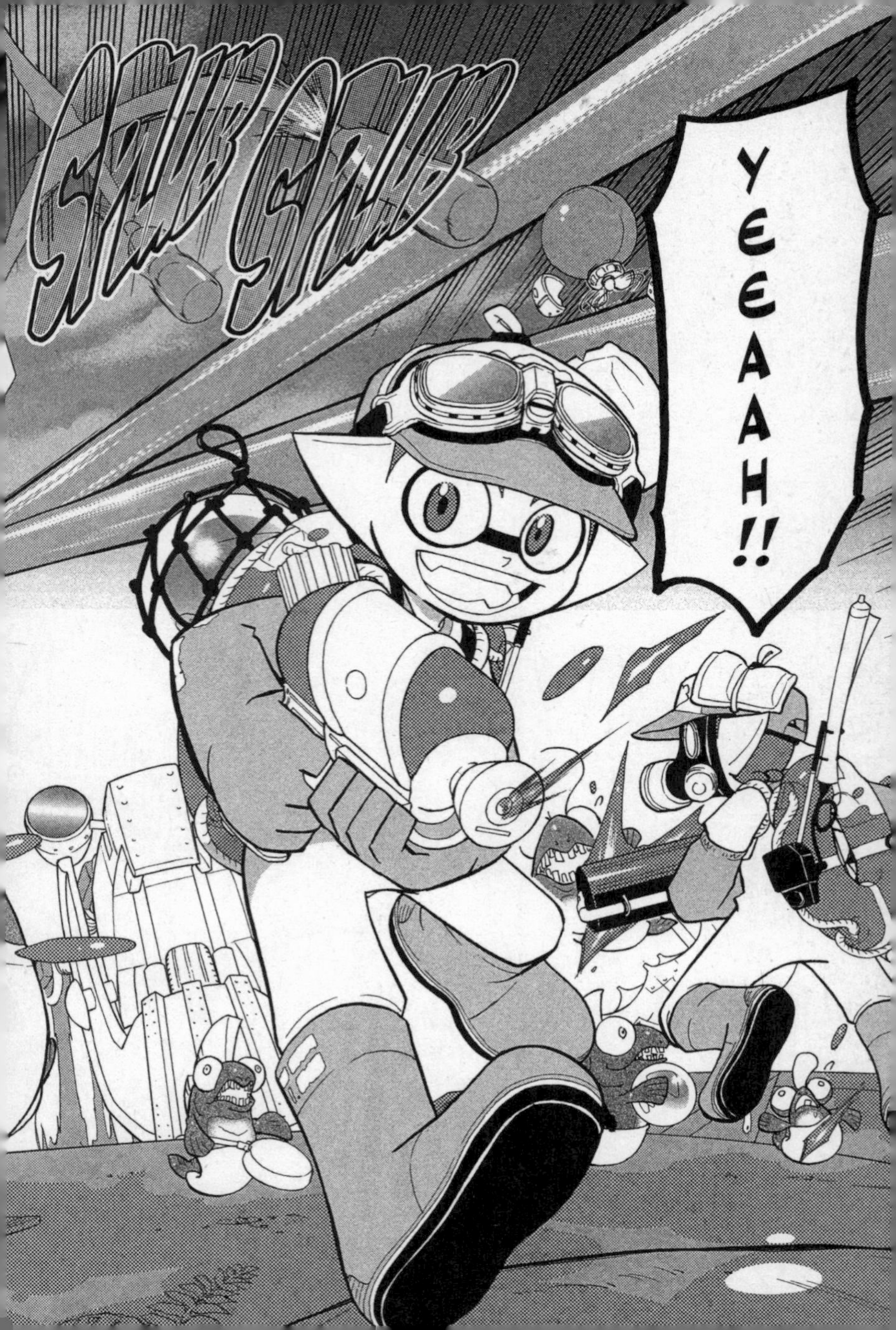
YEEAAH!!

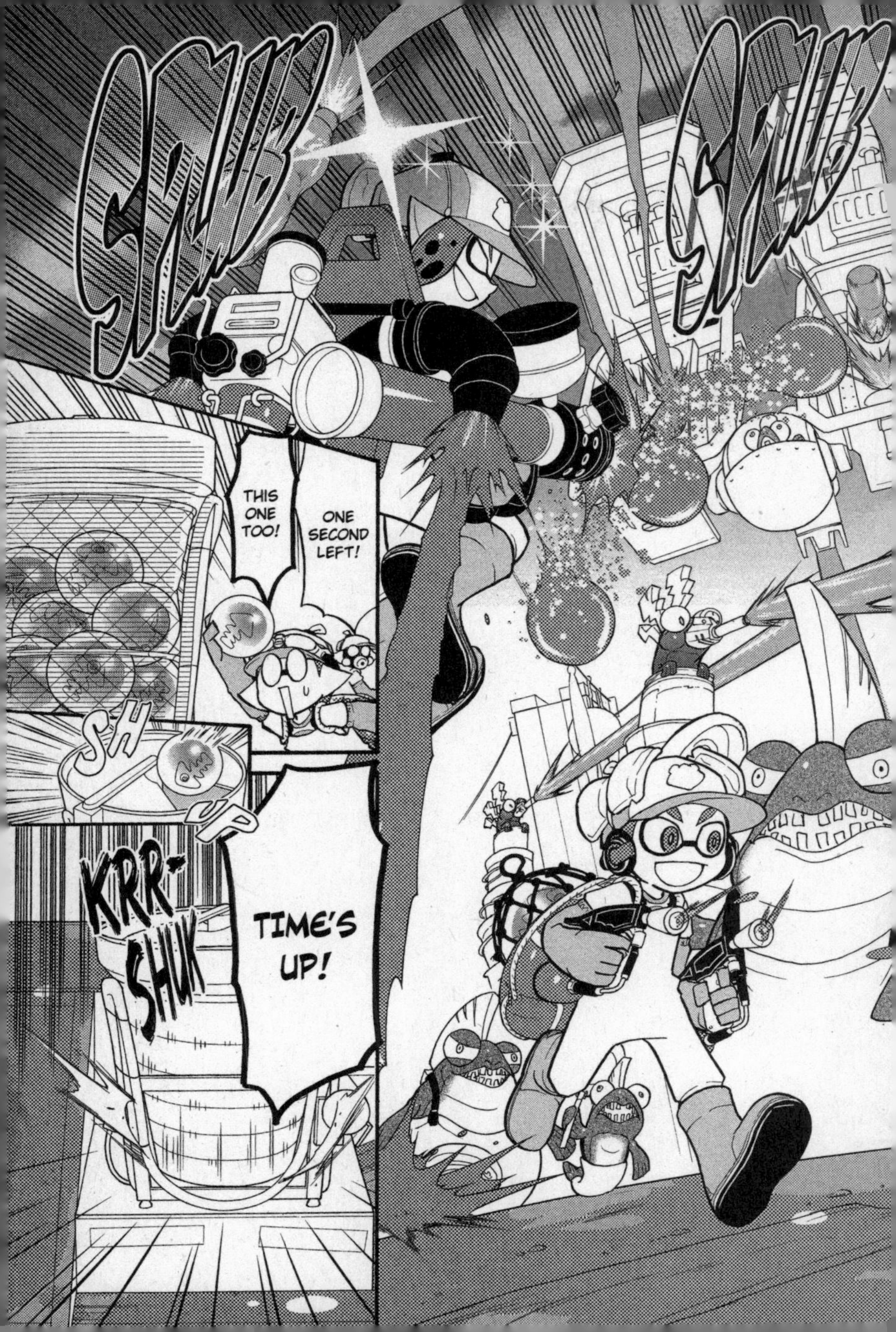
ONE SECOND LEFT!
THIS ONE TOO!
SH UP
TIME'S UP!
KRR-SHUK

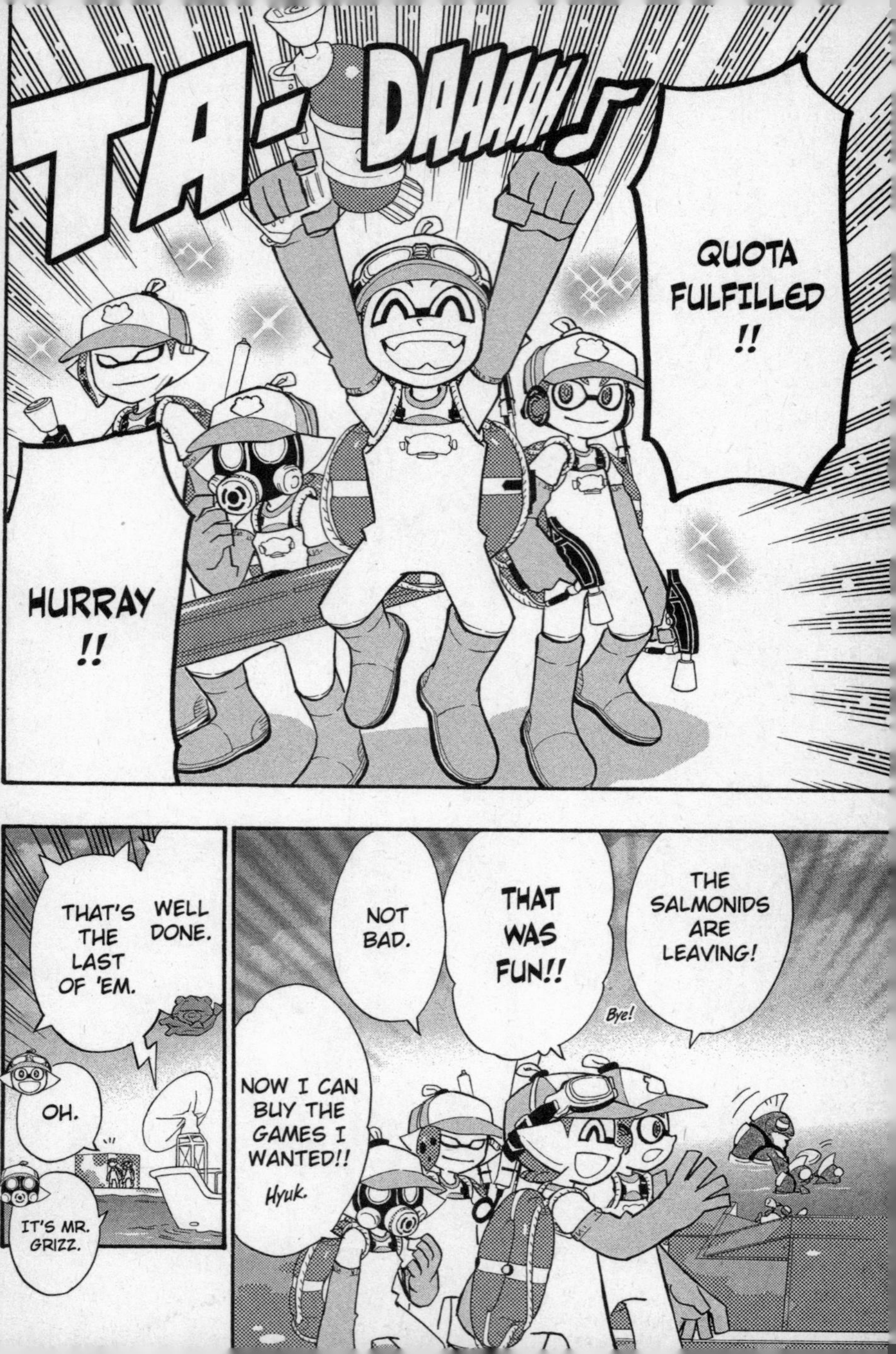
T.A.-DAAAAH♪
QUOTA FULFILLED!!
HURRAY!!
THE SALMONIDS ARE LEAVING!
Bye!
THAT WAS FUN!!
NOT BAD.
NOW I CAN BUY THE GAMES I WANTED!!
Hyuk.
WELL DONE.
THAT'S THE LAST OF 'EM.
OH.
IT'S MR. GRIZZ.

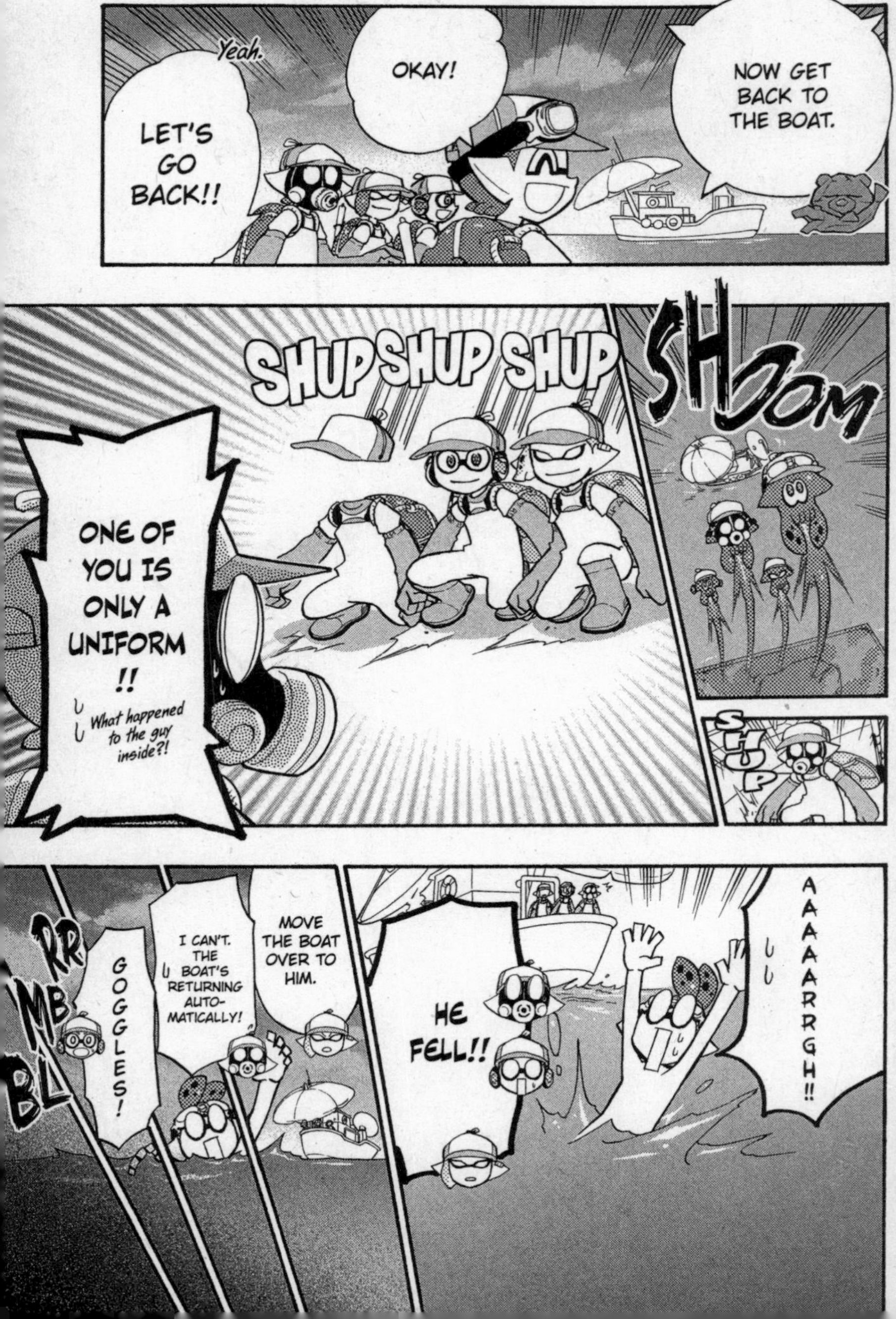
NOW GET BACK TO THE BOAT.
OKAY!
Yeah.
LET'S GO BACK!!
SHOOM
SHUP
SHUP SHUP SHUP
ONE OF YOU IS ONLY A UNIFORM!!
What happened to the guy inside?!
AAAAARRGH!!
HE FELL!!
MOVE THE BOAT OVER TO HIM.
I CAN'T. THE BOAT'S RETURNING AUTO-MATICALLY!
GOGGLES!
RRMBBL

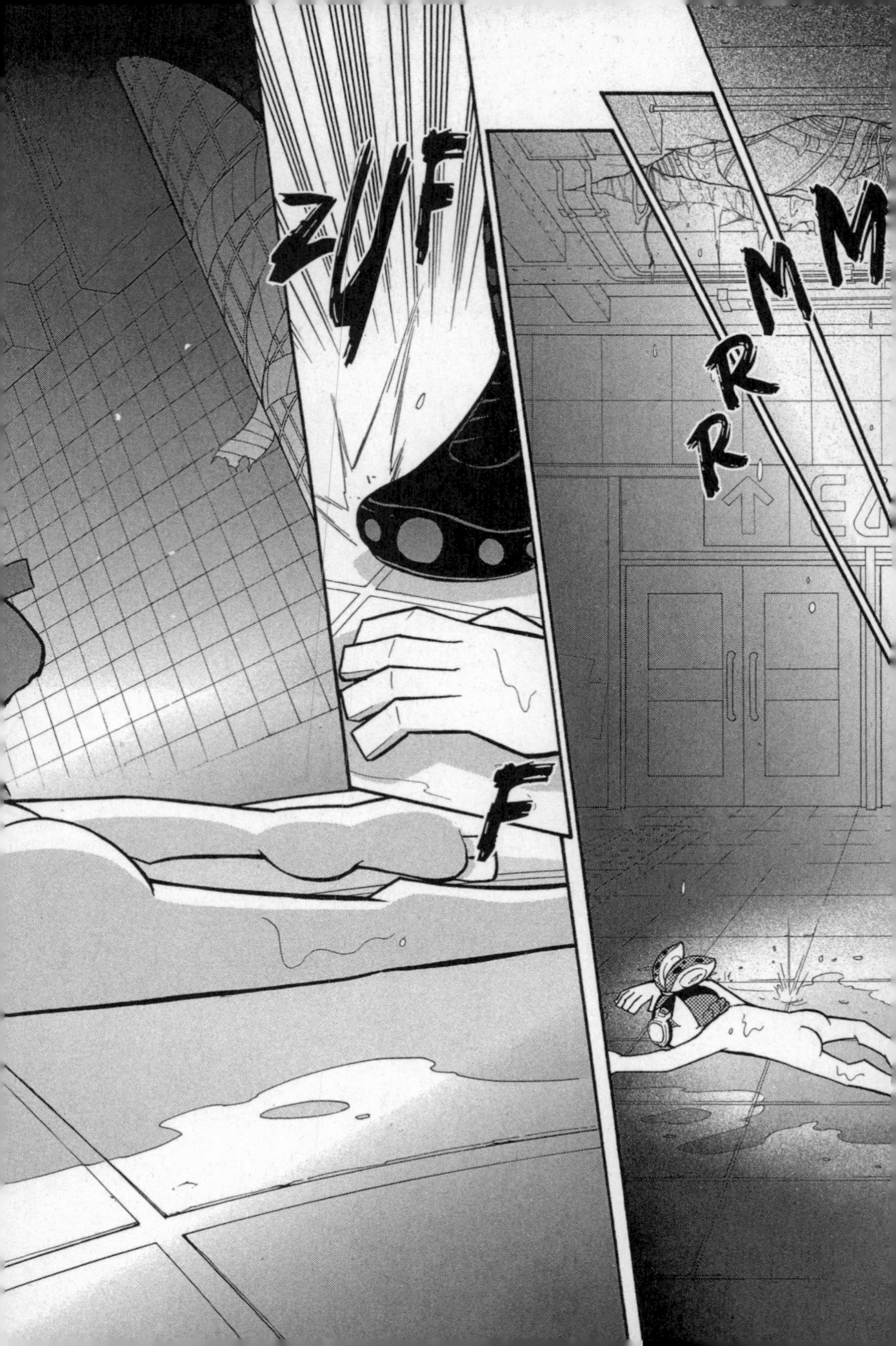
RRMM
ZUFF

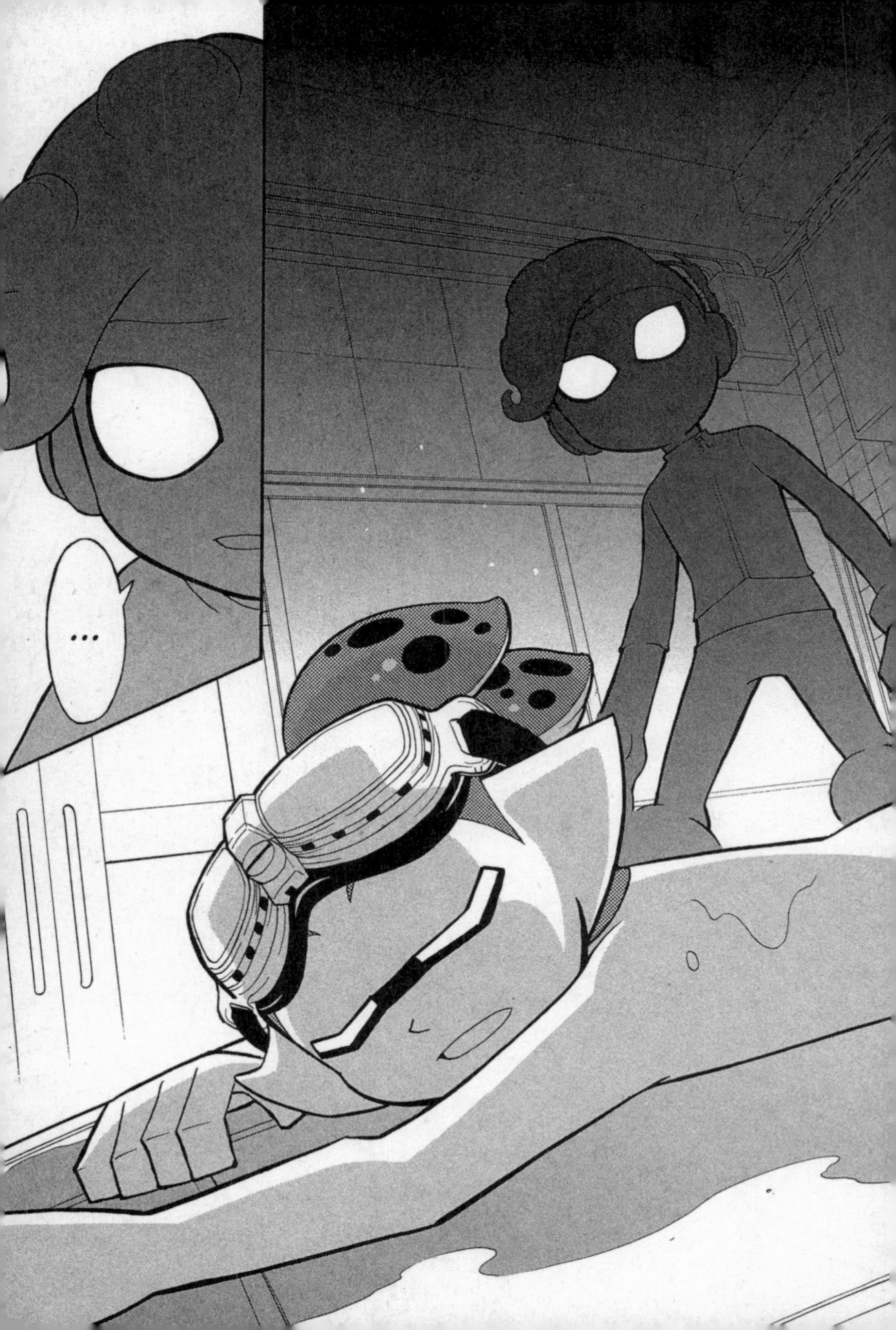
...

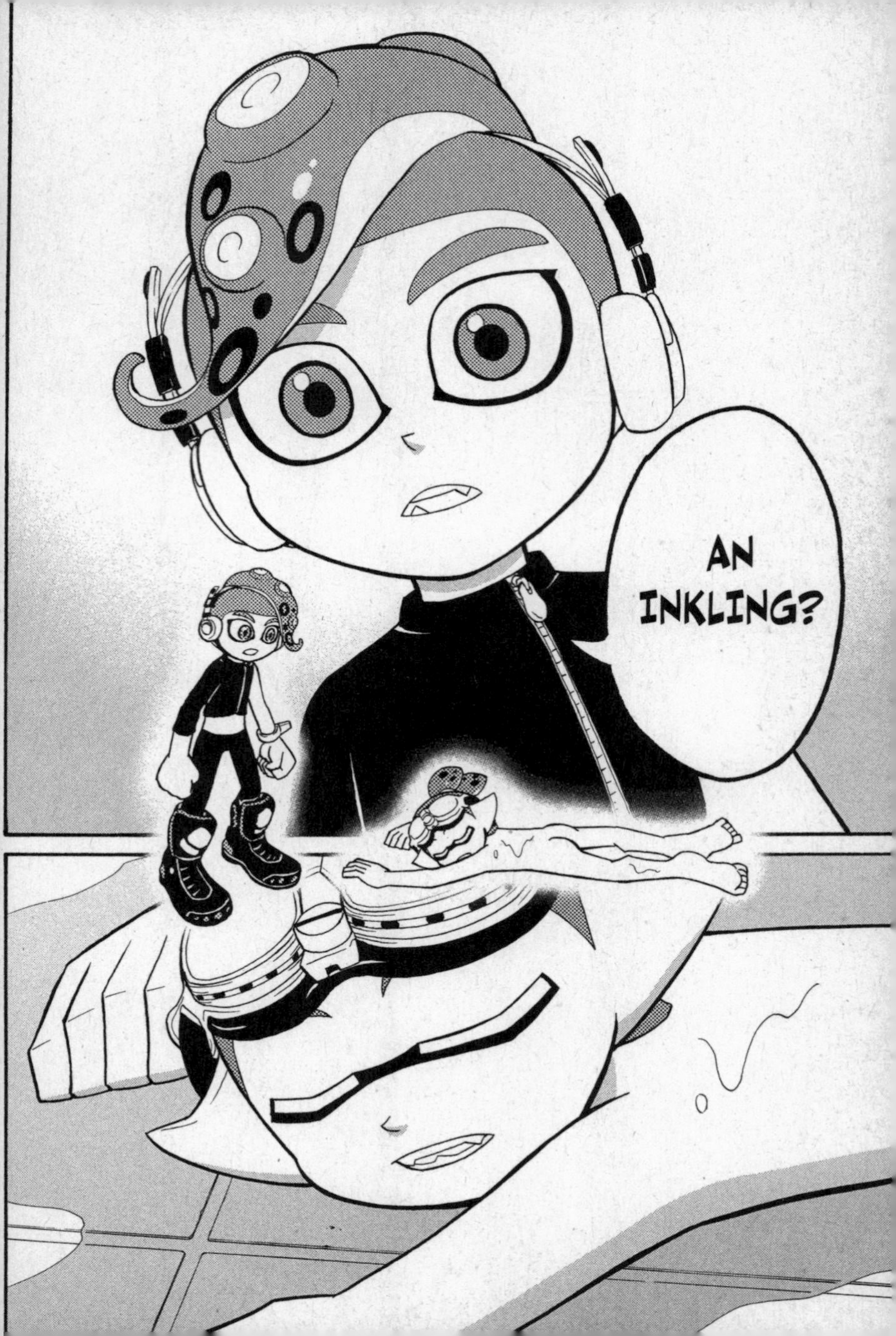
AN INKLING?

Next volume,
the new
Octo Arc
begins!!!

SPLATOON VOLUME 6 END / CONTINUED IN VOLUME 7

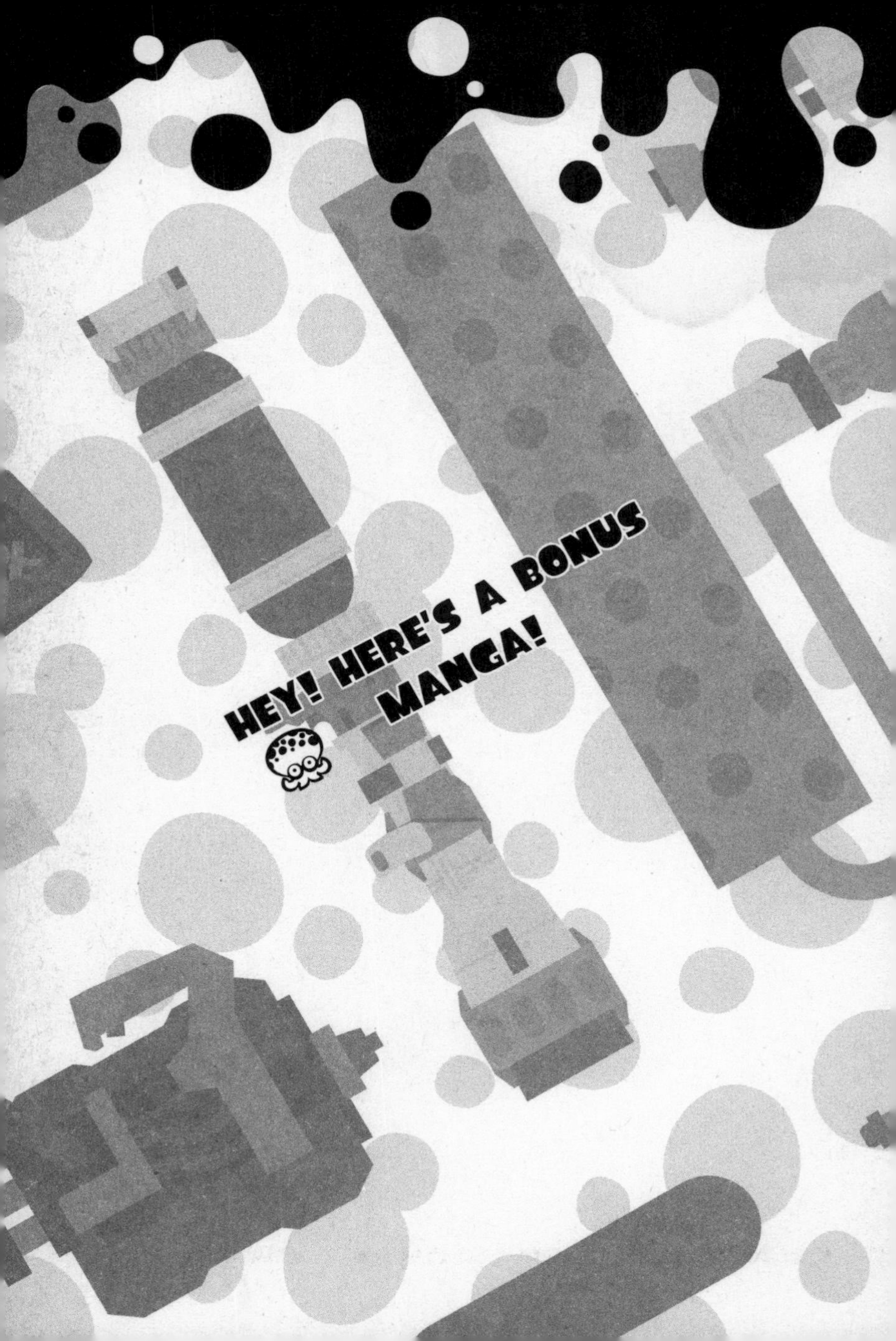
HEY! HERE'S A BONUS MANGA!

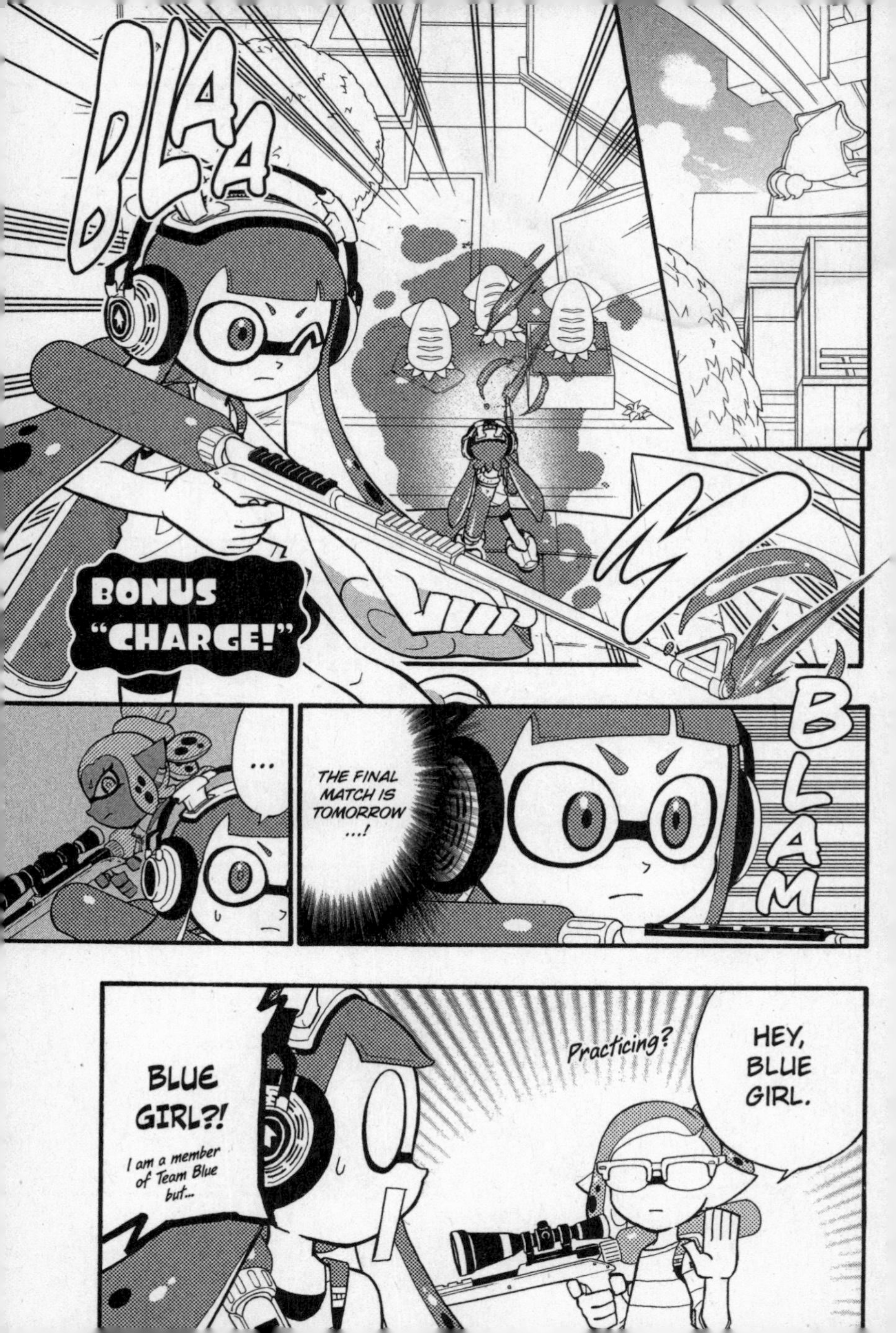
M
BLAA
BONUS "CHARGE!"
BLAM
THE FINAL MATCH IS TOMORROW ...!
...
HEY, BLUE GIRL.
Practicing?
BLUE GIRL?!
I am a member of Team Blue but...

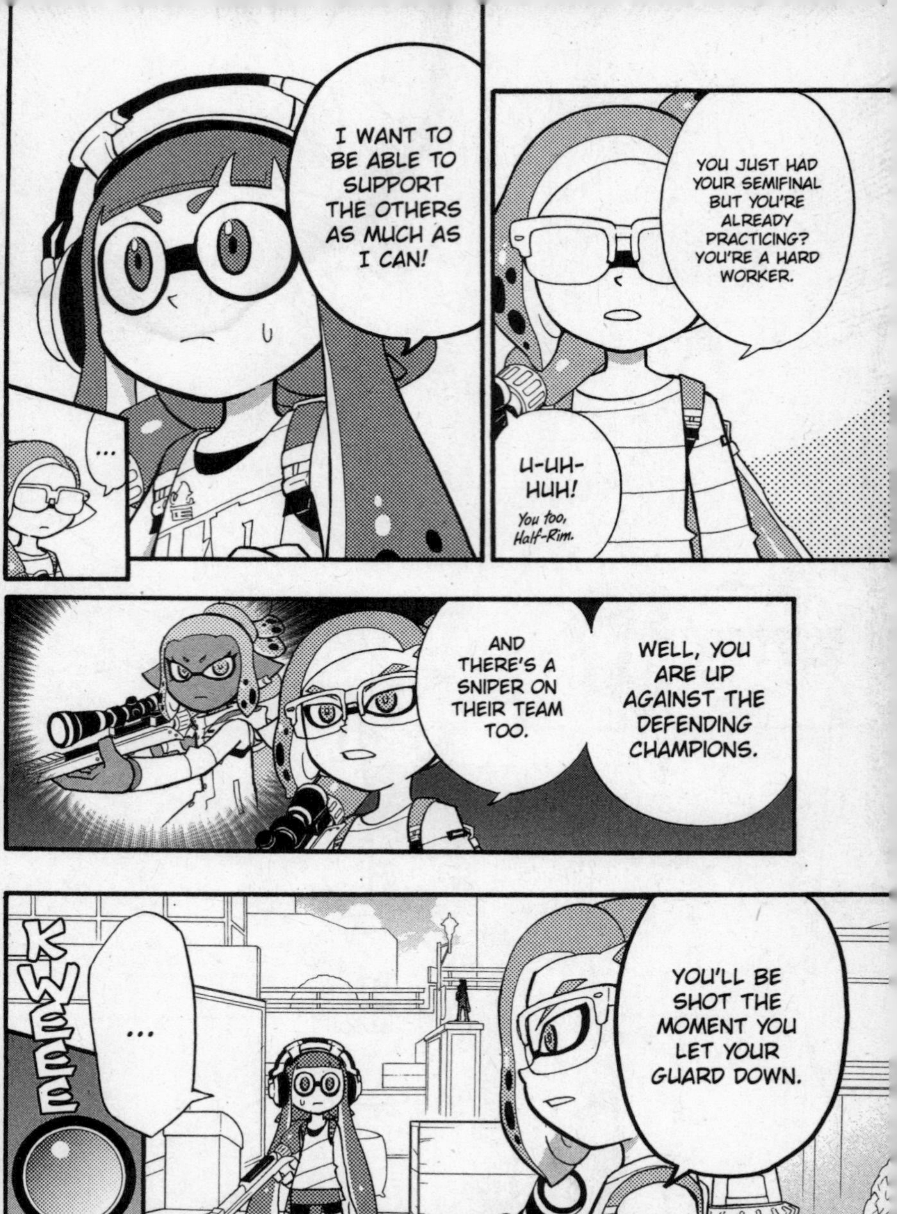
YOU JUST HAD YOUR SEMIFINAL BUT YOU'RE ALREADY PRACTICING? YOU'RE A HARD WORKER.
U-UH-HUH!
You too, Half-Rim.
I WANT TO BE ABLE TO SUPPORT THE OTHERS AS MUCH AS I CAN!
...
WELL, YOU ARE UP AGAINST THE DEFENDING CHAMPIONS.
AND THERE'S A SNIPER ON THEIR TEAM TOO.
YOU'LL BE SHOT THE MOMENT YOU LET YOUR GUARD DOWN.
...
KWEEE

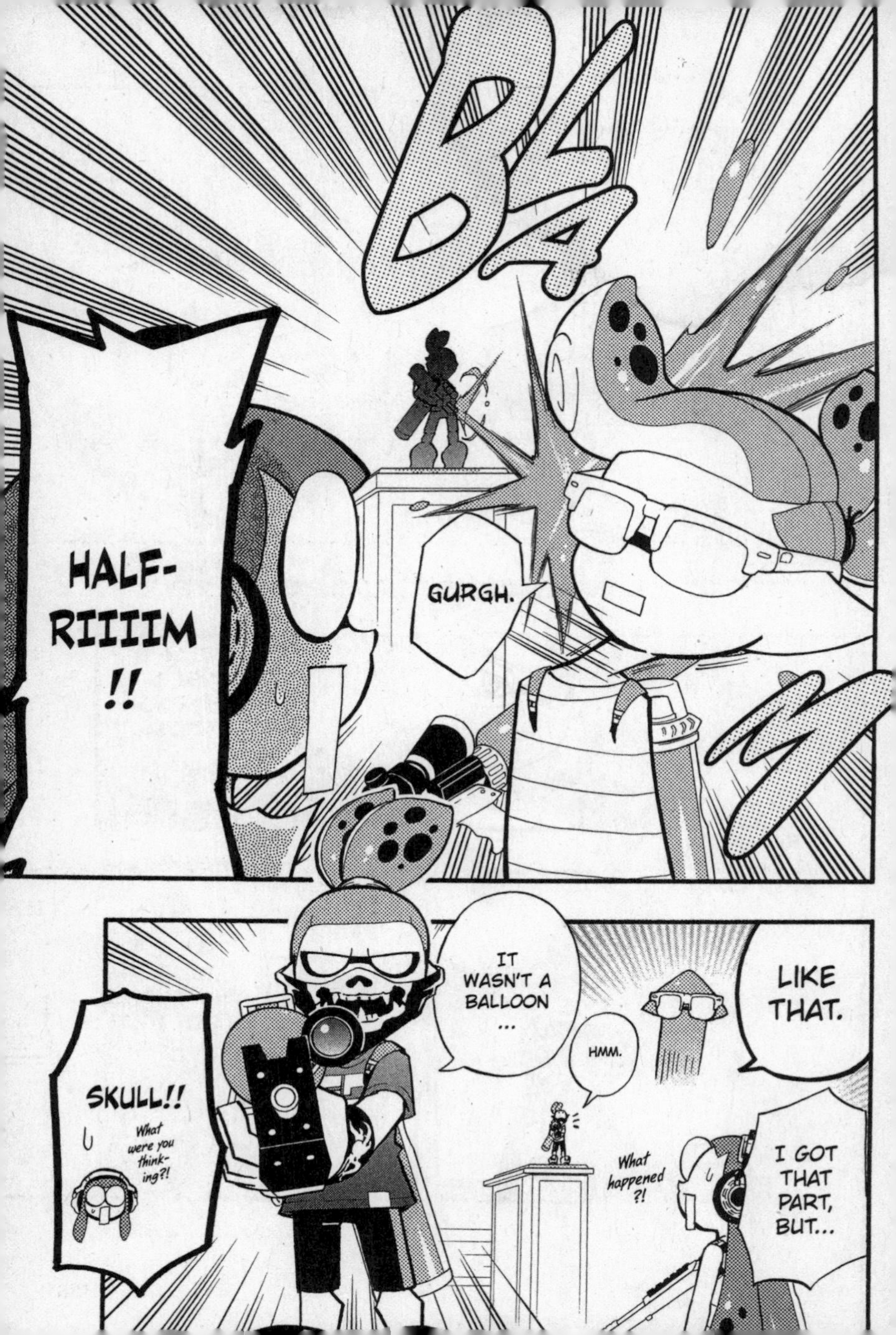
BLAM
GURGH.
HALF-RIIIIM!!
LIKE THAT.
IT WASN'T A BALLOON...
HMM.
I GOT THAT PART, BUT...
What happened?!
SKULL!!
What were you thinking?!

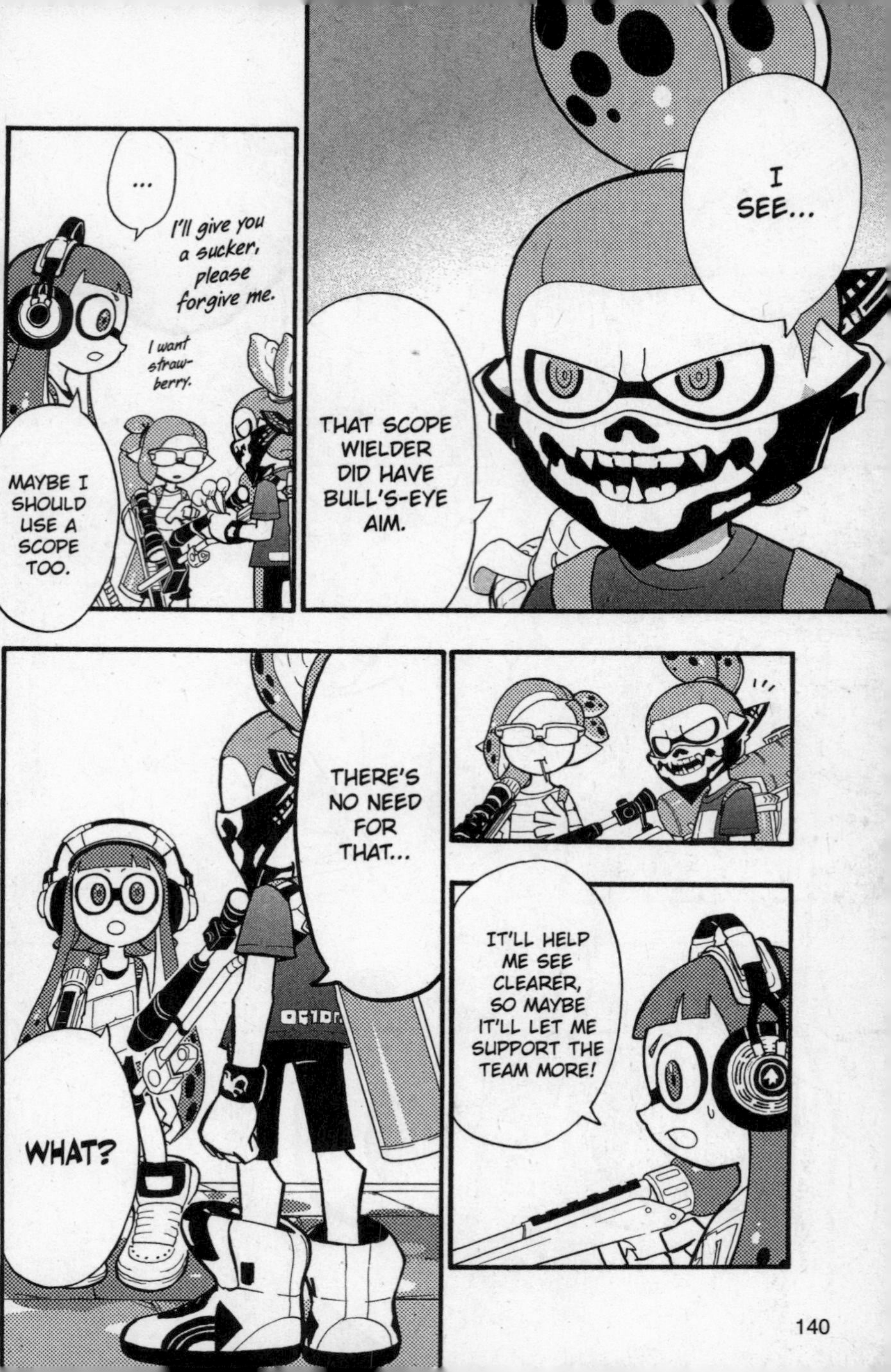
I SEE...
THAT SCOPE WIELDER DID HAVE BULL'S-EYE AIM.
...
I'll give you a sucker, please forgive me.
I want straw-berry.
MAYBE I SHOULD USE A SCOPE TOO.
IT'LL HELP ME SEE CLEARER, SO MAYBE IT'LL LET ME SUPPORT THE TEAM MORE!
THERE'S NO NEED FOR THAT...
WHAT?

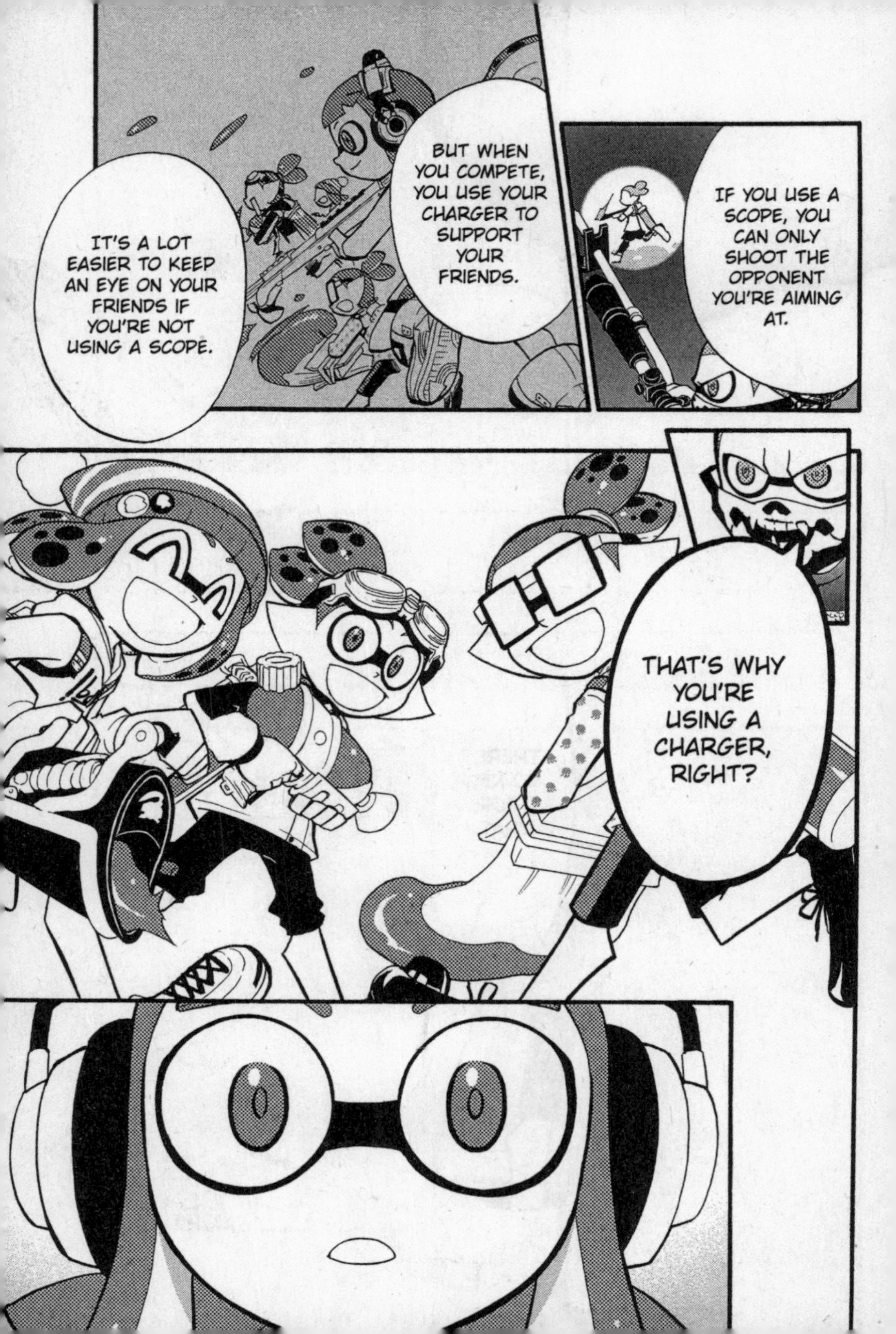
IF YOU USE A SCOPE, YOU CAN ONLY SHOOT THE OPPONENT YOU'RE AIMING AT.
BUT WHEN YOU COMPETE, YOU USE YOUR CHARGER TO SUPPORT YOUR FRIENDS.
IT'S A LOT EASIER TO KEEP AN EYE ON YOUR FRIENDS IF YOU'RE NOT USING A SCOPE.
THAT'S WHY YOU'RE USING A CHARGER, RIGHT?

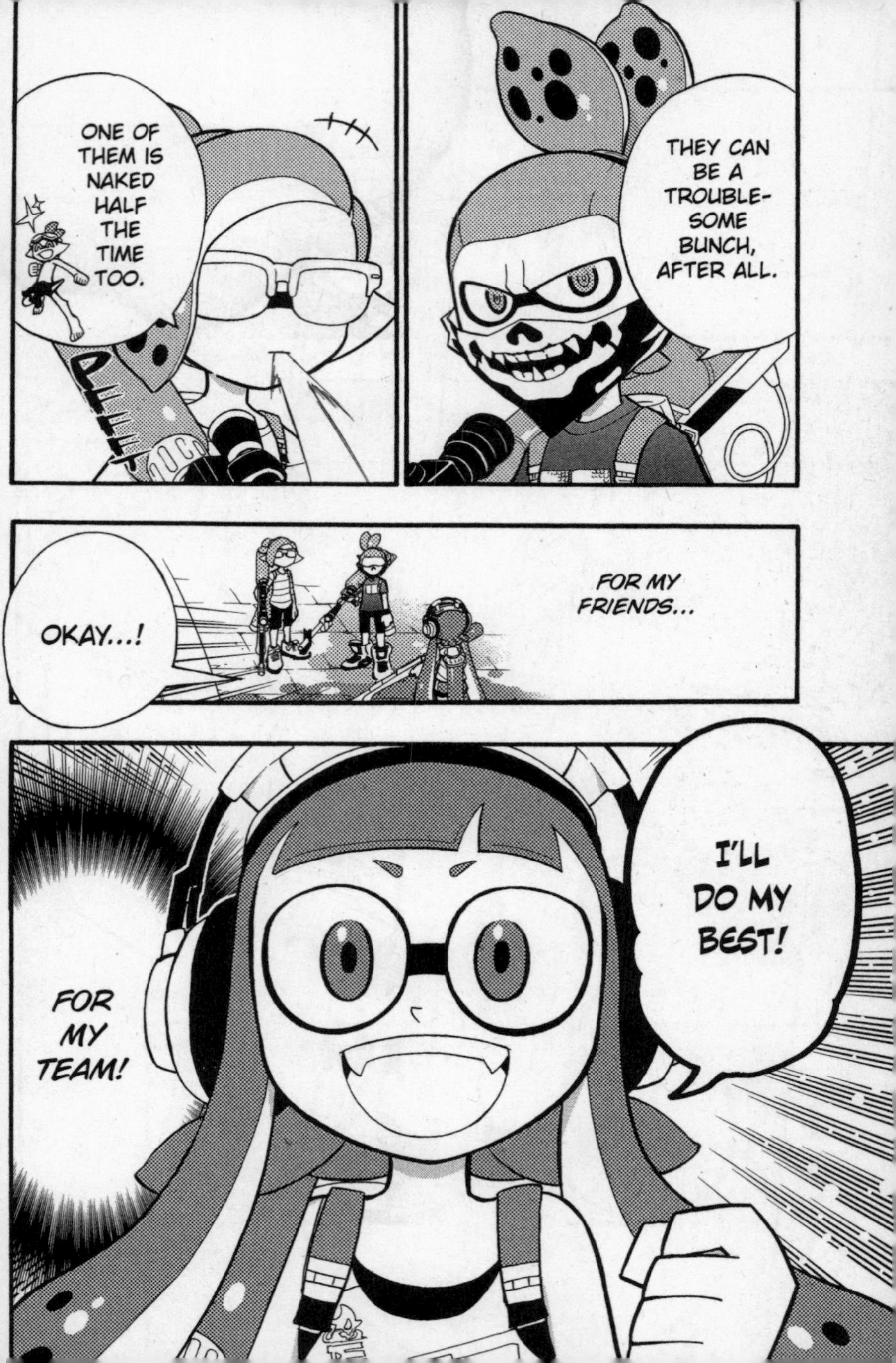
THEY CAN BE A TROUBLE-SOME BUNCH, AFTER ALL.
ONE OF THEM IS NAKED HALF THE TIME TOO.
FOR MY FRIENDS...
OKAY...!
I'LL DO MY BEST!
FOR MY TEAM!

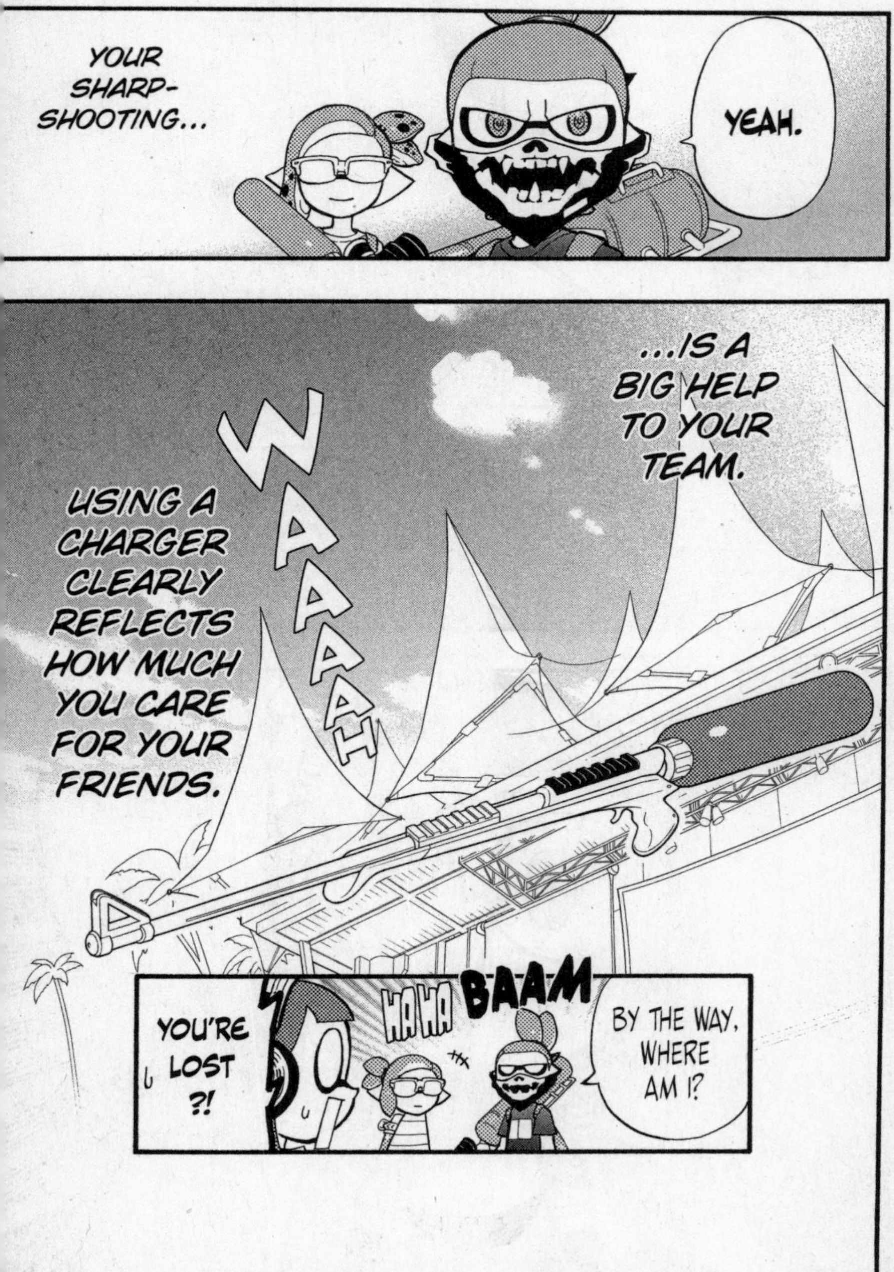
YEAH.
YOUR SHARP-SHOOTING...
...IS A BIG HELP TO YOUR TEAM.
WAAAAAH
USING A CHARGER CLEARLY REFLECTS HOW MUCH YOU CARE FOR YOUR FRIENDS.
BY THE WAY, WHERE AM I?
BAAM
HA HA
YOU'RE LOST ?!

SPLATTERSHOT

THANK YOU!
I KNOW YOU'LL GIVE IT A GOOD HOME.
GIVE IT A GOOD HOME?
GIVE IT A GOOD HOME...
Z Z Z...
Okay!
I'LL GO GET IT A SOCCER BALL!
YOU'LL WHAT ?!
A soccer ball?

SPLAT DUALIES

SPLAT DUALIES!
THEY LET YOU PERFORM SLIDES. A GREAT FEATURE!
EVEN WHEN YOU'RE IN A HURRY TO GET TO THE BATHROOM.
BWOOSH
BWOOSH
YOU SLIDE OVER TO IT?!
KRCHK
Phew
NGKT
THU
YOU CAN ALWAYS MOVE AROUND IN A COOL WAY!
THAT WASN'T COOL!!

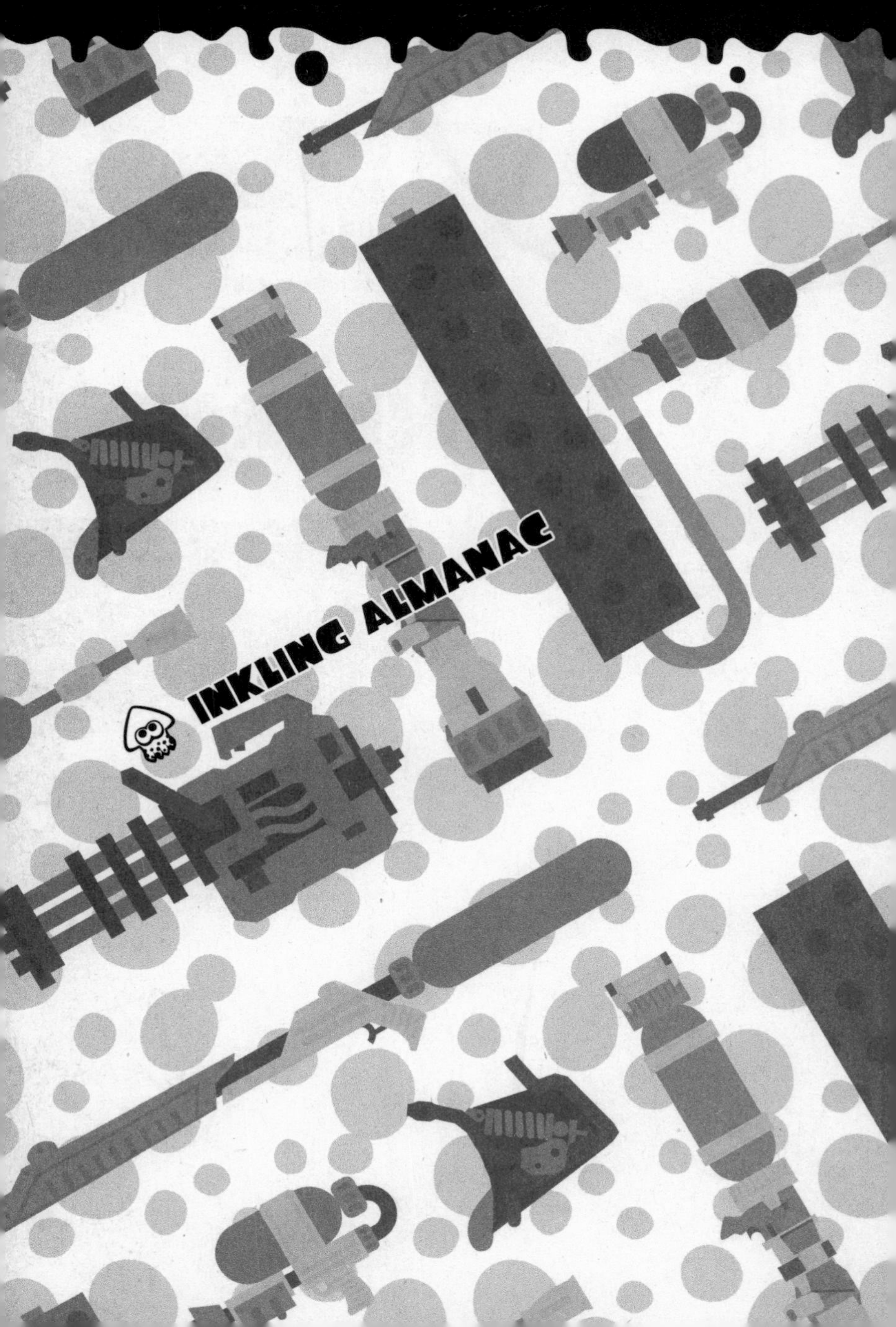
INKLING ALMANAC

TEAM EMPEROR

(INK COLOR: SUN YELLOW)

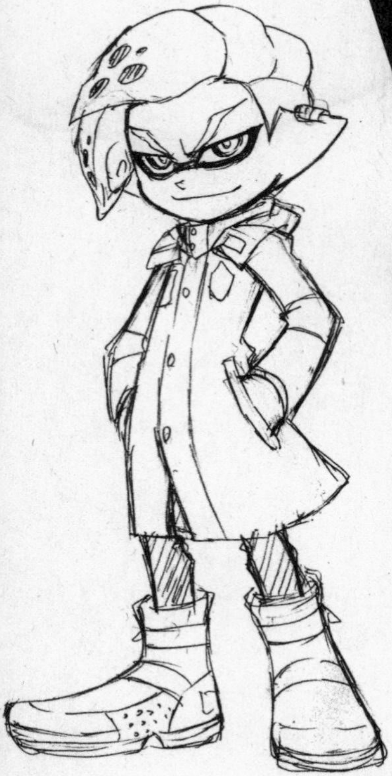

EMPEROR

Weapon:	Enperry Splat Dualies
Headgear:	Eminence Cuff
Clothing:	Milky Eminence Jacket
Shoes:	Milky Enperrials

INFO

- His family is apparently rich.
- He has been enjoying himself lately since he has discovered things of interest outside the Turf Wars.

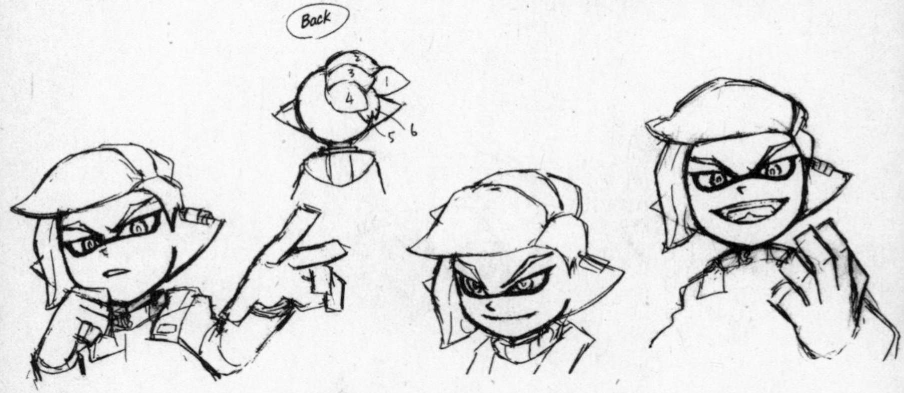
Back

PRINZ

Weapon: Enperry Splat Dualies
Headgear: Eminence Cuff
Clothing: Milky Eminence Jacket
Shoes: Milky Enperrials

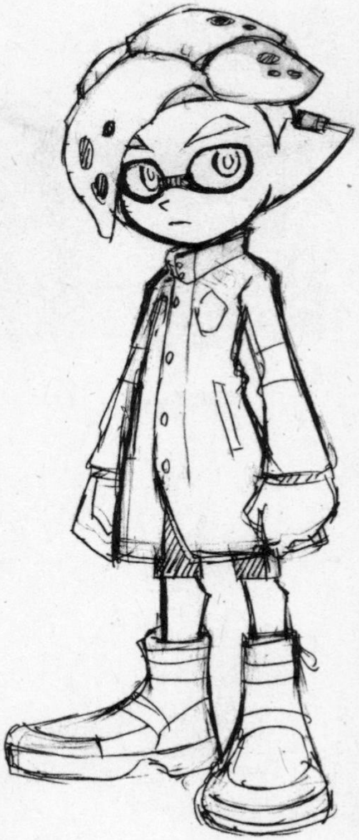

INFO

- He takes good care of the things he is given.

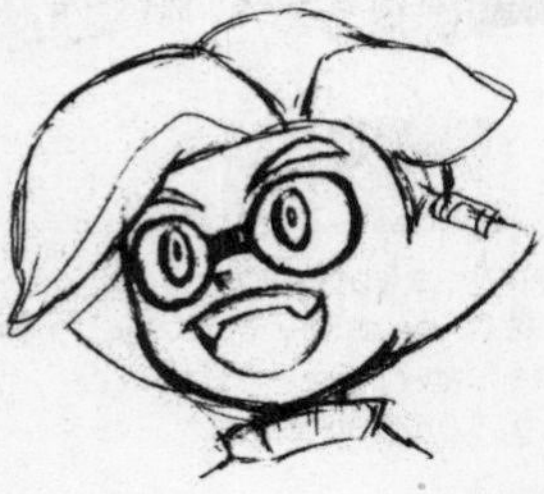

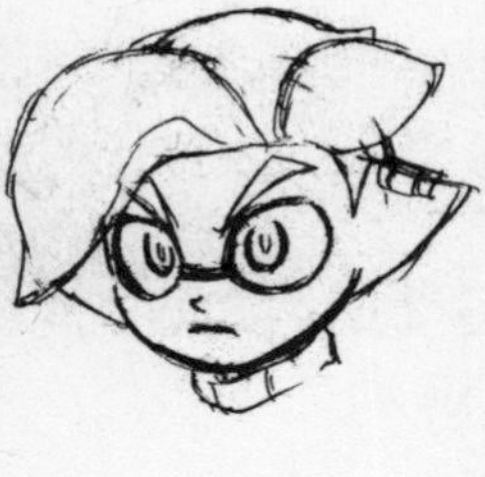

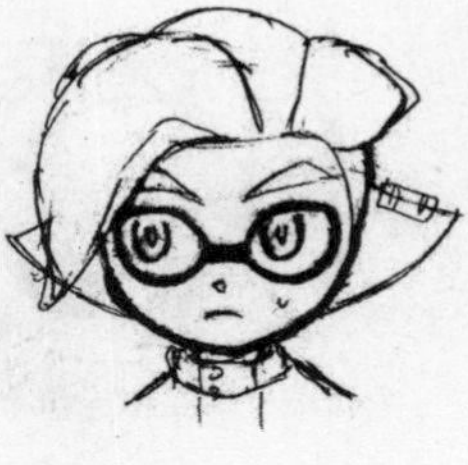

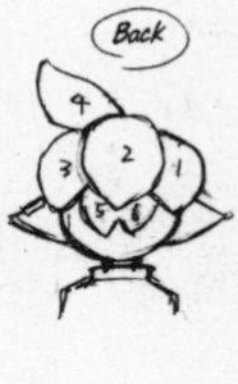
Back

SQUIDKID JR.

Weapon: Clash Blaster
Headgear: Eminence Cuff
Clothing: Milky Eminence Jacket
Shoes: Red & Black Squidkid IV

INFO

• He gave his favorite shoes to Prinz, but Prinz hasn't been wearing them.

Phweee,
not bad.

TEAM
EMPEROR

(INK COLOR: SUN YELLOW)

N-PACER

Weapon: Splatterscope
Headgear: Eminence Cuff
Clothing: Milky Eminence Jacket
Shoes: N-Pacer Ag

INFO

• She likes to drink tea while listening to her teammates chat.

TEAM INFO

• Team Emperor's parents have known each other since the old days.
• Even if Emperor doesn't say anything, the team members will naturally gather to practice together.

RESEARCH MATERIAL

TEAM EMPEROR PROTOTYPE

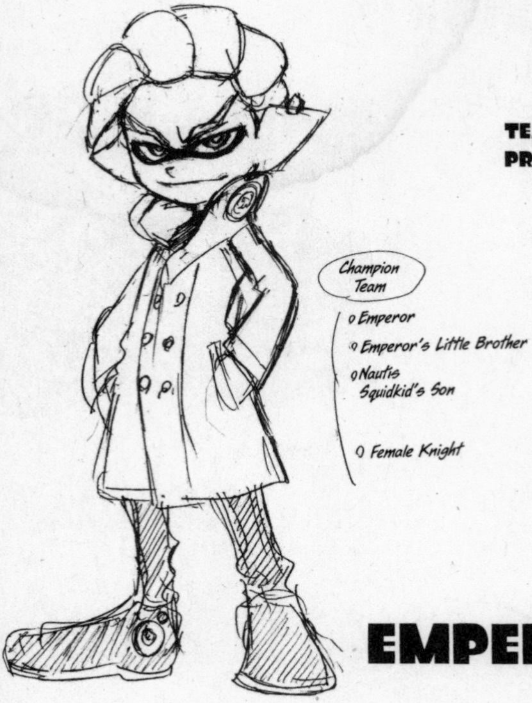
Champion Team
Emperor
Emperor's Little Brother
Nautis Squidkid's Son
Female Knight

EMPEROR

· I USED THE RESEARCH MATERIAL PROVIDED TO ME BY THE SQUID RESEARCH LAB TO CREATE THE FINAL IMAGES OF SQUIDKID JR., N-PACER AND PRINZ.

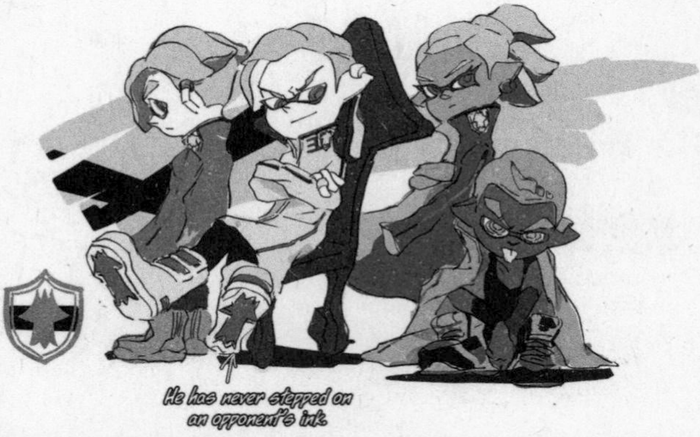
He has never stepped on an opponent's ink.

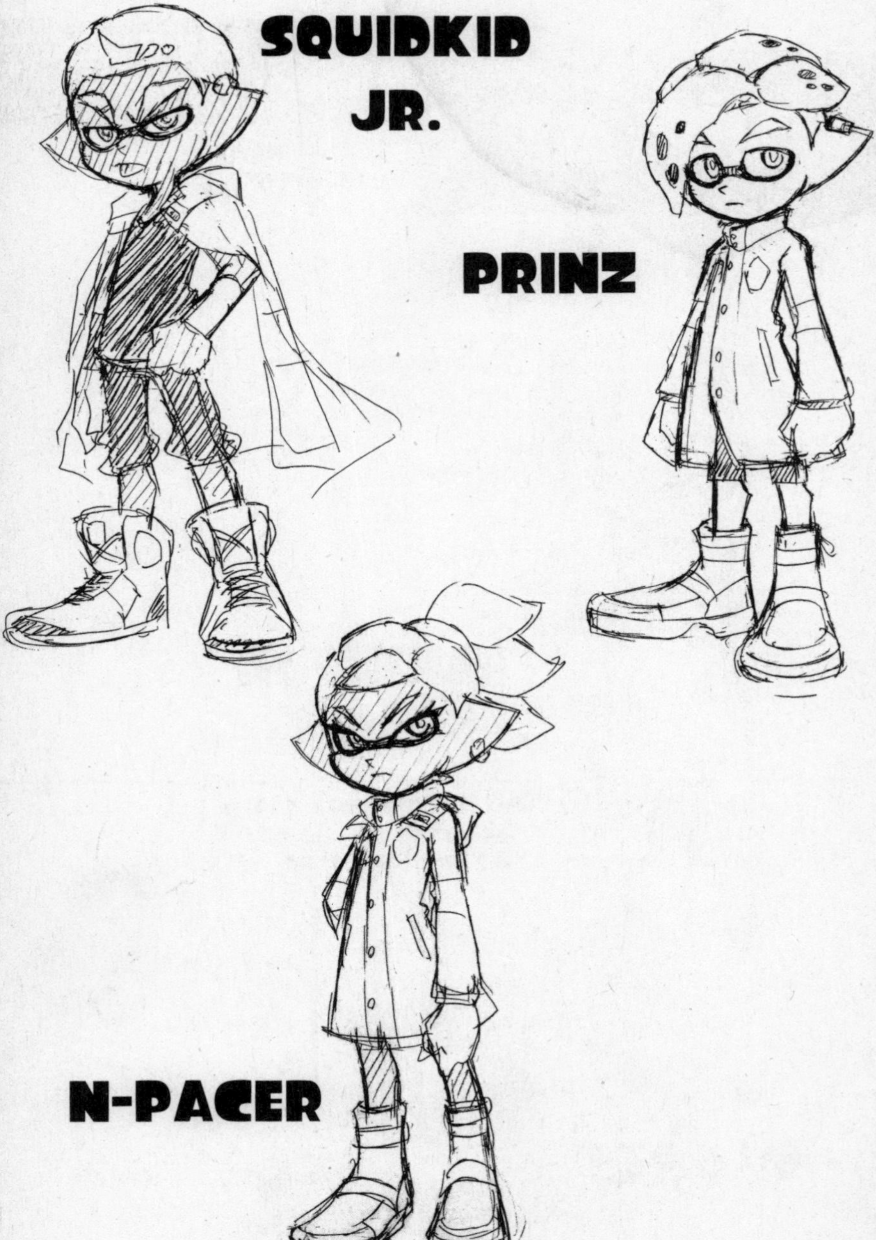
SQUIDKID JR.
PRINZ
N-PACER

RUN ARC

GLOVES

GOGGLES

SALMON

MASK

EMPEROR

Splatoon 6

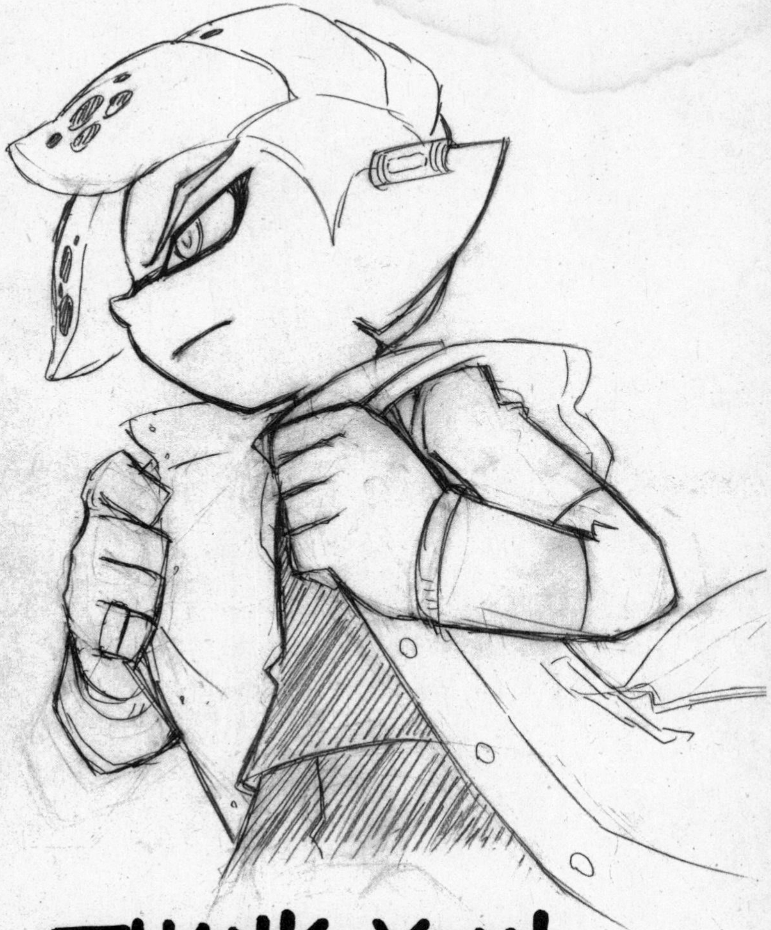

THANK YOU!

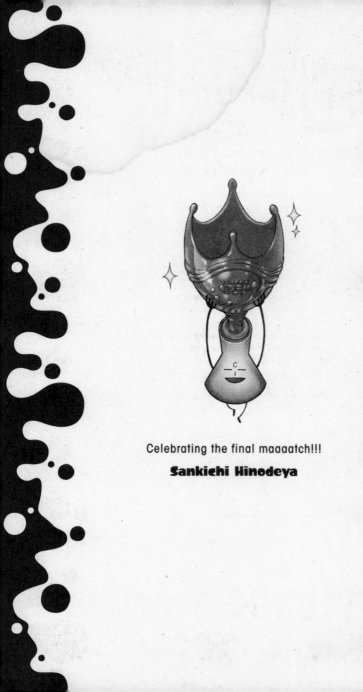

Celebrating the final maaaatch!!!

Sankichi Hinodeya

Volume 6
VIZ Media Edition

Story and Art by
Sankichi Hinodeya

Translation **Tetsuichiro Miyaki**
English Adaptation **Jason A. Hurley**
Lettering **John Hunt**
Design **Shawn Carrico**
Editor **Joel Enos**

SPLATOON Vol. 6 by Sankichi HINODEYA
© 2016 Sankichi HINODEYA
All rights reserved.
Original Japanese edition published by SHOGAKUKAN.
English translation rights in the United States of America,
Canada, the United Kingdom, Ireland, Australia and
New Zealand arranged with SHOGAKUKAN.

The stories, characters and incidents mentioned
in this publication are entirely fictional.

Original Design **100percent**

Printed in the U.S.A.

Published by VIZ Media, LLC
P.O. Box 77010
San Francisco, CA 94107

10 9 8 7 6 5 4 3 2 1
First printing, June 2019

PARENTAL ADVISORY
SPLATOON is rated A and is
suitable for readers of all ages.

graphic
novel.

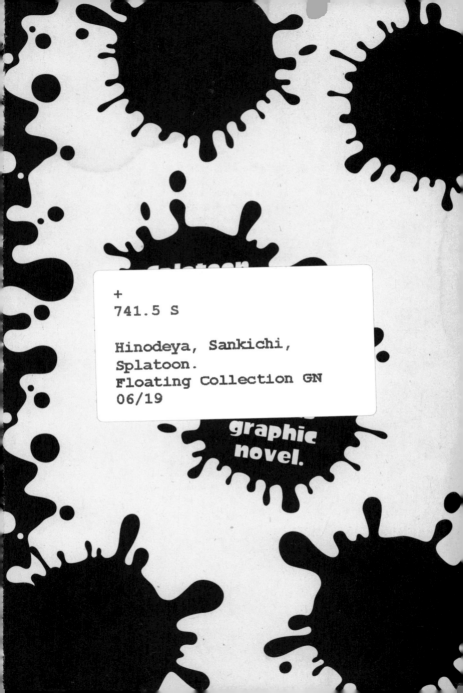